Sense and Stigma in the Gospels

BIBLICAL REFIGURATIONS

General Editors: James Crossley and Francesca Stavrakopoulou

This innovative series offers new perspectives on the textual, cultural, and interpretative contexts of particular biblical characters, inviting readers to take a fresh look at the methodologies of biblical studies. Individual volumes employ different critical methods including social-scientific criticism, critical theory, historical criticism, reception history, postcolonialism, and gender studies, while subjects include both prominent and lesser known figures from the Hebrew Bible and the New Testament.

Published Titles Include:

Jeremy Schipper *Disability and Isaiah's Suffering Servant*
Keith Bodner *Jeroboam's Royal Drama*
Mark Leuchter *Samuel and the Shaping of Tradition*

SENSE AND STIGMA IN THE GOSPELS

Depictions of Sensory-Disabled Characters

LOUISE J. LAWRENCE

Great Clarendon Street, Oxford OX2 6DP
United Kingdom

Oxford University Press is a department of the University of Oxford.
It furthers the University's objective of excellence in research, scholarship,
and education by publishing worldwide. Oxford is a registered trade mark of
Oxford University Press in the UK and in certain other countries

First Edition published in 2013
Reprinted 2014

Published in the United States of America by Oxford University Press
198 Madison Avenue, New York, NY 10016, United States of America

British Library Cataloguing in Publication Data
Data available

Library of Congress Cataloging in Publication Data
Data available

ISBN 978-0-19-959009-4

Acknowledgements

This book is the culmination of a research project funded by the British Academy, to whom I am extremely grateful. Their funding facilitated not only fieldwork with Deaf participants at the 2010 'Signs of God Conference' and interviews with blind interpreters, but also research trips to Cambridge University and the Concordia Sensoria Research Team (CONSERT) in Montreal, Canada. I am particularly indebted to Professor David Howes at Concordia University, not only for his warm reception of my project and direction in all things sensory and anthropological, but also his generous hospitality to my family and allowing me to participate in CONSERT events during my stay. These memorably included eating mushrooms in a cemetery, printmaking through sounds, and a doctoral student presentation in a greenhouse at the top of a multi-story building!

I am also thankful to Tom Perridge and Elizabeth Robottom, editors at Oxford University Press, and Professor Francesca Stavrakopoulou and Professor James Crossley, respectively editors of the Biblical Refigurations series, for their enthusiastic reception of my proposal and invaluable support throughout the production process. Francesca in particular, as both valued colleague and friend, has read drafts at various stages of completion with her characteristic sharpness, insight, and charm. The anonymous reader of the manuscript likewise gave invaluable advice. Professor David Horrell has also commented on draft chapters. As the years go by, I am ever more appreciative of his wisdom, knowledge, good judgement, modesty, and friendship.

The front cover of this book features Anthony Falbo's cubist artwork 'Who Touched Me?' I am really grateful to him for allowing me to use his painting for this purpose. It fitted, like no other, the theme of this book in its displacing of sensory organs and putting the agency of the 'sensory-disabled' woman at the centre of the encounter.

On a personal note, writing this book has been accompanied by a 'sensorial revolution' of sorts with the arrival of our baby boy: Andrew Lawrence Morgan. Without the support of my amazing mum and dad (aka super-nana and super-papa) and my fantastic husband

Dan—whatever would I do without you?—this book would certainly never have got beyond the planning stage. Not that in the great scheme of things I suppose that would have mattered much, for I count Andrew as my four-star 'output' not only of the last four years, but of a lifetime!

Both Dan and I feel so blessed and privileged to have 'little lover' in our lives and for his daily reminders to us of appreciating everything and every minute. So with all my love, hugs, and kisses, this book is affectionately dedicated to darling Andrew: 'How wonderful life is, now you're in the world.'

Louise Joy Lawrence
Advent, 2012

Contents

List of Abbreviations

AIAN	*Annual Indian Academy of Neurology*
AmEthn	*American Ethnologist*
AmQ	*American Quarterly*
ARA	*Annual Review of Anthropology*
BibInt	*Biblical Interpretation*
BT	*Bible Translator*
CA	*Current Anthropology*
CADAAD	*Critical Approaches to Discourse Analysis Across Disciplines*
Crit. Inquiry	*Critical Inquiry*
CultAnth	*Cultural Anthropology*
CW	*Classical World*
DSQ	*Disability Studies Quarterly*
EpilepsyBehav.	*Epilepsy and Behaviour*
ET	*Expository Times*
Ethnos	*Ethnos: Journal of Anthropology*
FemTh	*Feminist Theology*
ISSJ	*International Social Science Journal*
JAmHist	*Journal of American History*
JBL	*Journal of Biblical Literature*
JFSR	*Journal of Feminist Studies of Religion*
JHS	*Journal of Hebrew Scriptures*
JIWS	*Journal of International Women's Studies*
JLCDS	*Journal of Literary and Cultural Disability Studies*
JSNT	*Journal for the Study of the New Testament*
JSOT	*Journal for the Study of the Old Testament*
MAQ	*Medical Anthropology Quarterly*
MedAnth	*Medical Anthropology: Cross-Cultural Studies in Health and Illness*
NIV	*New International Version*
NKJV	*New King James Version*
NLH	*New Literary History*
NLT	*New Living Translation*

NovT	*Novum Testamentum*
NRSV	*New Revised Standard Version*
NTS	*New Testament Studies*
NWSAJ	*National Women's Studies Association Journal*
REB	*Revised English Bible*
SBL	*Society of Biblical Literature*
SenSoc	*Senses and Society*
VT	*Vetus Testamentum*

Introduction: Sense
and Stigma

How one 'senses'—engages with and understands the world—has deep ramifications for not only one's personal identity but also how one is regarded and treated by others. Those who are perceived to lack particular dimensions of sensory experience are frequently branded as 'disabled' in one way or another. In the pages of the gospels, characters with sensory 'disabilities'[1] are curiously 'everywhere' and 'nowhere'. 'Everywhere' in the sense that those who are deaf, blind, untouchable, and 'out of their senses' in demon-possessed states form the numerous stock props in tales of messianic healings; but 'nowhere' in that no meaningful identity, agency, or complexity is attributed to them beyond formulaic and flat character traits. In such processes, these characters are literally defaced: 'marked, marginalized, and muted...on the basis of bodily difference'.[2] As a result, biblical scholars have understood characters with sensory disabilities either as nothing more than objectified beneficiaries of divine healing or, in contrast, 'defiled evildoer[s]'[3] in need of physical and spiritual therapy. In both cases, the characters are not important in themselves, but only as part of the larger plot or theological schema in which they feature. Indeed through healings these characters' sensory disabilities are often expediently eliminated from the narrative stage. Their sensory 'abnormalities' and the chaos they respectively represent, are quelled, subdued, and normalized.

David Mitchell and Sharon Snyder's thesis that characters with disabilities frequently function within literary texts as cultural 'others', the anti-types of social norms, is particularly relevant in this respect. An able body 'still largely masquerades as a non-identity, as the natural order of things'[4] and thus passes without comment, whereas the disabled body stands out as odd, problematic, and needing to be reckoned with.[5] This certainly rings true in relation to such characters in the gospels. Their sensory disability encapsulates their identity and marks them out as 'deviant', excluding them from participation in realms in which 'normal' others are more openly incorporated. As a result their condition regularly features as the subject of metaphorical discourses used to denigrate and reject certain persons, ideologies, and beliefs.

Erving Goffman was particularly sensitive to the ways in which the perception of deviance from a 'norm' marked out an individual or group as stigmatized and evoked negative and castigatory reactions from others. The stigmatized individual was 'reduced…from a whole and usual person to a tainted, discounted one'.[6] Moreover, these destructive correlations were internalized by the stigmatized, and interactions with 'normals' were accordingly adjusted: many chose to conceal their irregular features, others fled and isolated themselves to avoid enduring more shame, and only a few fought to aggressively dispute the stigma imposed upon them. As Thomas Reynolds explains, 'stigma is not the property of an individual body but rather the result of complex social projections that represent bodies, lumping them into general stereotypes insofar as they display undesired qualities'.[7] Whilst Goffman's thesis has since been criticized for its lack of interest in the dynamics of power and the stigmatized subject's forms of resistance, his overall thesis that stigma is an applied 'deviant identity' manifested and performed in social exchanges, rather than a static condition dependent on biomedical factors, continues to be largely influential.

In this book I will initiate a variety of interdisciplinary dialogues with disability studies and sensory anthropology in a quest to refigure characters with sensory disabilities featured in the gospels and provide alternative interpretations of their conditions and social interactions. In each instance I will try to reclaim the identity of those stigmatized as 'other' (according to particular physiological, social, and cultural 'norms') by exploring ethnographic accounts which document the stories of those experiencing similar rejection on account of perceived sensory 'difference' in diverse cross-cultural settings. Through this process these 'disabled' characters will be recast as individuals capable of employing strategies to destabilize the stigma imposed upon them and tactical performers who can subversively achieve their social goals. By way of introduction here I briefly lay out the disciplinary terrains I will be exploring: 'Embodiment and Performance', 'Disability Studies', and 'Sensory Anthropology'.

Embodiment and Performance

Embodiment and performance will be two central concepts to 'think with' throughout this book. 'Making sense' is a bodily, fleshly and emergent process, played out by individuals and groups, from one situation to another. Thus sensory perception is 'not passive...but *acts* that shape a sense of bodily self and ground that sense of self into experienced and re-livable sensations'.[8] Indeed even when stereotypical traits are employed within biblical literature, one can still question, through sustained engagement with particular narratives, how characters variously impact, echo, or resist the dominant cultural consciousness of the text in which they appear. Such considerations challenge the essentialist binary of 'normal' and 'disabled' which is often tritely rehearsed. For as Petra Kuppers states, 'there is no pure body, no pure self, no pure social world, and a theory of touching and texture which acknowledges the positionality and interweaving of knowledge is called for'.[9]

Performance studies likewise understands categories such as gender, race, sexuality, ethnicity, and latterly disability not as a 'static fact of the body'[10] but rather a purposefully enacted role-play. As such the performer herself is not a 'passive specimen on display' but rather 'an active maker of meaning'.[11] Performance is at base a verb not a noun and as such it signifies 'what one does' rather than 'what one is'.[12] In this respect, performance takes seriously the ways in which individuals can influence, control, and tactically convert the stereotypes and stigmas so 'deeply entrenched in the cultural imagination',[13] notwithstanding the fact that alternative models may seem, at first sight, exasperatingly limited.

Disability Studies

Lennard Davis declared in 1997 that 'Disability Studies is a field of study whose time has come'.[14] Now, over a decade later, disability perspectives are fully established and used in history, politics, social science, literary studies, and more recently, biblical interpretation.

Hector Avalos, Sarah Melcher, and Jeremy Schipper's landmark work, *This Abled Body: Rethinking Disabilities in Biblical Studies* (2007) offers the following definition of the aims of a disability-critical standpoint:

> Disability studies foregrounds an awareness of how the particular discourse(s) one uses (including theological, medical, social-scientific discourses and so on) influences the way in which one conceptualizes the term 'disability'. This approach draws on the tools of various disciplines to examine how social, literary and institutional discourses produce and represent a conception of disability…such scholarship opens up the study of disability as a subject of critical enquiry. It promotes the need for critical theorization of disability just as scholars in the humanities and social sciences have critically theorized race, gender, sexuality and other identity markers.[15]

Three models of disability are frequently cited within the literature. First is the medical perspective, which views a disability as a functional or biological defect in a body which is in need of diagnosis and treatment.[16] Of course the biomedical model is culturally remote from the biblical world, which tends to view disability not primarily as pathology but rather, in the words of Jeremy Schipper, as a 'social, political, cultic, sexual, moral, theological, or military issue'.[17] Second is the social model of disability which does not primarily view a physical 'impairment' as disabling, but rather the social context the individual inhabits. The social model unveils the 'ableist' discrimination which is encoded in social, religious, and environmental structures disallowing certain individuals' full participation in their communities. This model has been the most dominant paradigm in biblical studies hitherto. Its weakness is the exclusion of the actual experiences of people with 'disabilities' within its considerations. Third is the cultural or 'minority group' model which takes seriously the views of those labelled as disabled and seeks to get an 'insider' view of complex personal identities and shared rich sub-cultural heritages. In Gill Green's terms it is this perspective which most readily holds promise for the transformation of stigma. In her opinion,

> We are witnessing a realignment of social relationships—the old order in which the sick and disabled are disempowered and marginalized is being replaced by a world characterized by their increasing confidence and reassertion of their personhood. In contrast to the traditional notion of a long-term condition defining a person and their identity, people living with long term

conditions are increasingly resisting such labels and are actively defining their illness in relation to who they are.[18]

Of course, in biblical studies we are dealing with ancient and alien cultural evidence which does not seem to document the experience or autobiographies of those it deems 'disabled'. That is not to say however, that, what Mark Osteen terms 'an empathetic scholarship'[19] is a theoretical impossibility. We can imaginatively speak *with*, rather than *for* those who cannot speak for themselves, by immersing ourselves in the experiences and stories of those in other cross-cultural settings who have experienced similar marginalization on account of their perceived sensory disabilities. Sensory anthropology seems one particularly promising disciplinary context to explore in this respect.

Sensory Anthropology

There has, in the last decade, been what some regard as a 'sensual revolution' in the arts and humanities.[20] Largely based on insights from sensory anthropology, this transformation has hailed the senses not as given biological phenomena, but rather as cultural constructs, dynamic and fluid, enacted and performed. David Howes accordingly submits that 'sensation is not just a matter of physiological response and personal experience. It is the most fundamental domain of cultural expression, the medium through which all values and practices of society are enacted.'[21] Thus social hierarchies, structures, race, gender, class and social norms are all 'learned' through the senses.

Sensory anthropology not only reveals the social construction of sensory models but also that cross-culturally functional competencies may be valued very differently; indeed a characteristic is only conceived as a deficiency or disability in those situations in which an alternative dominant model is operative. Constance Classen illustrates the cultural relativity of sensory frameworks when she states:

When we examine the meanings associated with various sensory faculties and sensations in different cultures we find a cornucopia of potent sensory symbolism. Sight may be linked to reason or to witchcraft, taste may be used...for sexual experience, an odour may signify...social exclusion. Together these sensory meanings and values form the sensory models used by a society, according to which the members of that society 'make sense of' the world, or translate sensory perceptions and concepts into a particular 'worldview'. There will likely be challenges to this model from within a society, persons or groups who differ on certain sensory values, yet this model will provide the basic perceptual paradigm to be followed or resisted.[22]

Howes and Classen have accordingly offered pointers in approaching the 'sensorium'—'the sensory apparatus or faculties considered as a whole'[23]—operative in different cultural contexts. Here I flesh their categories in reference to sensory disability as outlined by Elizabeth Keating and Neil Hadder in their cross-cultural work on this theme.[24]

(a) The sensorium which a Euro-centric cultural approach promotes (an Aristotelian five-fold model of the senses in which sight is highly valued) is not necessarily the model that other cultures share. Moreover, who and what is considered 'abnormal', 'deficient', 'dangerous', or 'other' is different in different cultures. For example, the Hausa of Nigeria mark two senses, sight and experience (which includes emotion and intuition along with smell, hearing, touch), but celebrate taste in particular. In this context the loss of 'taste' would be particularly serious though other sensory losses may not necessarily be viewed as 'disabling' to such an extent.

(b) The sensory priorities and relationships shared (intersensorality) between senses within a specific cultural context need to be considered carefully. For instance, the Columbian Desana where smell is central, talk about the 'odour' of music, thus showing an alternative sensory perception to 'hearing'. Similarly, persons with sensory disabilities may share sensory discourses, but the actual perception may be markedly different. For example musical vibrations would be 'felt' by a person who could hear as well as a person with hearing impairments. However the former would also experience 'audio', whereas for the latter, vibration would constitute the sound of the music. Also, whilst a particular sense may be celebrated in one culture, another sense may be conceived as dangerous. Howes and Classen use the example of vision in Islamic societies where the suppression of the visual ensuing from aniconic norms which prohibit visual displays of God or creation correspondingly leads to evil eye accusations, which 'would seem to be designed to emphasize hearing (and obeying or "submitting" to) the *word* of God'.[25]

(c) Senses which are used widely for functional purposes may hold different sorts of symbolic capital within particular cultural contexts. Howes and Classen note that some sensory data enshrined in language or myth and ritual may actually be remnants from previously held sensory frameworks. They cite Cheever Mackenzie-Brown's work on Hinduism as an example of a context in which sight and vision eclipsed hearing as the predominant sensory medium to experience Hindu scriptures. In some instances, of course, knowledge of previous sensorial orders may be lacking, so one can only imaginatively reconstruct what one sensory register may be building upon, or reacting to.

(d) Sensory models are not constant and unchanging, but rather fluid and dynamic. They adopt and adapt over time within different circumstances, social hierarchies, and contexts. Likewise sensory disabilities are only considered as such in contexts in which particular individuals or groups are marginalized or excluded from full participation. Martha's Vineyard, an island south of Cape Cod in Massachusetts, famously has a high incidence of genetic deafness. This lessened and rendered invisible the distinction between hearing and deaf as most inhabitants could communicate in sign language.[26]

In many ways sensory anthropology takes seriously the challenge set by the cultural or minority group model in disability studies. Namely, it does not disparage alternative ways of knowing, including those performed by individuals with different cultural sensory perceptions, nor does it judge those epistemologies by ableist Euro-centric principles. Anthropology's main strength has always been to empathize and share the space of 'the other' in order to gain an insider's view of particular cultural experiences and perceptions; such insights are crucial in imaginatively sharing a space with characters with sensory 'disabilities' in ancient texts such as the gospels.

Overview of Book

The main aim of the following chapters is to refigure various 'sensory-disabled' characters from a disability consciousness perspective, informed particularly by ethnographic studies; this hopefully will allow some of their strategies, agencies, and identities, which are so often lost behind a label of 'disability', to come to the fore. The first chapter conducts not only a review of works which have taken the 'senses' in biblical traditions as their main theme, but also a disciplinary profile of biblical studies in which its eye-centricity and textocentrism is exposed. Pointers for reimagining the exegetical task in accord with other sensory frameworks, particularly as these are evidenced by the 'sensory-disabled', are proposed.[27]

Each subsequent chapter takes as its focus particular characters with sensory disabilities. Chapter 2 explores the metaphorical symbolization of blindness as spiritual darkness and sin. It also 'unveils' the use of blind characters as props in various indirect characterizations of Peter, the disciples, and the Jewish leaders. In imaginatively refiguring these negative associations, biographical material from the sightless/'blind' is used to question the centricity of the eye and its epistemological stability and reinstate the importance of sound and touch in renegotiating social hierarchies.

Chapter 3 reimagines the interaction between Jesus and a 'deaf mute' not as the fulfilment of Isaiah's 'audio-centric' messianic prophecy (Isa. 35: 5–6), but rather a subversive and evocative performance of Deaf World Arts which disrupts any neat equivalence between hearing, spoken words, and knowledge.

Chapter 4 creatively reads characters that are subject to haptic (sense of touch) and olfactory (sense of smell) censure within the gospels alongside ethnographic studies of untouchable groups in India. It is the 'stench' (both physical and ideological) of pollution which ironically arms them with 'poisoned weapons' which they use tactically to question the oppressive systems which mark them out as not-touch-able.

Chapter 5 utilizes ethnographic evidence of the narrative dynamics of seizure events to reconceptualize the incident as a strategic, multidimensional illness narrative in which not only the boy and his father, but also the crowd, disciples, and Jesus have key roles to play. Finally, in conclusion, some attention is given to how the interpretations in this book could refigure understandings of God and Jesus through a 'sensory disability' consciousness and deconstruct the abled/disabled binary so common in contemporary discourse.

Avalos, Melcher, and Schipper identify three main ways in which biblical scholars can approach biblical texts concerning disability.[28]

First, there are 'redemptionist' approaches in which a biblical text is 'redeemed' for modern application and 'rescue[d]…from the mis- interpretations of modern scholars with normate views'. Second, a 'rejectionist' approach unveils culturally distant and negative portray- als of disability which should not in any way 'provide normate val- ues today'. Third are 'historicist' methodologies, in which ideological landscapes of the history and interpretation of disability in the Bible are unveiled. Whilst selected elements drawn from these approaches will be evident in my own discussions, I do not favour a monolithic perspective or interpretive agenda which could easily be aligned with rejectionist, reformist, or historicist positions. Rather I wish to imagi- natively and creatively bring together inter-disciplinary perspectives drawn from sensory anthropology and disability studies, to offer not only salutary exposés of oppressive interpretations of characters with sensory disabilities, but also at times new and cathartic interpreta- tions which reconfigure the profiles of these flat and often silent characters in fresh and innovative ways. These novel readings will not only emphasize new dimensions of sensory-disabled characters, but also help exegetes acknowledge their own sensorial biases and norms which have prejudiced their interpretations and closed off the means to engage with the multidimensional natures of other sensory worlds.

Looking through a Glass Darkly: Sensing Disabilities of Biblical Studies

Most biblical commentaries and monographs are, I suspect, written in hushed university libraries where sensory experiences beyond vision and texts are strictly prohibited. Cautionary signs read 'Silence Must Be Observed At All Times', 'No Eating Or Drinking', 'No Running', and in one notable case 'No Offensive Body Odors'.[1] Academia it would seem can be quite 'sniffy' about the sensory. The *Oxford English Dictionary* records that 'sense' evokes a twofold meaning. First, a faculty through which bodies respond to an external stimulus; and second, a method of comprehension; literally the means by which one 'make[s] sense of' and interprets phenomena.[2] These channels of 'making sense' are of course never innocent. Quite the contrary, they can silence other ways of sensing including those employed on the margins of society. George Roeder, an American historian, bemoans a similar predicament in his own field when he links narrow sensory interests to perceptions of social hierarchies based on gender, race, class, and social status.[3] He provocatively questions whether historians have overlooked sensory dimensions beyond the visual for some of the same snobbish reasons that well-mannered and 'deodorized' Western (white, male, able-bodied) elites find body odours distasteful:

Not the nation's leaders, but their wives, used perfume. Not managers but manual labourers had the jobs and the living conditions most likely to give them body odor. Historians seldom sweat for their profession, and I think of us as quite normal, rather than arrogant or malicious, when I note that we have sometimes taken pride in this, and this pride may have had some influence on how we regarded the historical role of sensory experience. This does not mean that most historians treated the sensory dimensions of history as they did because they thought this would help protect the existing social order. They wrote and taught as they did because sensory experience did not seem particularly pertinent to the study of political, economic, diplomatic, military and intellectual history, as traditionally defined. [4]

Mark Smith likewise gave voice to this trend when he bemoaned the fact that Western scholars have 'tended to ignore the so-called "lower" senses…through a largely unconscious occularcentrist or retinaphilic "lens" which…has informed scholarly "perspective" and tethered rational truth to a stable, cool, authenticating eye'.[5]

In this initial chapter I do not seek to refigure a sensory-disabled character but rather refigure the character of biblical criticism and its 'sense-making' methodologies. My agenda is threefold: first, to offer a brief review of the handful of works in biblical studies which have taken the senses as their central theme. Second, to illustrate scholarly trends in biblical studies in which 'sight-centricity' is central and other sensory perceptions are largely bypassed. I will use as an example the ocular 'honour and shame' complex which has frequently been used to 'look down upon' those perceived as 'other', including the 'sensory-disabled'. Sensory anthropology will be employed as a specific example of an alternative construction of these values. This sort of enquiry offers a distinct interpretation of the cultural construction of senses and associated sensory 'disabilities' in particular contexts. Third, I will initiate a general sensory-profile of the discipline of biblical studies and consider how this could be transformed with reference to a cultural consciousness model of disability. Contextual interpretation and recent work on embodiment and performance will be brought into conversation with groups and minority cultures perceived by mainstream biblical studies as 'sensory-disabled' in some way.

The Senses in Biblical Studies

Whilst Robert Jütte opens his magisterial study of the *History of the Senses from Antiquity to Cyberspace* (2005) with the statement that 'interest in the body…[and] everyday culture…[means] senses are back in fashion',[6] it is true to say that in biblical studies this trend has not been largely followed. There are only a small number of studies which take 'the senses' as their central subject matter and among them, those which mention sensory disabilities, if they do so at all, do so rather cursorily.

Dorothy Lee for example has conducted a narrative survey of 'The Gospel of John and the Five Senses' to explore how the evangelist uses sensory symbolism to positively furnish his faith ideals.[7] Many others have taken one particular sense and traced it in narrative terms through particular biblical passages or books. Isaac Kalimi for instance, has investigated the sense of sound as a literary trope which enables the reader to be transported from one location or context to another in traditions as diverse as the Joseph story, ark narrative, and throne succession accounts.[8] Dominika Kurek-Chomycz has also employed a literary-theological methodology in her exploration of olfactory dimensions of 2 Corinthians 2: 14–16, linking the fragrance of the gospel to the cult of wisdom.[9] She has also probed the tradition of the anointing of Jesus by Mary of Bethany in the Gospel of John and contends that this character's fragrance is used to appropriate social order in John's world and thus functions as an important means to bolster her positive depiction.[10] In such studies however, little consideration is given to the place of one sense *vis-à-vis* others. For example, is it an ideological accident that 'olfactory' imagery should be used in reference to a female (rather than male) character in John? How is smell or sound valued in comparison to touch, sight, or kinaesthesia ('awareness of the position and movement of the parts of the body by means of sensory organs in the muscles and joints')[11] in the biblical worlds surveyed?

Steven Weitzman, in his essay 'Sensory Reform in Deuteronomy', goes some way to considering the sensorium as a whole when he probes the 'training of the senses' in Deuteronomy.[12] In spite of the fact that Israel had heard God's words and seen his supernatural activity, they still did not fully 'make sense of' them (Deut. 29: 1–4). Thus, Weitzman proposes, Deuteronomy initiates 'an unprecedented attempt to reform through…"regimen of perception"—a set of practices by which to discipline, train and refocus Israel's senses'.[13] Furthermore he suggests that Deuteronomy may be an example of the education of the senses long before Foucault would document such processes: 'one that seeks to reshape how the self relates to the world by teaching the senses that mediate between them—the eyes, ears, and the tongue—to act in new ways'.[14] Within this schooling of the senses, Weitzmann contends that sight is particularly policed in order that the memory of God's works may be cultivated and visible idols may be rejected.[15]

All the above studies to some degree replicate the Aristotelian five-fold Western models in their literary appropriations of the sensory. Ian Ritchie in his study of smell in Isaiah 11: 3 is a notable exception. He proposes that smell both as a means and metaphor of knowledge in the Hebrew Bible has often been sidelined in favour of sight or hearing.[16] Building on his cross-cultural work in Africa, he takes to task both translators and commentators for obscuring olfactory cognition and simply assuming an Aristotelian hierarchy.

Taking such critiques seriously, Meier Malul in his *Knowledge, Control and Sex* (2002) accordingly abandoned a fivefold scheme and instead proposed an eightfold model of the senses: sight, hearing, speech, smell, taste, touch, mobility, and the sexual sense. In relation to the latter he states, 'the sex organs may be regarded as part and parcel of the human epistemic sensorial apparatus, besides such "classic" senses as sight, hearing, taste and smell, the sex organs coming closer to the tactile sense in their operation in the process of carnal knowledge...sexual activity would then be perceived as an epistemic activity as much as the activities of looking, hearing and touching'.[17] For Malul, thinking in the Hebrew Bible should not be considered apart from specific physical embodiments, moreover, the pre-eminent sense throughout scriptural tradition is, he proposes, touch.[18]

Avalos's development of a so-called sensory criticism helpfully theorizes some of the prompts in both Weitzman's and Malul's work, in that rather than focusing on a preordained sensory model, or each sense individually, he designs a method whereby one can plot the ways in which biblical texts comparatively evaluate different senses and 'sensory disabilities'. Avalos maintains that differential privileging of senses can be detected by, among other methods, contrasting expressions of valuation, e.g. 'hearing is better than seeing', documenting 'expressions of antipathy toward particular senses', and identifying 'narratives about the performance of valued tasks and functions in the absence or diminution of certain senses'.[19] Avalos's framework allows biblical interpreters to achieve an enhanced understanding of how biblical authors portray and regard human embodiment and use it to forward particular political, social, and religious agendas; it can also go some way to perceiving the respective severity of sensory disabilities in particular contexts.

Avalos's work was the main inspiration behind my own recent plotting of a sense-scape of the Gospel of Mark.[20] I established that Mark was an audio-centric text. This likely reflects the reality and dependence on orality to communicate the gospel among Mark's audiences. His was a gospel that was primarily heard and not seen. Accordingly, the gravest sensory impairment within Mark's world was to be deaf and without speech, for speech itself should be considered as a sensory phenomenon in Mark's world. Sight, although statistically an important sense, was shown to give insufficient data to attain true insight. The audio-centric nature of Mark's sensorium may well have openly challenged 'visiocentric' forms of imperial propaganda prominent at the time.[21]

The only book-length project on senses in biblical traditions hitherto is Yael Avrahami's newly published PhD thesis from the University of Haifa, *The Senses of Scripture: Sensory Perception in the Hebrew Bible* (2012).[22] Well versed in sensory anthropology,[23] Avrahami constructs a sevenfold sensory model from material in the Hebrew Bible: sight, hearing, kinaesthesia, speech, taste, touch, and smell. She notes how collectively this sensorium is used to furnish 'metaphors for life' and 'ability and sovereignty' within the texts she surveys[24] and how sensory disabilities are used to signify an inability to act or create life. Thus the powerful sensory disabling metaphors are used to castigate inanimate idols: 'the message is clear: creative abilities belong to God alone, God has created the senses and he is the source of ability'.[25]

Opposing general statements that hearing must be central, due to aniconism and the centrality of law in Jewish history, she seeks to cut through sensory hierarchies, but states that 'if force[d] to choose a side in the age-old dispute of the supremacy of sight vs. hearing in biblical epistemology one must choose sight'.[26] This is based on her close reading of associative patterns within literary texts, where eyes and heart are frequently paired and used in reference to learning and education and where sight and smell are coupled in terms of moral judgement so much so that 'the appearance of blindness in the context of the elderly [and] punishment creates an associative link between [these] and foolishness'.[27] Kinaethesia and sight are also coupled in moral formation, for 'walking in the light' functions as a dominant metaphor for righteous following of commandments.[28]

Avrahami does devote one small subsection in a chapter on 'Theology of the Senses' to sensory disability, or what she elsewhere terms 'non-functioning sensorium', as she believes these not only 'indicate lack of ability and lack of independence'[29] but also 'the absence of any real existence or power'[30] in the world of the Hebrew Bible. In Avrahami's view there are primarily two main complexes of knowledge which can be retrieved surrounding sensory disabilities. First, actual information about day-to-day difficulties of those 'who have been cast to the margins of society' in social, political, legal, and practical terms on account of their sensory lack or loss. Second, the prejudicial contexts in which sensory disabilities feature, namely divine punishment and rejection of opponents.[31] Divine chastisement for example was often meted out through the senses (Deut. 28: 28–9) and warriors too sought to inflict physical damage on sense organs to indicate 'the loser's surrender and inferiority'.[32] For Avrahami therefore, the lack of a particular sense can be nothing more than socially debilitating. No alternative sensory frameworks are proposed for such characters. Rather, the sensory-disabled are in effect rendered as 'non-persons', for 'like all marginalised people, they are betwixt and between, part person, part non-person, between life and death, between society and the outside'.[33]

The works briefly surveyed here all take as pre-eminent a largely literary methodology in their survey of respective biblical presentations of the sensory and try in part to illustrate that social relationships and experiences are mediated through a variety of sensual means in biblical texts. Moreover, sense experience extends to both divinities and idols; the living and the dead and the embodied and disembodied. Whilst cumulatively providing important pointers for 'sensitizing' biblical scholarship to the senses, perhaps the overriding drawback of such approaches is that the observing 'eye' tends to flatten these literary texts into neat sensory compartments. A narrative-critical approach is after all, irrevocably bound to the visual medium of written and 'viewed' texts. Ian Ritchie's comments are apropos in this respect:

The bias of modern scholarship stems from the sensorial paradigm shift between the modern Western 'worldview' and the life world of the ancient Hebrews. The modern paradigm, Edward Said has so ably indicated in his work entitled *Orientalism*, is profoundly visualist and textualist. This paradigm assumes the priority of the visual mode of knowledge and equates seeing, especially the seeing of texts, with knowing. Modern discourse profoundly embeds this priority that the uses of non-visual senses, in connection with modes of knowing, are made to appear 'non-sensical'.[34]

Moreover, in reference to characters with sensory disabilities, such studies tend to stigmatize and alienate such individuals, attributing them with little or no agency and not attempting to flesh out their alternative sensory models and 'ways of making sense'. Thus, the subversive social powers that these other sensory experiences may provide are also bypassed.

Biblical Studies: A 'Sight-Centric' and 'Textocentric' Discipline

Biblical studies is of course a 'bookish' industry; its primary evidence and focus are textual and literary, as illustrated by the methods of the studies perused hitherto. Over the last four decades however, there has been a growing interest in 'fleshing out' and 'embodying' understandings of biblical traditions through the adoption of various socio-cultural perspectives drawn from anthropology. Whilst the critical hub of such studies is not limited to textual evidence, but includes reconstructions of the social contexts of authors and/or recipients, still an ocular-centric and 'wordy' metaphor persists at the heart of the endeavour. Cultures are 'seen' as a textual phenomenon, and people and social movements are 'read' accordingly.[35] Deciphering a world-*view* often remains the dominant concern.

   In recent years anthropology has itself had to confront its predominantly 'visual' and 'textual' bias to incorporate what Paul Stoller has termed a more 'sensuous scholarship'.[36] This does not mean a plethora of studies which take 'senses' as their main topic (as reviewed above in biblical studies) but rather a methodology that sees senses as critical dimensions of all arenas of social life. Such perspectives seek to remember the fact that not all wisdom is spoken or written. Moreover, the agency and sensory perceptions of individuals differ according to their placing in social hierarchies. As Dwight Conquerwood, an ethnographer who worked among refugees in South-East Asia and Gaza evocatively states, 'the white man researcher is a fool not because he values literacy, but because he valorized it to the exclusion of other media, other modes of knowing. I want to be very clear about this point: *textocentrism—not texts—is the problem*'.[37] Conquerwood sardonically contrasts the 'textual knowledge' of the Western scholar with the embodied 'local know-how' of community memory and practice when he states: 'it is the choice between science and "old wives' tales" (note how the disqualified knowledge is gendered as feminine)'.[38] He exposes the 'blind spots' of epistemologies which link knowing with sight alone and also unveils the domination of the textual over other 'unlettered' forms of meaning. He cites John and Jean Comaroff's ethnography of colonialism in South Africa as an example of how Tswana peoples exercised social agency extra-linguistically:

They excavate spaces of agency and struggle from everyday performance practices—clothing, gardening, healing, trading, worshipping, architecture, and homemaking—to reveal an impressive repertoire of conscious, creative, critical, contrapuntal responses to the imperialist project that exceeded the verbal. The Comaroffs intervene in an academically fashionable textual fundamentalism and fetish of the (verbal) archive where 'text—a sad proxy for life—becomes all'.[39]

Sensory anthropology, a pursuit which itself grew out of a dissatisfaction with what Howes termed 'the incorporeality of conventional academic writing',[40] likewise encouraged anthropologists to engage more broadly with other sensory experiences (aural, kinaesthetic, dramatic, olfactory, and such like). Howes recounts how on ritual occasions, for example, much is consciously performed and communicated by multisensory media without words.[41] Also, the cultures of the marginalized that often do not inhabit a visual space 'require gustation, listening, feeling, smelling, and other sensory attention to become evident'.[42] Stoller similarly contends that in many African contexts wisdom is interpreted not in terms of 'reading' or 'writing' but rather physical ingestion: 'people are transformed through their internal digestive processes'.[43] For Stoller such understandings are significant, especially in the ethnographic accounts of cultures in which 'the Eurocentric notion of text and of textual interpretations—is not important'.[44]

To give just one example where sight-centric and textocentric constructions have been adopted and utilized in social-scientific criticism of the Bible, let us consider the values of honour and shame. The adoption of cultural 'scripts' which try to identify dominant assumptions and values held by the cultures producing and receiving biblical texts have supposedly enabled biblical interpreters to consciously evade the hazards of ethnocentrism (judging all contexts from one's own cultural standpoint) and anachronism (chronological misplacement of ideas) within their work. It has also put embodied experiences at the heart of exegetical projects. Such approaches presuppose that biblical texts are 'high context' literature in which many elements are assumed to be self-evident by the author and original receivers (e.g. collectivistic, group-orientated, and anti-introspective elements) but when encountered in a different context may not be understood in quite the same way.[45]

In reference to this book's theme, honour and shame are also two values which have often been employed as binary pairings to plot 'ability' and 'wholeness' (honour) as opposed to 'disability' and 'disintegration' (shame). Saul Olyan makes this point when he states that biblical depictions of disability are 'in part the product of the operations of a number of native dual oppositions...clean/unclean, honoured/shamed'.[46] Moreover these oppositions respectively mark 'discourses of valorisation and stigmatization'.[47] Avrahami similarly constructs the 'associative space' occupied between 'the vocabulary of sensory disability' and 'fear, shame and inferiority'. In her opinion, 'the use of such vocabulary in these contexts contributes to the semantic marginalisation of the sensorially disabled'.[48] Carol Fontaine also in her comments on Leviticus 21: 16–22 notes that in general terms the 'honourable' person is a fecund male, who is modified by circumcision, bears no physical or sensory imperfection and who is accordingly able to offer sacrifice. For in her words: 'in the paradigm of honor and shame being less than fully male is certain cause for self-loathing'.[49] Bruce Malina sees the rationale of townspeople, neighbours, and kin who petition on behalf of 'disabled' persons in the gospels in terms of honour and shame; the blind, deaf, demon-possessed 'pointed to a defective family' and thus posed threats of disintegration to the entire group.[50]

The model of honour and shame was largely drawn from the British anthropologist, Julian Pitt-Rivers's construction of honour as an ocular value, denoting 'the value of the person in his/her own *eyes*' and 'the *eyes* of the society',[51] resulting in large part from a sight-centric ethnographic perspective. It was that which could be 'seen' and 'surveyed' which was ultimately fixed as knowledge. Many of the subsequent criticisms of the Mediterranean construct in anthropology can be perceived, at base, to be criticisms of the 'hegemony' of sight which seeks to control, dominate, and objectify the 'observed'. The 'objectifying' of the area identified by Michael Herzfeld, and summed up in his term 'Mediterraneanism' as an adjunct to Said's 'Orientalism', demonstrated the reification of the area into an 'exotic other' by ethnocentric observers.[52] The forced isolation of characteristic themes such as honour and shame as the 'quintessential and dominant questions of interest in the region'[53] not only artificially limited anthropological theorizing about the area but also exposed the dominating and reductive power of the participant observer's eye. This was coupled with the suspicion that a political agenda was at play in the 'eyes' of Anglo-American anthropologists in forging difference and distance from dwellers of the Mediterranean region.[54] In biblical studies a similar argument has recently been forwarded by James Crossley who, utilizing the insights of Noam Chomsky, Edward Herman, and Edward Said, has taken to task those employing a Mediterranean cultural script in New Testament Studies for their latent racism. Crossley argues that stereotypical pictures (note the ocular metaphor) of Arab cultures 'covering vast cultural areas…smack of old-fashioned imperialistic anthropology'[55] in which the imperial power 'looked down upon' the colonized.

Feminist critics similarly focused on how the socially marginal and muted females, often under-represented in the ethnographic record, do not neatly enact or support the constructed social systems of which they are assumed to be a part.[56] Their experiences, largely in the 'private' realm, were 'out of sight' of the gaze of the Western male ethnographer. Lila Abu Lughod's study of Bedouin women in the Western Desert of Egypt,[57] for example, unveiled a very different sensory register from the sight-centric, male honour model of Mediterranean anthropology which pictured women, to a certain degree, as 'disabled' in the public realm, without voice, modest, and shameful. She showed however that in oral poetry (*ghinnawas*), an audio-centric medium, women unmasked their sexuality and love and expressed their interpersonal emotions. Nadia Seremetakis in *The Last Word: Women, Death and Divination in Inner Mani* (1991) in a similar vein reveals the 'acoustic' role of females in Greek mourning rituals. The women exert autonomy and power through their 'sounds' which function as instances of 'gendered cultural resistance' in a predominantly ocular-centric, patriarchal culture. Mourning is a uniquely female activity and therefore becomes one place in which dominant male patterns can be challenged. The main force of the women's power though is crucially not words, but rather a vocal, 'antiphonal' lament of obscene language—'in the laments they could kill a person with language'[58]—and ends in undifferentiated screaming. Sound 'constructs the space of death and the separation from the everyday social order....The acoustic pain of singing is self-inflicted corporeal violence, like scratching the face and pulling out hair.'[59] Seremetakis goes on to describe how these screaming soundscapes dramatize and subvert the 'polluting' orifice imagery of the female body (and the corpse) so prominent in male discourse.[60]

A similar appeal about the silence of honour and shame constructions with respect to those perceived as sensory 'disabled' could also be made.[61] Shlomo Deshen's 1992 ethnography, *Blind People: The Private and Public Lives of Sightless Israelis*, which will be discussed more fully in Chapter 2, for example, documents the experience and performance of visual impairment. Deshen, by virtue of his ethnographic subject matter, unsurprisingly evokes a world that is 'other' to sight-centric models and in which cultural values such as 'honour' are subversively resisted. In contrast to honour's collective group nature, kin and group identities are shunned, for the blind want to escape the stigma they acquire in family groups and can only do this by becoming more independent.[62]

In light of such dissenting voices from the margins, it has been said that honour, once the 'mainstay of Mediterranean anthropology', has now become its 'virtual bogeyman',[63] a symptom of a largely dated approach in which the anthropological observer 'visualized' values which were errantly 'read' into the lives of diverse peoples and regions. Criticisms such as these powerfully jolt interpreters into acknowledging their own social location and the sensory epistemologies they may uncritically assume. In Nadia Seremetakis's words, knowledge is 'extralinguistic and revealed through expression, performance, material culture and conditions of embodiment'.[64] This realization has been particularly evocative in relation to anthropological 'sensing' of the whole social order: the bodily, banal, underside and everyday is now viewed as just as significant as the elite, textual, and literate. Moreover, it has made ethnographers aware that the dominant sight-centric models and frameworks of the mid-twentieth century are themselves reflective of elite sensory paradigms and prompted them to question how particular individuals may reflect, challenge, or subvert aspects of the dominant sensory order of which they are a part.

'Textocentrism' in disciplines like sensory anthropology is as a result of these trends being supplanted by more performative conceptions of culture, which take seriously other sensuous elements and construct meaning as collective, participatory, and embodied.[65] Conquerwood proposes a 'hermeneutics of experience, relocation, humility and vulnerability', 'listening to and being touched' by everyday performances and imaginatively trying to 'occupy spaces' of the other. In this respect, 'proximity, not objectivity, becomes an epistemological point of departure and return'.[66] Herzfeld accordingly urges that sensory studies should therefore not be consigned to the margins as a singular field;[67] rather, understandings of character, cultural traditions, memory, and material culture are all membranes through which sensory elements pass.

It is not coincidental that the adoption of a performance methodology is also emerging within biblical studies and this could hold great promise for unearthing alternative sensory experiences 'from below'. David Rhoads in a programmatic essay proposes performance as a fundamental part of all early Christian reception of New Testament traditions. Indeed these written compositions may be transcriptions of what were first, oral performances.[68] Gospel 'readers' were in fact 'listeners', 'observers', and 'co-dramatists'[69] and whilst manuscripts may have been important vehicles for the spread of Christianity, these were 'not central to the experience of the early church'.[70] Rhoads, now voicing a consensus, relays how ancient contexts were 'oral': speech and hearing were the dominant forms of communication and literacy was the reserve of a small, elite minority. Rhoads estimates only 5–8 per cent at most could read, with still fewer being able to write. Meir Bar-Ilan's estimations are even slimmer: he contends that in the Maccabean period literacy rates for Jews were '1.5% if not lower'.[71]

Such statistics deal a powerful blow to those who contend that the New Testament grew within what could be understood as a predominantly 'scribal' context.

One of the important contributions that 'performance theory' offers exegesis is that performers themselves became key 'interpreters' as well as 'mediums' of tradition. They would 'put their own take on the story'; 'fit it to the immediate audience and situation and even adjust it to the responses of the audience in the very course of performing'.[72] The recipients' are also not cast as passive receptors but rather active co-dramatists. Building on Tom Boomershine's work, Rhoads argues that the performers always took on the character of the individual or group who had direct speech. They did not use onstage focus. Thus, the audience were always directly addressed by the character the actor voiced. They would also therefore 'play' the disciples, the crowds, the ill and disabled, Jesus, even God—they would in short be part of the drama.[73] This sort of direct agency also makes kinetic, non-verbal, emotional, and sensory elements, which could be seen as mere incidentals in our textual readings, much more important. [74]

A Sensory Profiling of Biblical Studies: Disabilities and Possibilities

For sensory anthropologists the senses are to be conceived in reference to culture, not just physical organs. They would concur that 'knowledge [likewise] is not a given, but a culturally and historically embodied language'. [75] Research is a 'sensory process' which, like other such practices, propagates and hallows certain ways of 'making sense' and in the process rejects or ignores alternatives.

A number of recent works which have attempted to delineate the nature of biblical studies, and its teaching and research methodologies, attest to a largely historical-critical, textocentric, and ocular-centric discipline.[76] Whilst acknowledging the astounding proliferation of exegetical 'lenses' developed in recent years (literary, narrative, feminist, postcolonial, queer, liberation, African-American, Dalit, etc.), historical criticism still remains at least implicitly prevalent within the guild, as does an 'assumed "normate" context' modelled by an 'able-bodied, white Protestant [heterosexual] male'.[77]

Elisabeth Schüssler Fiorenza and Kent Harold Richards, in
their delineation of the 'ethos' of the biblical studies discipline, thus
acknowledge at the outset of their project 'the still dominant Euro-
American scientist ethos'.[78] Dale Martin in his review of the pedagogy of the Bible similarly concludes that 'one would have to say that
in spite of recent innovations which move away from teaching only
historical criticism, that method is still the dominant one taught'.[79]
In their *Invention of the Biblical Scholar: A Critical Manifesto* (2011)
Stephen Moore and Yvonne Sherwood likewise bemoan the fact
that even 'reader-response' approaches all too often conceive of texts
'shackled to their hypothetical historical contexts'; thus reader-orien-
tated practice becomes another 'exercise in historical criticism', albeit
one 'performed in wig and dark sunglasses'.[80]

Purposefully, ironically, and jarringly using a colonial metaphor,
Moore and Sherwood state that 'theory's empire' if conceived rela-
tively in the world of biblical studies, would 'approximately [be] the
size of Tobago or the Falklands Islands' such is its 'underwhelming
reality'[81] in relation to the expansive dominance of Western historical approaches. The relative size of 'disability's empire' would
be even smaller: probably comparable in size to the Faroe Islands,
most people may have heard of it, but few could pinpoint its specific
locale or nature.[82] It is also true to say that the historical critical paradigm has colonized works at this interdisciplinary interface. Candida
Moss and Jeremy Schipper confess as much when they state:

Biblical scholarship on disability focuses on close readings of the textual representation of disability rather than trying to reconstruct the lived experience of people with disabilities in antiquity. Although these biblical texts
may indicate that people with disabilities suffered social stigmas in antiquity,
they provide little, if any, information about the actual living conditions or
the everyday experiences of people with disabilities. While these texts do not
provide a clear window into the past or help us distinguish medical impairments from social discrimination on the basis of a social model, a focus on
their representations of disability may increase our understanding of how
these texts both reflect and reinforce ancient cultural ideas about identity and
social organization. In this sense, disability studies can help biblical scholars
better understand the ancient cultural contexts of biblical literature.[83]

Such narrow interests are frequently lamented by more advocacy-
orientated disability practitioners. Amos Yong in his recent review of

Moss and Schipper's volume, for example, states that a focus on the 'social model' of disability as evidenced within a particular historical context, in effect just individualizes, privatizes and flatly stigmatizes conditions. Whilst such works do acknowledge 'the condition of being positioned as "disabled" to be conceptualized as oppression, rather than an unproblematic description of the characteristics and functioning of the bodies of some individuals',[84] nonetheless readings which try and imbue interpretations with a 'disability' cultural consciousness are largely lacking, precisely because 'literary' evidence documenting such experiences is virtually non-existent from the ancient world. Thus, as Olyan illustrates, 'association[s] of disability with weakness, vulnerability, dependence and ineffectuality [which] constitute an exceedingly widespread *literary topos* in biblical texts'[85] *de facto* remain the dominant picture in disability analyses. Commentators, whilst paying lip service to stigma, often have no means to challenge it and thus end up perpetuating rather than confronting assumptions of the texts *vis-à-vis* disability. Yong accordingly states,

Perhaps this is precisely what objective biblical scholarship is supposed to do: merely describe the historical effects of scriptural reception, without rendering theological judgment. The latter is inevitably subjective or perhaps would be indistinguishable from this or that ideological stance, both outcomes of which biblical scholars have been trained to assiduously avoid.[86]

However, Yong employs the example of feminism as a pursuit not just equipped for recording women's roles within a text, but also actively criticizing 'normative theological commitments' surrounding gender in texts. This latter element seems largely undeveloped in many disability readings, yet in his opinion:

The field of disability studies is similarly committed to championing the rights of people with disabilities against their marginalization from the dominant, ableist culture. So if disability studies are to inform contemporary readings of the biblical literature, is there not a presumption here in favor of a resistance toward ableist or normate readings of the Bible? Is it not also the case that disability is not negative and disability studies readings of the image of the cripple (or whatever other impairing condition) ought to critically interrogate the effects of such associations? If so, is not the emancipation and liberation of those with disabilities an underlying goal, and in this case, readings that intentionally engage the theological dimensions of the biblical texts would not only be appropriate, but also in some sense be required?[87]

In a similar vein, in analysing the 'ethos' of graduate biblical education, Fiorenza and Richards petition for the construction of a dynamic 'disciplinary space' which should be remodelled according to 'different social and geographical locations and in light of different experiences of the ethos of biblical studies'.[88] This call for a democratic space populated with voices which are largely unheard in biblical studies is also an important rallying call for disability studies. Sensory anthropology likewise appeals for different 'democratic spaces' which show diverse ways of belonging to cultures and forming identities. Howes and Classen in their sensory-profiling strategy probe among other elements 'Metaphors and Language' and 'Artefacts, Aesthetics and Media of Communication' in different contexts.[89] If these categories are applied in very broad brush strokes to the academic discipline of biblical studies, and reimagined according to a disability consciousness, what sort of patterns would emerge?

Language and Metaphors

Howes and Classen first ask ethnographers to note how words, metaphors, and turns of phrase belie how particular sensory organs or sensory functions are evaluated. In biblical studies the frequently employed metaphor of the biblical 'text as a window' through which one either looks 'behind', 'at', or 'in front of' belies the sight-centricity of exegetical 'outlooks', 'lenses', and 'perspectives'. Pheme Perkins demonstrates the employment of a visual metaphor in reference to one of the prime media of exegesis, the biblical commentary, when she writes, 'I like to think of commentaries as windows into the world presented by the biblical text.'[90] In such volumes, the cultural consciousness of the 'commentator' is often screened out, for the purposes of 'scholarly [objective?] perspective' and their 'discerning eye'. In a typically sardonic description of the 'epistemological decorum' of a biblical commentator, Moore and Sherwood testify:

This self-effacing reader does not write, but as his name implies merely comments. He is a civil servant of the text....For hundreds of pages at a time, there's little or nothing on his own text to indicate that it was written by a living, breathing human being....He lives vicariously through the text and willingly under its thrall.[91]

Commentaries as a genre of course 'self-reflectively witness to the success of the historical critical paradigm'[92] and have often in the words of Gordon Fee, as 'good technicians of the text', avoided other theological, ethical, or consciousness concerns 'like the plague'.[93] Whilst a new wave of commentaries documenting positions from the margins based on race, gender, or social class have been forthcoming in recent years, disability studies still rarely features in such genres. Bruce Birch gives voice to this when he notes how in writing commentaries on the Books of Samuel, and reading references to the blind and lame, he just skipped 'blindly' over them, completely unaware of their relevance. He sees this as a 'disability' of biblical scholarship itself:

> I have been trained in Biblical scholarship with a limited awareness and understanding that has allowed me to spend decades in studying and teaching the Bible without noticing or paying any particular attention to the large number of references to impairment/disability in the biblical witness....It is socially easier not to notice such persons, and I suppose it has been easier for biblical scholars to give texts referencing impairment/disability only the general descriptive treatment accorded to a disabled character that enters the story or the minimal explanation given to a reference to impairment that crops up in a text.[94]

It would seem that the language and metaphors of the discipline thus link the eyes with knowledge. One of the great contributions of postmodernism however, has been to acknowledge and celebrate diverse forms and media of knowledge. To give just one example, reading with subalterns in India (Dalit peoples, etc.), Sathianathan Clarke has commended a 'multimodal' approach that encourages oppressed groups to 'perform' transformation in response to biblical narrative and images. In oral cultures interpretations are 'corporately weaved together'[95] and frequently represented in 'media other than writing'[96]—the Dalits for instance use drumming, dancing, spinning, weaving, painting, and carving in their hermeneutics and, as will be seen in Chapter 5, make political protests through bodily senses. Clarke urges mainstream biblical studies to literally 'come to its senses' and acknowledge the great contribution that cultures which speak with their hands, rather than words and written texts, can offer.[97]

Such analyses cumulatively question the epistemological centrality of the observer's eye. Moreover they disorder and disrupt simplistic equations between sense organs and sense perception. One may see with one's ears, speak with one's nose, smell with one's touch, and hear with one's tongue.

Artefacts, Aesthetics, and Media of Communication

Howes and Classen's second category is the use and appreciation of cultural objects, relics, and the media through which sense is conveyed. The key artefacts within biblical studies are of course ancient texts; and given this textual focus, disciplinary linguistic skills are essential. As Martin reveals,

Students are taught Hebrew and Greek…introduced to reference books such as analytical concordances, bible dictionaries, and books that display different English translations side by side…students are taught to outline passages and books to analyze the rhetorical devices such as chiasm and parallelism, to recognize different genres of literature…[and develop] the practice of comparing different manuscripts [and traditions].[98]

In such disciplinary training, 'meaning [is conceived as] inherent in [language] and text'[99] and 'eisegesis' is seen as the diametric opposite of '"responsible" historically sensitive interpretation'.[100] A disability consciousness however may well prompt interpreters to acknowledge that for some 'the limits of language' are not the 'limits of the world'.[101] In a similar vein the postcolonial feminist, Musa Dube, initiates contextual interpretations of biblical stories among African readers and revels in the dictum offered by one participant that 'God never opened the Bible'. This graphically illustrates the fact that God was active and dynamic, not contained in, or contained by, particular written directives in printed texts. The deaf community which use sign language likewise 'retell and weave their own stories of healing and empowerment'[102] through not words but bodily gestures, and experience 'sound' as vibrations, all elements which will be expounded more in Chapter 3. A similar trajectory could be traced in relation to comprehension through the fingers in Braille or the ears in audio or sound recognition technologies.

Stephen Tyler has as a result, petitioned scholarship to literally 'de-scribe' and resist the limiting power structures of the written word, for in his opinion such moves stultify the possibilities of the imagination: 'writing puts everything in the past, it has no future'; 'the past is the incurable illness of writing'.[103] He submits that oral cultures provide a resistance to this 'algebraism—shufflings of meaningless signs'.[104] In his opinion, 'our redemption in/from this tale of loss and liberation is not in sight nor in hand [by which he means scribal practice] could it be just on the tips of our tongues? [or more specifically in the actions of our body]?'[105] Oral and performative cultures also often appropriate a text to a cultural context shared by others: 'Sometimes the story is framed in a new context, or the ending changed, or variants suggested alongside the original story'.[106] Peter McDonough's study of issues of translation of gospel stories into sign language found that what the deaf community and the hearing community valued as good translations differed significantly. For the deaf, the most important criteria were that translations were 'embodied in [their] own culture and colloquial idiom'. In contrast, for the hearing the most important element was a 'direct and true translation of biblical texts'.[107]

Janet Lees, a speech therapist and minister, in her essay, 'Enabling the Body', is also alive to the problems that the 'wordy' artefacts and media of biblical studies can pose to 'those of us who cannot speak, read, or turn over the pages'.[108] More importantly she sees 'marginal characters' within stories as important touchstones for 'sensitising' interpreters to different knowledge bases and ways of making sense. She cites the case of Andrew who has cerebral palsy and his review of visiting Jerusalem as a pilgrim in his wheelchair. He got out of his chair and sat on the floor amidst dust, feet, legs, and cries out so he is not crushed. Lees accordingly writes, 'Andrew's view of what these early Christian communities looked like to disabled people is from the floor.'[109] Palm Sunday looks very different when told from this dusty and quite literal 'view from below'.

In contextual interpretations, the medium of communication is also changed from depersonalised 'comment' to a story encapsulating personal experience. Holly Toensig for example, uses the exorcism of Legion narrative to articulate her own feelings about 'guarding the tomb' and memory of her brother who committed suicide due to paranoid schizophrenia. Legion in her reading therefore primarily represents not as perhaps expected her schizoid brother but rather herself. She jarringly claims: 'I am the demoniac living among the tombs, shrieking in personal mourning, unwilling to give my brother into hands so bent on delivering him to hell.'[110] Through critically contextualizing the biblical character in her own experiences she feels that 'Mark 5 provides a means to "visit that place" so often avoided.'[111] She contends that 'viewing the text only through a [historical] lens at the exclusion or denigration of other perspectives threatens the idea that biblical texts are living traditions that are challenged and renewed by lived experience'.[112] She sees personal narratives as a central tool in which people can variously listen, tell, and share stories of struggle and more importantly 'find and name the numerous commonalities between people'.[113] In short, artefacts and media of communication take on very different characteristics when conceived from a space which takes a disability consciousness seriously.

Biblical Studies: Disabilities and Possibilities

Classen has identified 'sightseeing' as a major Western tourist occupation,[114] for what is 'seen' is ultimately 'valued'. In many ways this short survey of the senses of biblical studies has also confirmed the value placed upon sight above other forms of knowledge production. Those works which had as their main focus 'senses and the sensory' ofttimes replicated an Aristotelian hierarchical ordering of sensory perception; other studies that did propose alternative sensory models for biblical worlds still nevertheless tended to compress and conceive of the sensory-disabled as entirely 'other' on account of their perceived difference. Their alternative sensory experiences were not explored or valued whatsoever.

Mitchell and Snyder rail against the tendency to reify sensory patterns and close down difference. Arrestingly they state: 'eugenics offered a form of redemption that would solve social crises through the eradication rather than accommodation of human variation'.[115] In order to encompass variation in human capacities we must question and distort so-called 'similitude' in 'understanding[s] of ourselves as social and biological animals'.[116] In light of such critiques, it seems timely to probe ethnographies that adopt alternative sensory positions and consciously seek to rehabilitate experiences 'from below' which were under-represented in previous studies. The continuum of structure and agency is necessarily refigured for each individual according to their hierarchical and ideological place within social structures, since the ability of individuals to exercise transformative agency depends on their position.[117]

Whilst an ethnographer may well choose to ignore all previous studies of an area if he/she has plentiful data of her own from face-to-face participation and engagement, for the biblical scholar this is not an option. One cannot live among or interview the peoples we meet in the Bible, especially not those considered disabled who often leave little documentary evidence. Thus, in the words of Seth Schwartz, 'we are not looking for analytical tools...[but alternative ways] of providing ourselves with sets of social-historical assumptions (in the absence of real information) against which we can measure the exiguous fragments of information we do have'.[118] In short, we need evocative resources to juxtapose with our texts, if not to reach 'reality' then at least to generate new questions. Sensory anthropology, which charts the sensory lives of those so often under-represented by previous ableist, Euro-centric suppositions, I contend, offers such a resource.

Imagination is of course key in such undertakings, but this has always been true of anthropology which has sought to conjure a shared space with 'the other'. Lees similarly believes that 'the move toward including people with disabilities as research partners rather than the object of research'[119] is central. For whilst the voiceless, or those whose stories are not encased solely in texts and literature are often hard to access, ethnographic material which witnesses to their experiences (albeit often by proxy through an ethnographer's hand) does allow a certain sensitizing and opening up of their lives. In short, sight-centric methodologies disable the scholar who with them inevitably 'look[s] through a glass darkly'; however by creatively sharing the space of another, they are enabled to feel, hear, smell, touch, and move 'face to face'. This is surely reason enough to engage with the sensory strategies to be explored in the following chapters of this book.

| 2

Blind Spots and Metaphors: Refiguring Sightless Characters in the Gospels

One need not delve too deeply into the gospels to witness what Susan Sontag terms the 'lurid metaphors' of impairment which occupy social worlds, most prominently the metaphorical link between blindness, misunderstanding, and dispositions unbecoming of a would-be disciple.[1] Perhaps even more damaging, however, has been the unquestioning echoing and perpetuation of these biblical themes by biblical scholars who have also rendered sightless characters as nothing more than metaphors in indirect portrayals of sighted characters' dispositions, variously representing spiritual darkness and sin. By reducing a character solely to an expression or illustration of something or someone else, any other potential agency or identity outside that metaphor is completely eclipsed.

Throughout this chapter I follow Shlomo Deshen's ethnographic framework which seeks to juxtapose the different ideological stances evoked by the terms 'sightlessness', a largely medical term denoting physical delimitation of sight, and 'blindness', a cultural term which contains within it a 'rich context of attributes—beliefs, prejudices, fears—that culture has associated with sightlessness in many (perhaps most) times and places'.[2] My particular focus in this chapter will be on blindness metaphors in general, and on sightless characters in particular, namely, the man at Bethsaida (Mark 8: 22–6), Bartimaeus (Mark 10: 46–52), and the man born blind (John 9: 1–34). First, I will probe the widespread use of blindness as a metaphorical trope

frequently used as a tool of social rejection and how sightless characters have variously been construed as 'metaphorical' within biblical
interpretation, particularly through indirect characterization of Peter
and the disciples. Second, I will introduce some sensory-anthropolog-
ical work on corporeal metaphors surrounding illness and disability.
Third, I will attempt to bring new insights to bear on the metaphorical interpretations outlined through interaction with ethnographic
and biographical insights from 'blind' interpreters. These readings will
not only emphasize new dimensions of sightless characters, but also
help exegetes acknowledge their own interpretive 'blind spots', places
where sight-centric norms have led to damaging misunderstandings
and prejudices concerning sightlessness.

Blindness as a Metaphorical Tool of Rejection

In the contemporary West, blindness's metaphorical status as a master trope is well established. The *Oxford English Dictionary* reveals that
'blind' can refer not only to the inability to see, but also to that which
'lacks perception, awareness or judgment'.[3] Individuals are commended for their 'clear-sightedness' and 'vision', whilst others, often
those with whom we 'do not see eye to eye', are chastised for their
'blind obedience', 'blinkered opinions', and wanderings down 'blind
alleys'. Pierre Fontanier, a French rhetorician suggests:

> Blindness must have at first referred only to the deprivation of the sense of
> sight; but he who does not clearly distinguish ideas and their relationships;
> he whose reason is disturbed, obscured, does he not slightly resemble the
> blind man who does not perceive physical objects? The word blindness came
> naturally to hand to also express this deprivation of moral sight.[4]

Mitchell and Snyder's important book, *Narrative Prosthesis: Disability
and the Dependencies of Discourse* (2000), begins with the question: 'why does the "visual" spectacle of so many disabilities become
a predominating trope in the non-visual textual mediums of literary
narratives?'[5] They contend that one of the primary functions of disability is to provide 'an opportunistic metaphorical device' which is
used to denote 'social and individual collapse'. In their words, 'disability acts as a metaphor and fleshly example of the body's unruly resistance to the cultural desire to enforce normalcy…the able body has

no definitional core (it poses as transparently "average" or "normal"), the disabled body surfaces as anybody capable of being narrated as "outside the norm."'[6] They contend that disability has, as a result, been used as a 'crutch upon which literary narratives lean for their representational power'[7] and a potent site for metaphorical compositions.

This certainly seems true in relation to blindness metaphors within biblical traditions. Deuteronomy warns 'The Lord will afflict you with madness, blindness and confusion of the mind; you shall grope about at noon as blind people grope in darkness, but you shall be unable to find your way' (Deut. 28: 28–9). Similarly, *The Damascus Document* from Qumran pictures Israel's repentant remnant before the advent of the Teacher of Righteousness, as 'blind persons…who grope the way for twenty years' (CD 1: 8–11).[8] The Psalmist and Jeremiah cast false idols as blind and devoid of the sensory agency enjoyed by Yahweh (Psalm 115: 5–8; Jer. 10: 5).[9] Isaiah, a text widely used by the gospel writers, links blindness with a lack of knowledge and outright rejection of God's word (Isa. 6: 9–10). The blind also came to be ideologically associated with the dead in certain Jewish traditions, hence their potential to represent darkness, loss, mortality, impurity, impotence, and lack of knowledge, literally being 'kept in the dark of the tomb'. Lamentations, for example, bemoans that 'he has made me sit in darkness like the dead long ago' (Lam. 3: 6).

Gospel blindness metaphors also develop this theme. 'The blind leading the blind' accusation comes up in Matthew in the context of a controversy surrounding ritual cleanliness (Matt. 15: 4). Historical and social-scientific critics have noted a typically stark sectarian contrast set up between 'creaturely teachings' of the Jews and Jesus' teaching. Jesus exposes the error of the Pharisees' ways by unmasking their teachings as unbiblical (Matt. 15: 3–6) and labelling them 'hypocrites', literally stage players, whose faces (and eyes) tell a different story from their inner dispositions and intentions.[10] Ironically, in their case, physiognomic thinking seems not to unveil the truth about their personalities, but rather, the leaders' exterior bodily form acts as a cloak for their diseased and corrupt dispositions. Jesus finally castigates the Jewish leaders as 'blind leaders of the blind', picking up on prophetic warnings against false leadership (see Isa. 3: 12; 9: 16). Redaction critics note how Matthew transplants Luke's singular to the plural so as to pointedly castigate the Pharisees as an ignorant group who are polar opposites of his own disciples.[11] The plural use of the metaphor tends towards essentializing the whole out-group with the same negative traits. Critics also note that falling into a pit is frequently used to denote chaos, catastrophe, the underworld (Ps. 7: 15; Prov. 26: 27), and punishment for the wicked (Isa. 24: 18; Jer. 48: 44), hence the metaphor represents their ultimate judgement.[12] The metaphorical marginalization of the Pharisees as a group continues in Matthew 23: 16–26 in which they are characterized no less than five times as blind. This set of derogatory, deviance labels—'blind guides' (23: 16, 24), 'fools and blind' (23: 17, 19), and 'You blind Pharisee' (23: 26)—fall in the context of the woes against the Pharisees, which once again centre on the accusations that Pharisaic teaching is obsessed with the practicalities of the law, but misses the weightier matters of justice, mercy, and love. Warren Carter hence emphasizes that 'name calling is not intended to reform the other group. It is for internal consumption, affirming a group's identity as distinct from other groups. Chapter 23 affirms the community of disciples in its commitment to Jesus and in practices that differ from those attacked in this chapter.'[13] Luke's version of 'the blind leading the blind' parable (Luke 6: 39) is likewise set in the context of a lengthy discourse surrounding discipleship ethics, attitudes, and the construction of group identity. Judith Lieu notes that this parable may indicate the importance of developing disciples equipped to lead others properly, again in marked contrast to the 'blindness' of false authority.[14]

Similar metaphorical tropes can be discerned in relation to the interpretation of specific sightless characters presented in other gospel traditions. The man at Bethsaida (Mark 8: 22–6) and Bartimaeus (Mark 10: 46–52) have, for example, throughout the history of interpretation frequently been seen as nothing more than metaphors or analogues for Peter and the disciples' spiritual blindness. Sandwiching as they do the great declaration of Peter at Caesarea Philippi (Mark 8: 27–33), which at once sees him commended for recognizing Jesus' messiahship but also rejected as 'Satan' for failing to see the importance and inevitability of Jesus' death to his mission, these blind characters are presumed to act as interpretive cameos illustrating misapprehension. Elizabeth Struthers Malbon, in her study of characterization in Mark, for example, renders these 'minor' characters as 'indirect characterisations' of the lead apostle's spiritual blindness. For

Malbon, the man who is blind at Bethsaida and Bartimaeus enable the 'implied audience to reflect on the gift of insight. The half sight/ half blindness of the Bethsaida man as he sees trees walking is immediately paralleled by Peter's half sight/half blindness as he sees Jesus as only a powerful Christ and not also a suffering servant.'[15] A similar conclusion is drawn by Willem Vorster, when he submits that 'there is a good reason to think that the healing of the blind man at Bethsaida is a metaphorical narrative about the same theme. Initially the man can see only vaguely (Mk 8: 24) and Jesus has to lay his hands on his eyes again before he can see properly.'[16] Marcus Borg likewise renders the healing narratives of the two Markan sightless characters as metaphors. In his words 'by placing these stories where he does, the author of Mark gives them a metaphorical meaning, even as one or both of them may reflect history remembered. Namely, gaining one's sight— seeing again—is seeing the way of Jesus. That way, that path, involves journeying with him from Galilee to Jerusalem, the place of death and resurrection, of endings and beginnings.'[17] A similar trajectory has been drawn within the interpretation of the character born blind in John 9, who has also been read as a metaphorical symbol of darkness, rejection, and sin. His physical blindness becomes the metaphorical referent for the Pharisees' inner blindness. In Bruce Morhill's words, 'Jesus' healing of the man born blind sets up the conflict exposing the real metaphorical blindness of the Pharisees, who reject Jesus' claim to authority and reject the healed man from the community. The irony is that the one who from the start is considered as good as dead ends up coming to know the true light (life) that has come from God, joining the fellowship of Jesus and his followers.'[18] The blind man's healing thus also becomes a metaphor for Jesus' enlightenment of the world. Jesus' command to the man to wash his eyes in the pool of Siloam (which the text declares means 'sent') has been seen by many commentators to give a sacramental analogue, namely the washing away of sin at baptism by following the one 'sent from above'.[19] He opens the blinded eyes to witness salvation, enlightenment, and belief.

Thus scholars have uncritically echoed biblical traditions in identifying blindness as a metaphor to signify not only misapprehension but also inner darkness and transgression. This is in stark contrast to 'seeing' which metaphorically represents perception and salvation.[20] It is perhaps unsurprising therefore that, as Mosche Barasch reveals, images of the healing of the blind were frequently put on early Christian sarcophagi. Here, the action is not celebrated as a healing or miracle, rather it symbolizes salvation: 'the blind person to whom sight is restored is an image of the transition from bondage to salvation…from death to eternal life'.[21] All these metaphorical illustrations belie, underscore, and habituate ableist suppositions in trying to convince in-group readers and viewers that they can develop spiritual sightedness, whereas those considered false leaders and enemies, or traits considered unworthy of a would-be disciple, are cast as dimsighted and blind. What needs further thought now is why sensory impairment becomes such a prevalent and potent metaphorical motif in the texts and interpretations outlined.

Corporeal Metaphors: Illness and Disability

George Lakoff and Mark Johnson in their celebrated *Metaphors we Live by* (1980) traced how metaphors contributed to the landscapes of our minds and constructions of our ideologies. They viewed truth not as objective, but rather as experiential and conceptualized through culturally relevant metaphors which orientate our mental maps and influence how we think and act.[22] Metaphors were consequently understood to have two particular functions in discourse: first, making complex matters comprehensible to a community and second to justify ideas of a particular group. In this respect, metaphors could both promote consensus but also cloak reality in the perceptions of those constructing the discourse. However, whilst the meaning of the metaphors outlined above may ultimately be to establish differences between in-group and out-group, righteous and unrighteous, saved and condemned, the actual subject matter of the metaphors considers the sighted body as the norm and the sightless body as a deviation from it.[23]

The body itself has of course been a 'rich vein' of metaphors throughout history. Paul Ricoeur identified the phrase 'a figure of speech' as a fitting idiom to demonstrate how the corporeal literally embodies ideas.[24] Mary Douglas likewise emphasized the importance of the physical body as a metaphor for the social body.[25] The 'body politic' is widely known from Graeco-Roman literature in which the physical body imaged the populace and social problems were frequently characterized as diseases. The symbolic meanings of these disease metaphors often aligned with dominant and domineering positions in conceiving of the marginal or lower classes as threatening the health of the whole polis.[26] To take a more recent example, Hitler used the body metaphor for the German nation 'infected' by Jewish 'parasites' in *Mein Kampf.* This Nazi metaphor system, in Andreas Musolff's words, initiated 'wider parts of the German populace into the implications of the illness-cure scenario as a blueprint for genocide. The Nazi anti-Semitic metaphor system thus provides a unique example of the cognitive forces that can be unleashed in the service of racist stigmatization and dehumanization.'[27] It is not insignificant that, whilst an 'able' body often escapes explicit comment, the disabled or ill body, as the above examples illustrate, often endures a more developed schematization in metaphorical constructions. Mitchell and Snyder conclude that the reasons why disability features in metaphorical images are twofold: first 'overheated symbolic imagery' and second disability's role 'as a pervasive tool of artistic characterisation'.[28]

Sontag also shows how metaphors are part of the 'arsenal' which equips people with the power to label and stigmatize certain individuals as 'other' and how illnesses and impairments can consequently be adopted to represent the malevolent in all sorts of domains and discourses. Disease metaphors used in situations of conflict or rejection only add to the suffering and marginalization of those who physically have the conditions. Once a cure has been found for a certain disease, Sontag argues it is demystified, however, until that time incurable ailments and disorders are always laden with metaphorical potential, with disease metaphors frequently employed as commentaries on rejected moral positions. This is perhaps particularly true in relation to the ancient world, where the discipline of physiognomy linked an individual's physical form with their inner disposition.[29] Many have tried to rationalize such difficult symbols or motifs by stating that, because cures for eye conditions were virtually non-existent at the time, it is not surprising that the eyes were frequently part of this physiognomic commentary.

Dale Allison outlines the ancient optical theory of 'extramission'[30] in which the eye was seen to emit its own particles of light which touched the external world and accordingly facilitated sight. This, he argues, lay behind Jesus' metaphorical statement that 'the eye is the lamp of the body' (Matt. 6: 22–3; Luke 6: 34–6). Joel Marcus also applied the theory to the healing of the man with blindness at Bethsaida: 'at the conclusion of our Markan narrative the formerly blind man is able to see clearly because his vision [has] become far beaming i.e. the internal light beams have been freed of the impediments that restricted them, so that they can travel the necessary distance to objects in the external world, and vision can ensue'.[31] The corollary of an understanding of the eye as an instrument which emits light is a blinded eye which emits darkness. Charles Hartsock consequently maintains that, given the importance of eyes in interacting with the world, 'it is not a far step to recognize the importance of the *lack* of eyesight and the largely negative conclusions that might be drawn from one whose eyes are as far from perfect as possible. [Moreover]...such a physiognomic assumption would further contribute to the rejection and fear of the blind in the ancient world.'[32] Those theorists adopting cross-cultural anthropology surrounding the 'evil eye' concept also support the extramission theory, in which an eye can cast spells on another in its sight. Evil eye is seen to be the result of envy and greed and potentially dangerous to others, an ophthalmic phenomenon which is symptomatic of 'a heart hardened and a hand shut to a neighbour in need'.[33]

Whilst Sontag focused on illness and disease, Naomi Schor (who herself experienced visual impairment) focused on disablement, in particular blindness, in her work on metaphors. She writes, 'I would add disablement and disfigurement to this register of bodily metaphors that void words of their charge of pain and sorrow, dread and death, and invest them with the language of stigma and shame and burden them with negativity.'[34] However, unlike Sontag who wished to break the knots which tied metaphor to illness, Schor submits that to disentangle them would be near impossible. Rather, she petitions that such metaphors should try to break free from the 'othering' tendencies which are destructive and negative and realize that defect and deficiency is more often than not the 'norm' for the physical (and social) body. In her words:

Any impairment of the five senses cannot be viewed as anything but a challenge, any loss of sensual apprehension of the world as anything but a catastrophic diminution of human potential. But as long as the dysfunction or deprivation of vision is metaphorized, viewed as monstrous...representation is placed in the service of ideology and blindness, naturalized. The time has come for a new body language, one which would emanate from a sensorium that is grasped in its de-idealized reality, in its full range of complexity.[35]

In short, defining individuals solely by a dominant trait such as blindness is akin to defining individuals exclusively on the basis of skin colour, sexuality, or gender. Such categories act not as descriptive definitions but rather as essentialist labels. Moreover this tends to reduce 'blindness' to nothing more than a binary opposite of 'sight' rather than acknowledge the embodied intricacies of sensory differences. What remains to be seen now is how, if at all, one can start, first, to expose the ableist frameworks within biblical texts and interpretations which stigmatize and stultify the sightless characters as 'blind' through negative metaphorical associations, and second, explore ways to take seriously the diverse agencies (physical, emotional, and social) of the sightless and attempt to construct alternative readings involving these composite and multifarious dimensions of their experience.

The Metaphor's Referent: Sightlessness, Stereotypes, and Stigma

When flesh and blood referents of metaphors are considered, namely individuals without physical sight, references to blindness are reconfigured not as innocent turns of phrase but rather ideologically laden statements which reveal much about a particular user's conceptions of the 'normal'. Whilst these ableist metaphors which adopt sensory impairment as their signifiers pepper biblical evidence, modern commentators have often not questioned these assumptions either and have oppressively reproduced such associations. The exposure of ableism as an ideology which prejudices the 'able-bodied' in cultural discourses and sustains what Stanley Hauerwas has aptly termed the 'tyranny of normality'[36] is vitally important in unmasking discriminatory suppositions. For such analysis sensitizes one to biases which have become naturalized in one's thinking and functioned literally as interpretive 'blind spots'.

There is much to support the idea that 'blindness' has been 'naturalized' in this way in the gospel narratives' portrayals of characters with visual impairments. Barasch's work on the characterization of blindness in literature and art of antiquity identifies three main 'levels' which are in turn instructive as regards the image's stigmatizing and exclusionary nature. The first is that 'blindness is perceived as a grave personal injury'.[37] Postures, walking, guides, sticks, and external appearances of blind characters are all recorded to bolster this impression. Expressions of pity are also frequently seen. The blind man of Bethsaida fits this mould. He does not petition for his own cause, rather others bring him to Jesus and appeal on his behalf (Mark 8: 22). Bartimaeus likewise encompasses the 'personal injury' of family dislocation. He is a destitute beggar, decked with the apparel of blindness including a beggar's cloak (Mark 10: 50). The man born blind in John's Gospel also indirectly assumes the appearance or posture of congenital blindness, for we are simply told 'he [Jesus] saw a man blind from birth' (John 9: 1), perhaps on a roadside begging. In short, these characters are in certain ways portrayed as 'dependent, childlike, passive…less competent than people who do not have disabilities'. [38]

Barasch's second level involves the explanations about the causes of the condition. Despite a whole gamut of eye conditions being experienced as a result of battle, dust, old age, etc. (and many not being particularly noted or stigmatized in any way) he notes that in literature and art of the ancient world many explanations would veer into supernatural domains. The condition is due to gods or demons and frequently is seen as 'a punishment for transgression of basic natural, moral or religious law'; thus the sightless one is perceived as 'a delinquent, and his blindness always reminds us of his grave guilt'.[39] The physical condition is thus seen to arise from an underlying social problem. Negative construction of this human sensory anomaly is central to all depictions of characters with blindness in the gospels. The people beg at Bethsaida for Jesus to touch the man (Mark 8: 22); Bartimaeus pleads for mercy (Mark 10: 48); and the congenitally blind man evokes an unprompted reaction from the disciples: 'Rabbi who sinned, this man or his parents, that he was born blind?' (John 9: 2). The third level for Barasch involves belief and meaning, including that blindness has some inherent significance in itself. This is where the link between the physical and metaphorical comes into play and one could rehearse again the aforementioned associations between blindness, sin, and death in contrast to sight's association with salvation and life.

Rather than swallowing the metaphorical discourse surrounding illness and sense-impairment wholesale, one needs to acknowledge that ableism itself is a fiction, particularly when dealing with sources from the ancient world, where corporeal diversity was 'the norm' rather than the exception for many. Whilst the study of the particular subculture and ideologies of the raft of people suffering from ophthalmic complaints in the ancient world may be lost to us, nonetheless, the multiple identities and minority group consciousness of sightless people today can offer important insights into their own reception of texts which use their condition as an ideological symbol. Historically, sightless people have had little chance, with various social and political powers silencing their voices, to articulate their own alternative sensory experiences. It is in listening to such voices however, that a playful and at times cathartic refiguring of sightlessness in literature and history can potentially be achieved.

Biographical Insights from Blind Interpreters

If one listens to authors who themselves have experience of disability one can trace how their experiences impact particular interpretations. Mitchell and Snyder talk about a 'disability consciousness' that is at play in such works. Others have noted how individuals who are disabled can 'put certain images, especially the tragic and fatalistic ones, in perspective',[40] through reference to their own experiences. Such studies are thin on the ground in biblical studies, a point recognized by Birch who labels this lack as an 'impairment' of the discipline.[41] One notable exception however is John Hull, who lost his sight in 1980 and has since devoted his entire career to exposing the sight-centricity of biblical texts and interpretation and forwarding a non-sighted response to them.[42] Hull stands at one with those who expose negative metaphorical interpretations of characters as disabling—'Yes, I know that you only meant it metaphorically but it is not very nice to be regarded as a metaphor for sin and unbelief'[43]—and condemns the sight-centricity of Jesus and the gospels. In response to the Gospel of John for example, Hull declares, 'the symbolism made me feel uneasy and I soon came to realize that this book was not written for people like me but for sighted people. No other book of the Bible is so dominated by the contrast between light and darkness, and blindness is the symbol of darkness.'[44] Hull is instructive in his non-sighted interpretations; not only does he reject the negative use of the label 'blind', he also rejects the ways in which non-sighted experience becomes the force of the meaning of the metaphor. For example, in reference to the deviant label of 'blind guides' given to the Pharisees in Matthew 23, he questions the logic on which the ascription is given. One charge levelled against the Pharisees is that they are too embroiled in the minutiae of law abidance to 'see' the whole picture. This is graphically illustrated by the saying that they strain out a gnat but swallow a camel (Matt. 23: 24). Hull counters this criticism in relation to the experience of sightless people which, by necessity, concentrates on immediate objects and concerns without necessarily gaining a 'vision' of the whole. He writes, 'If you sat with me at a table, Jesus, would you notice that although I managed to eat the last pea on the plate, I completely ignored my glass of wine because no-one had told me it was there?'[45] He takes a similar practical non-sighted approach in reference to the charge that Pharisees clean the outside of a cup but ignore the inside (Matt. 23: 25). He mentions how viewing the cleanliness of a cup is not an option for the sightless rather they have to feel the inside of a cup for stains and in Hull's own words:

> These techniques illustrate the difficulty of cleaning the inside as well as the outside. The fact that these observations are coupled with the accusation of blindness indicates that the word 'blind' is not used casually or accidentally, but arises from detailed observation of the behaviour of blind people. Oh dear, that makes it worse.[46]

The metaphor of the 'blind leading the blind' is also given an entirely new reading when interpreted biographically by a non-sighted person. Hull mentions that elsewhere in Matthew (Matt. 9: 27–31) two blind men navigate their way into a house to catch up with Jesus and do not come to any harm on their journey. He questions whether sighted people, like the evangelists, truly based their metaphors on observations of the sightless. For, in Hull's opinion, a sightless person familiar with a terrain would always help another sightless person unfamiliar with it. In his words, 'I have myself led blind people many times, and have in turn been led. We have never fallen into ditches, been run over on the road, or fallen down stairs.'[47] Moreover, Hull turns the metaphor on its head by actually playing it back on the sighted who do not always make the most dependable guides.[48]

Perhaps one of the fiercest criticisms that Hull reserves for the construction of discourses which marginalize the blind through metaphor is the fact that no blind followers are portrayed within the gospels, hence they are by default those physically considered 'outside' fledgling Christianity. Hull bemoans the fact that other major categories of the marginalized in gender or racial terms do find some models in characters like Mary the mother of Jesus, Mary Magdalene, Simon from Africa who carried the cross, and the Ethiopian traveller in Acts, but there are no such examples in relation to the blind. Whilst blind people often exemplify faith, such as Bartimaeus, they always become sighted. In Hull's words, 'This is why there was not a blind person amongst your disciples and why there could not have been one: you would have restored their sight and then they would no longer be blind.'[9] In commenting on John 9 he writes, 'when you spoke of God's works being revealed in the blind man, you were not referring to his blindness, but to the restoration of his sight. The implication is that God's works cannot be seen in a blind person but only in a blind person becoming sighted.'[50] The blind's status as 'representative others' so central in the metaphors is also consolidated by the fact that blind characters populating the parable discourses are time and again coupled with social outcasts. For example, Luke 14: 13–14 states 'When you give a feast, invite the poor, the crippled, the lame, and the blind. And you will be blessed, because they cannot repay you, for you will be repaid at the resurrection of the righteous.' Hull vehemently resists the assumption that the blind were and are *de facto* economically and politically marginalized, just because in biblical texts they were often pictured as such:

We [the blind] are invited to the banquet precisely because we have nothing to offer. Would my hunger overcome my fear of being patronised in this way?...Blind people are invited because they can do nothing, offer nothing. What we have to offer is our weakness.[51]

In short, Hull is largely critical of the fact that Jesus' ministry as imaged in the gospels was focused on restoration of sight rather than affirmation, compassion, and friendship to the blind. Jesus as the evangelists construct him operates by sight-centric values and thus conceives of the blind as an alien out-group. As Hull poignantly states, 'You would have led me by the hand out of blindness but you would not have been my companion during my blindness.'[52]

Hull does retrieve some positive alliances however, between himself as a blind person with aspects of the gospels which could counter-balance the negative metaphors outlined above. Jesus' experience as the blindfolded fool, derided and ridiculed by his captors in the passion narratives (Mark 14: 65; Luke 22: 63–5), though not the same as blindness, is nevertheless an experience which renders him temporarily sightless and brings some solidarity with this state. Hull declares to the blindfolded Christ: 'You have become a partner in my world, one who shares my condition, my blind brother.'[53] Similarly, the darkness that covers the earth at the crucifixion is interpreted by Hull as being forsaken by a 'sighted people's God' but maybe somehow an appreciation of sightlessness is the result. Finally, he plays with the metaphorical sightedness in the Emmaus accounts, where two disciples are effectively 'blind' to Jesus' identity (Luke 24: 16) and only at the point of recognition actually lose sight of Jesus once more (Luke 24: 31). In such an episode 'they became blind as far as you were concerned, but now it is the blindness of recognition, no longer the blindness of a failure to recognise. Sight has become more paradoxical.'[54]

Offering another biographical compendium, Sandy Resendes's unpublished thesis at the University of Concordia, 'The World at your Fingertips: Understanding Blindness' (2004), focused on the lives and personal identities of a sample of Canadians who, though legally blind, went blind after birth and had to adapt from a visual to a more unseen environment and adopt a new 'blind' identity. Of the three gospel characters under review the man at Bethsaida potentially fits this category (though whether he has been blind from birth, or lost his sight later is not explicitly defined) and Bartimaeus probably does, as his plea is 'Let me see [again]' (*anablepw* denotes, *regaining* one's sight, as well as becoming able to see). Resendes particularly concentrates on how such individuals deal with the stigma of their acquired condition, particularly through adjusting performances of identity, which in turn involves display and concealment. First, are the 'isolates' who 'disconnect themselves from the world outside and avoid certain situations in their daily life'.[55] One could play with the idea that the man in Bethsaida was such an isolationist, brought to Jesus, perhaps unwillingly, by sighted others. He could be someone who chose to keep out of public space, internalizing the 'shame' of his acquired condition, or unlike the congenitally blind, he may not have learnt the means by which he can navigate space without sight, he thus avoids potentially embarrassing situations. The people who bring him to Jesus are not characterized as 'friends', 'neighbours', or 'kinsmen', however, this may be implied in the forcefulness of their petition (*parakalew* denoting begging, urging, and encouraging). They may be set on reincorporating this man into the sighted and social world once more. On the face of it, Bartimaeus is another 'isolation-ist' character, he disassociates himself from communal life and sits literally and ideologically at margins and crossroads (Mark 10: 46). However, he also takes on shades of what Resendes terms a 'rebel' response, namely, 'forthright in asserting dignity' to the point of being 'verbally or physically abusive'; whilst others order him to silence, Bartimaeus defiantly cries out even more loudly: 'Son of David have mercy on me' (Mark 10: 48). He is more proactive in his response to his dismissive treatment by sighted others.

Deshen's 1992 ethnography, *Blind People: The Private and Public Lives of Sightless Israelis*, also documents how identities, behaviours, and social performances of the visually impaired are carefully man-aged to accord with sighted norms and parameters for interaction.[56] He reveals a will, on the part of sightless Israelis, to be perceived as conforming, as much as possible, to the dominant sighted culture and consequently avoid being subject to social stigma as a result. He notes for example how sightless Israelis 'adopted the common aversion to tactility' widespread in sighted culture, based in large part on modesty. He relays how he asked one lady if she ever wanted to touch a person's face to imagine it, to which she replied '"No! Never! Only primitive people do that."' Far more frequent were tales of sightless people's abilities to navigate places through reference to sound, touch, texture, and smell. Indeed the only times when sightless Israelis would link hands was to negotiate public thoroughfares. However, as Deshen states, this 'importantly, does not constitute an exploratory action to overcome sightlessness'.[57] How interesting then that Jesus' healing of the blind man at Bethsaida and the healing of the man born blind both involve what would offer most enlightenment to a sightless per-son, embodied materiality through touch, with spitting on eyes and laying on of hands and washing in water (Mark 8: 22–5; John 9: 6–7).

Deshen also focuses on attitudes to mobility aids by blind people and the ways in which they shape their practices in particular ways which are perceived to be inoffensive to the sighted. White sticks were used but with care not to tap the ground too loudly to disturb the 'sighted' world's peace. Moreover, in attempting to assimilate themselves to sighted culture, sightless Israelis would often adopt sighted technologies, like television sets, within their homes, even though they were completely unsuited to their sightless experience. Deshen surmised that social practices were adjusted to the ascendant (sighted) social stratum: 'mobility aids are prone to symbolisation like other artifacts in the domestic environment…this symbolisation can lead people to stigmatise artifacts and shun them'.[58] In the story of Bartimaeus the 'prop' which is encountered is his cloak (Mark 10: 50), an object 'commonly spread out on the ground to receive alms',[59] which we are told he throws off in order to come to Jesus. Many, interpreting this story metaphorically, have seen this action as representative of a discipleship virtue, giving away all he has in order to follow Jesus. However, we could also see it, in light of Deshen's insights, as a move to assimilate to sighted norms and distance himself from the trappings of his condition. Bartimaeus' plea to 'see again' and the fact that he 'follows Jesus' (v. 52) completes his reincorporation into the 'sighted' mainstream.

Not all elements of Deshen's ethnography, however, demonstrate a will to emulate dominant sighted, social patterns. Unlike the traditional models of ascribed precedence and atomistic kinship, Deshen shows how parents of blind children 'play a role in inculcating stigma'.[60] Israeli sightless adults spoke about their family's demeaning attitudes towards them and the low expectations relatives held for them regarding marriage prospects and occupational success. Many of these young persons were, as a result, keen to move out of the family home and seek an autonomous lifestyle. In marked contrast to 'the dyadic Mediterranean personality' often assumed in biblical studies, 'people wanted to be independent, even though logistically this was often difficult for them'.[61] In both the healing of the blind man at Bethsaida (Mark 8: 22–26) and the healing of blind Bartimaeus (Mark 10: 46–52) we also witness sightless adults who are alone or accompanied by those who are not blood family. 'Bartimaeus', whose name itself witnesses ironically to his position as both 'son of honour' and disenfranchised 'blind beggar', perhaps most acutely symbolizes the ambivalent identities of the sightless as regards kin groups. Likewise in John 9, though the parents of the man born blind appear in the narrative later, it is unclear what status their relationship is to him, indeed the man is initially encountered as alone and is known to others as a 'beggar' (John 9: 8).

Biographical insights from 'blind' interpreters help to expose ocular-centrist power strategies which sustain fictions of the 'normal' and variously bear upon the practices of both sighted and sightless in gospel narratives and their interpretations. In Lennard Davis's words, 'the power of the gaze to control, limit, and patrol the disabled person is brought to the fore. Accompanying the gaze are a welter of powerful emotional responses [which include]...horror, fear, pity, compassion and avoidance.'[62] How if at all, though, can we utilize such material to militantly subvert sighted norms and hermeneutical frameworks?

Transgressive Reappropriation of Blind Characters

'Transgressive reappropriation' is a radical approach which attends to 'the subversive potential or the hyperbolic meanings invested in disabled figures'.[63] Just as the label 'Queer' whilst once perceived as derogatory has become a transgressive identity label, so disability also in its 'embrace of the denigrating terminology forces the dominant culture to face its own violence head on because the authority of devaluation has been claimed openly and ironically.'[64] 'Crip' from cripple is an oft-cited example of such subversive adoption of terminology. In effect such studies make the dominant culture aware of its 'normalizing' outlook. In this sense disability is conceived as a confrontational challenge to 'ableist' ideologies and unquestioned social structures.

Offering a transgressive biographical voice, Georgina Kleege, in her celebrated volume *Sight Unseen* (1999) provocatively begins with the statement 'Writing this book made me blind.'[65] 'Legally blind' since puberty, Kleege whilst partially sighted and having lived her life shying away from 'negative' blind stereotypes, trying to assimilate to sighted culture and pass as 'normal', tells how she has since learnt Braille, uses a white stick, and has at last embraced and celebrated a 'blind' identity. She invites her readers, playfully using the metaphor of her sense-impairment, 'to cast a blind eye on both vision and blindness, and to catch a glimpse of sight unseen'.[66] Kleege questions and relativizes the label 'blind' which she says for most sighted people denotes absolute darkness, though cautions that only about 10 per cent of people classified as 'legally blind' have total loss of sight. Kleege likewise sensitizes her sighted readers to how 'disabling' categories or labels are often linked to social environments. In her own words, 'The definition has more to do with the ability to read print or drive a car than with the ability to perceive colour, light, motion or form. If I lived in a different culture or a different age, no one would define me as blind, I could transport myself on foot or horseback, I could grow or gather my own food, relying on my other senses to detect ripeness, pests, soil quality.'[67] In short, only certain categories of people were rejected and objectified in discourse, however the majority of the sightless in any culture were still privy to negative repercussions of such formulations.

Kleege's project was not only to bring sightless experience into an equivalent relationship with sighted experience, but rather to deconstruct the power of the eye and celebrate alternative ways of 'seeing' including touch and sound. This twofold agenda is brought into conversation here with elements of the characterization of the three sightless characters in the gospels under review.

Disabling Eyesight

In Kleege's words, 'the sighted can be touchingly naive about vision'.[68] Accordingly one of her main aims is not to reclaim a correspondence between sight and blindness but rather, in the words of Susannah Mintz, 'to disable sightedness itself' and 'undermine its epistemological stability'.[69] In Kleege's opinion blindness narratives are often places in which the privileged status of sight is sustained. Her work facilitates some interesting juxtapositions with the story of the man born blind in John 9 on this point. This blind character, perhaps more than any other in the gospels, carries at the outset the weight of his condition's stigma. Indeed, the story opens with the disciples asking Jesus about the cause of his congenital disability, his own or his parents' sin? Moreover, caught as he is between the metaphorical images of light and darkness, night and day, sight and blindness, his narrative purpose is given as nothing more than that in him 'God's work might be revealed' (John 9: 3). This is generally accepted to denote that Jesus will illustrate, through the man's healing, his status as 'The Light of the World'. The path of interpretation which sees metaphorical sight and spiritual insight being gained following the healing is well-trodden, but Kleege's unveiling of sightedness as deception, and her rejection of sight as a reliable concept, can also find arresting resonances with the story. Kleege cites the example of being in a crowded station; if you are expecting someone you know you may mistake them for someone else from a distance. On another day when you are not expecting a certain person you may be completely unaware of their presence. In Mintz's terms, 'if the only proper way to see "is to take something in at a glance and possess it whole, comprehending all its complexities"', Kleege suggests then that her sidelong way of looking, '"circumambulating" objects becomes an ideological metaphor for displacing the eyes as the source of power and eyesight as a guarantor of knowledge and identity'.[70]

In John 9 the ambiguity of sight is mentioned at a number of points. In the aftermath of his healing, neighbours and 'those who had been seeing him' are shown as divided among themselves whether their eyes are deceiving them: 'Some were saying, "It is he," others were saying, "no, but it is someone like (*omoios*) him"' (John 9: 9). Likewise the religious leaders have to consult the parents about the identity of the man, but they too seem unclear and reticent about what they observe in their son (John 9: 18–23). In short, the man causes division in the sighted world and demonstrates for John that sight is not to be equated with knowledge.[71] Ironically the man born blind becomes the primary voice of revelation in the sequence. He speaks directly in nearly a third of the forty-one verses, and 'remains not only in the foreground but as the centre of attention for the entire chapter'.[72] Courageous and audacious in his exchange with the Jewish leaders, it is he that unmasks their limited field of vision: 'If this man were not from God, he could do nothing', which evokes the satirical response: 'You were born entirely in sins, and you are trying to teach us?' (John 9: 34). Indeed, later in their interaction with Jesus, it is with wretched paradox that the Jews ask, 'Surely we are not blind, are we?' (John 9: 40). Disrupting the equivalence between sight and knowledge the blind man, in the words of Cornelius Bennema, 'surprises the reader with his cognitive abilities and how he reaches an authentic understanding of Jesus in the face of persecution'.[73]

The blind man as representative of the Johannine community, expelled from the synagogue, is another quite widely held metaphorical trope. In *Seeing Politics Otherwise: Vision in Latin American and Iberian Fiction*, Patricia Vieira sets out to uncover the unitary 'worldviews' which dictatorships and oppressive regimes forward as 'all-encompassing' visions. She notes how subjects are accordingly 'blinded'; however, blindness can also enable new opportunities for reimagining collective socio-political lives. In her words, 'it turns into a condition of possibility for the subject's self-making, a re-creation of a new positive identity on the ruins of its shattered predecessor'.[74] Like the blind man in John, blindness offers a space to give voice to the experience of marginalized, shunned, or 'oppressed citizens'.

A similar ambivalence surrounding the ability of 'sight' to offer 'knowledge' occurs in the account of Bartimaeus. Barasch notes the frequent ambiguity surrounding blindness in ancient literature and art, namely that lack of physical sight is often balanced by alternative insight:

On the one hand, he is the unfortunate person deprived of sight, the most valuable of the senses; on the other he is often endowed with a mysterious supernatural ability. This ambiguity of the blind person's nature may explain how it is possible for audiences to have pity and compassion for him, but at the same time also to sense awe, perhaps anxiety in meeting him.[75]

In this respect Bartimaeus may have been understood by Mark's first hearers as just the opposite of obtuse and unperceptive. Building on the work of Eleftheria A. Bernidaki-Aldous, Mary Ann Beavis has traced the figure of the blind poet and seer in antiquity; the former often recited classic texts by heart and the latter was frequently sought out by people to attain wisdom.[76] Beavis goes on to suggest that the image of the wise blind-prophet in both Graeco-Roman and Hebrew traditions may provide a more suitable framework for interpreting this story. She notes the parallels between the narrative and recognition oracles; she also makes much of the fact that Bartimaeus shouts out the reverential address 'Son of David, have mercy on me' (Mark 10: 48) and acknowledges Jesus with the possessive, 'My teacher' (v. 51) *before* the actual healing. Beavis accordingly regards these words not as a suppliant outcry, but rather prophetic and 'inspired speech' which predicts Jesus' messianic role. In this reading sightlessness is not an intractable block against knowledge, quite the contrary, Bartimaeus emerges as a character who is to be admired for his knowledge and speech. Whilst this interpretation could be criticized on the grounds that it would be odd for Jesus to heal Bartimaeus if his blindness were central to his prophetic profile, and it also perhaps falls into other potentially disabling stereotypes of the sightless as 'endowed with a mysterious supernatural ability',[77] it does nonetheless serve to underline the importance of this character's unsighted oral declaration. This leads directly to the recognition of his additional sensory faculty namely, speech. Oral cultures distinguish sound as an intermediary of life, which in Mark's world-view is of course creation through the word and 'hearing the good news'. Jesus beckons people to follow him primarily through speech commands (Mark 1: 17) and effects healings, exorcisms, and dramatic acts of power over nature through speech (Mark 2: 9; 4: 39). He likewise beckons faith to be demonstrated through speech (Mark 11: 23). For Mark words have not only dramatic but also bodily force. Mark's God is envisioned in the citation from the Hebrew Bible as a God whose identity is revealed in voice rather than vision (Mark 12: 26). Speech can be felt within the body, it is not just cerebral. Echoing Western ocular-centric biases, our 'readings' of the gospels have all too often made us turn 'blind eyes' to alternative sensory faculties and alternative cultural 'visions'.[78]

Resistant Touch and More Reciprocal Relationships

In her own disabling of the pre-eminency of the eye, Kleege celebrates her different ways of 'seeing', namely hands and touch as primary modes of encounter with the world. Both of Kleege's parents were visual artists and from them she learnt that true sight involved more than just hastily glancing at an object with one's eyes. She talks engagingly about viewing brushstrokes and colours of paintings close up, and where possible using touch as a medium of knowledge, thus focusing on material details which eyes easily miss.[79] She accordingly implores others to acknowledge the 'empowering hand in place of eyes'.[80] One could also evoke Oliver Sacks's narrative of Virgil, a man who, after having his physical sight restored, did not seem to have the framework to interpret the refracted images from his retina. He thus continued to 'see' by means of sound and touch.[81] Moreover, in talking about welding her father's sculptures with him, their hands together, Keege shows that touch can often dissolve differences between individuals and refigure their relationships.

It is not accidental that 'touch' is also central to two of the three characters with blindness that we have been surveying. The people who bring the man to Jesus in Bethsaida beg Jesus 'to touch him' (Mark 8: 22) and in their encounter, Jesus 'puts saliva on his eyes' and 'lays his hands on him' (Mark 8: 23). Similarly the man born blind in John 9 is subject to Jesus' placing saliva and mud on his eyes and being washed in water (John 9: 6–7). A major trajectory has been to see Jesus' touch as one of authority, displaying power over the illness or powers that caused it. However, as Kleege argues, touch can also be defiant in reordering and subverting social hierarchies. She cites the example of Maurice Pervin, the protagonist of D. H. Lawrence's 'The Blind Man', who encounters his sighted love rival, Bertie, and subverts his adversary's potency through touch, narrating his short stature and youthful (and inexperienced) face. In Kleege's words, 'by forcing Bertie to experience his face as the blind do, through touch, Maurice forces him to recognize his own sensual deficiencies. Maurice triumphs in this physical intimacy while Bertie is shattered by it.'[82] This sort of hierarchical subversion could offer an interesting reinterpretation of the man at Bethsaida's two-stage healing. In response to Jesus' question, 'Can you see anything?' (Mark 8: 23), the man replies he 'can see people, but they look like trees walking' (Mark 8: 24). Following a second laying on of hands by Jesus, we are told 'his sight was restored and he saw everything clearly' (Mark 8: 25). So often, as outlined above, this narrative is seen to represent partial spiritual sight, then on second touch full understanding, previewing Peter's declaration at Caesarea Philippi. However, using Kleege's subversive touch which challenges hierarchies of dominant and dominated, is there any way we can read this narrative as reordering the relationships between healer and healed? Commentators have almost unanimously interpreted Jesus' question as 'Can you [physically] see anything?', but is there any mileage in interpreting this question as Jesus asking the blind man to reveal knowledge to him? One biblical commentator who perhaps comes nearer to this perspective than most is John Duncan Derrett who searches for possible meanings to the man's vision of 'people like trees walking' (Mark 8: 24). In his words, 'what the man says has *more to it than meets the eye*'. Whether in Hebrew or Aramaic trees include 'stakes' and 'walking' includes 'being made to move about'; Derrett connects these images of a forest to idiomatic marching of armies. Such a 'pseudo-messianic vision, of the end, the siege, the trees decamping to avoid the onslaught of Yahweh, in Bethsaida, the territory of Philip the Tetrarch, is potentially explosive and needs to be corrected'.[83] It is at this point that Derrett slips into line with the majority of commentators in seeing this blind man's vision as something which needs 'correction' by Jesus' second-touch therapy: 'the words of the not-yet-expelled spirit, or, if one prefers, of the man still subject to its power, are yet another attempt by the Evil one to embarrass the recruiting programme of Jesus. It is nothing other than a highly impressive piece of false prophecy' (cf. Ezek. 13: 6 LXX),[84] which 'would create such alarmed confusion as would jeopardise the very business which Jesus was about'.[85] However, demons in Mark are of course ironically known to be voices of truth within the narrative; they witness to Jesus' true identity from the very start, whilst acknowledging their eschatological demise. In this respect Derrett's work can be reversed to show the blind man's eschatological vision is actually one which coheres with Jesus' messianic vocation. No demon has told an untruth in Mark's story world hitherto, why should this instance be any different? Unlike Peter who does not recognize the force of his declaration, the blind man truthfully witnesses to the climactic place of Jesus within eschatological salvation. The reference to trees could also denote the cross and persecution that early Christians must themselves endure and brings to mind the power of trees as oracular, divine agents often associated with shamanic powers or knowledge (see Gen. 2). In this sense, the blind man does not echo Peter, but rather is his complete foil. He sees the necessity of death. Whatever the actual meaning of the vision, by refiguring Jesus' question to the man, as 'Tell me what you see', the hierarchical power relationship between healer and healed is less divisively plotted, for each learns from the other.

Such episodes also testify in part to Kleege's reinstatement of communication, not just based on the eye but also the hands, words, and movement. For in her words, 'it is only through the mutual interaction of embodied selves that the myriad seams of reality and identity'[86] can be perceived. Hannah Macpherson's recent study goes further in questioning the sighted world's conception of touch based on hands alone and extends it to include feet, thus challenging 'traditional coordinates of body knowledge'. Documenting imagery of a walk or path for the blind, Macpherson claims that touching 'the landscape with their hands was not stated to be a necessary or desirable component—rather, they drew attention to their feet as enabling…the navigation and appreciation of the terrain'.[87] Could such experiences be retrieved in the story of Bartimaeus concerning following the 'way' (Mark 10: 52) of Jesus, who is not 'seen' by recipients of the gospel, but rather his words 'travel' through others' itinerant mission and ministry? In a similar vein to Hull's rejection of the sighted logic behind the 'blind leading the blind' metaphor, Lakshmi Fjord likewise asserts that blind people's abilities to navigate places through reference to sound, touch, texture, and smell are a potent aid to sighted people in catastrophic landscapes, such as the London Blitz and Hurricane Katrina. In such chaotic contexts fictions of the 'able-bodied' are exposed as such and the differently abled assume much more importance.[88] Could the eschatological background of the gospel discourses likewise provide a context in which the 'differently abled' (including women, children, eunuchs, the sensory impaired) are valued more positively within Christian communities and constitute a challenge to those metaphors that assume the sighted, able body as the norm? In Mikael Parsons's words, '[T]he covenant messianic community…includes even, perhaps especially, those who do not themselves have, *in the eyes of the larger culture*, a "whole" body'.[89]

Blind Spots and Metaphors: Refiguring Sightless Characters in the Gospels

Sidonie Smith and Julie Watson in their work on postcolonial autobiography pose the difficult question: 'when people have encountered representations of themselves as the objects of the surveyor's gaze…how do they begin to assert cultural agency?'[90] In many ways this postcolonial conundrum applies equally to disability images within literature such as the gospels. As has been seen, metaphors surrounding sightless characters are socially as well as physically mortifying. They do not represent innocent physiognomic traits, but are burdened, for good and ill by cultural-historical presumptions. Sight and blindness as has been seen have frequently featured as vivid social analogues for group identities. Such metaphors are simplistic formulations, which objectify entire groups with similar traits and as such, in Lorraine Code's terminology, function as 'hegemonic imaginaries'.[91]

Literature on corporeal, disease, and disability metaphors has attested that incurable ailments were identified as powerful repositories for discourse. The diseased body was frequently used to represent faulty ideologies, practices, and politics and belied a heightened schematization of the 'abnormal' body in contrast to the seemingly invisible 'normal' body. Whilst at times such metaphors' power are derived from their inert simplification to make certain political points (e.g. poverty spread like a cancer), at the same time, as Geraldine Pratt cautions, we must 'continually remind ourselves of what we are closing off through these strategic closures; we must encourage this process of remembering'.[92]

By engaging emic perspectives on 'blindness' here, the sighted are made to forsake not only ableist metaphors but also their eye-centric epistemologies. Blindness is only made manifest in the realms of sightedness, but as Elizabeth Edwards and Kaushik Bhaumik attest there is 'no pure visual object as such but only uses of embodied and sensorially engaged sight'.[93] Whilst many of the practices of the sightless as featured in the gospels demonstrate certain assimilations to the dominant sighted norm, or isolation from it, certain rebellious traits 'shout out' at the sighted world. Transgressive reappropriations from blind perspectives, including the recovery of touch and the reordering of social relationships it involves (also sound, kinaesthesia, and speech),[94] refigure characters not as passive recipients of healing, but rather powerful agents who, in different ways, can, at times, educate Jesus and other sighted individuals they encounter.

Whilst we can probably never escape our use of 'blindness' tropes in discourse and knowledge (a point also made by Helen Keller, the famous deaf-blind author, when she stated that anyone who knows Latin would realize how hard it is to escape 'some etymological link to sight and hearing'[95]), we can at least be aware of some of the damaging and oppressive ideologies which lurk around its use. Homi Bhabha famously stated that stereotypes and stigmatizing labels relied on regular use and corroboration, for they were by their nature changeable and insecure.[96] If transgressive refigurations of the sort proposed here could be pursued, then the binary division between sight and blindness would likewise be destabilized and more inclusive 'visions' of the 'normal' could start to be developed. Such moves would be praxis and human focused rather than just linguistic and rhetorical. By breaking the ideology of ableism we can start to acknowledge our 'blind spots', empathize with the consciousness of sightlessness, and in so doing touch sight yet unseen.

Sounding Out a 'Deaf-Mute': Mark 7: 31–37 as Deaf World Performance

In the 1986 film *Children of a Lesser God,* James Leeds, a speech instructor at a school for the deaf, sets about trying to coach his deaf lover, Sarah Norman, to speak. The film exposes his attempts to assimilate her to his 'hearing' culture as stifling, paternal, and oppressive, eclipsing her deaf identity and signed language. Her silence is a powerful resistance to his verbal agenda which ironically 'mutes' her signed communication. To his onerously persistent request to 'Speak to me', Sarah violently delivers her sole verbal utterance in the picture: 'Here you go! Hear my words! Hear my voice! Ah, you want more than that? I'm gonna scream!'[1] In Michael Davidson's estimation: 'for the hearing educator, speech is the key to normalization in hearing culture; for the Deaf signer, speech is the sign of an alienating process that merely performance can make evident'.[2]

This cameo can, to a certain extent, be paralleled with interpretations of the character of the 'deaf-mute' in Mark 7: 31–7. Commentators have over again seen the main point of the story as the man's integration into the hearing/verbal world through Jesus' messianic healing and the consequent fulfilment of Isaiah's prophecy that the 'ears of the deaf will be unstopped' and 'the tongue of the speechless will sing for joy' (Isa. 35: 5–6). Like blindness, the faculty of hearing and the organ of the ear have frequently functioned figuratively for cognition and insight in biblical traditions: 'true hearing involves listening and understanding', thus 'to have deaf, heavy, or uncircumcised ears is to reject what is heard'.[3] However, just as Sarah's dramatic performance of shrieking when placed in the straitjacket of the hearing/verbal world jolts us into re-evaluating her Deaf identity (and reveals she can verbalize but specifically chooses not to) so here I will, through insights from Deaf world arts, specifically Aaron Williamson's 1999 performance piece, *Phantom Shifts,* and Peter Cook and Kenny Lerner's collaborative poem, '*I Am Ordered Now to Talk*', seek to refigure both Jesus and the 'deaf-mute' as Deaf performers. Such artists subvert tidy binary oppositions between hearing and deafness, silence and sound, muteness and voice, and embody a much more complex world in which communication is not just verbal or aural but also visual, tactile, vibrated, pressured, and breathed. The actual medium of the characters' interaction in Mark 7: 31–5 thus becomes the main axis of meaning in the story, rather than the theological input of the outcome of the exchange—'his ears were opened, his tongue released' (Mark 7: 35)—which has been the major focus of meaning in the story for so many biblical exegetes.

A note on language: 'deaf-mute' in my title and throughout this chapter is specifically put in inverted commas to highlight not only the frequent use of this epithet for the character in biblical translations and commentaries,[4] but also to indicate a certain distance from the label and its ideological associations. 'Mute' does not only mean 'without speech', though it is often narrowly conceived in this way, but also has damagingly been used to denote ignorance: 'Are you mute or something?' Mute can also be used to represent Deaf individuals who do not speak an oral language as their communication is primarily through sign, or others who opt not to verbalize due to damaging or unwelcome notice their speech will draw. The *Children of a Lesser God* character, Sarah Norman, was of course an example of this. The term 'deaf-mute' is currently seen by many as offensive and disparaging, retaining some of the insulting and belittling assumptions encapsulated in the now abandoned designation 'deaf and dumb'.[5] These varied connotations will be kept in mind throughout discussion here. Also, when speaking about Deaf world arts and performance I will employ the now standard capitalization of 'Deaf' to denote Deaf cultural identity and Deafhood—'an analytical category of subjectivity rather than labelling identities'[6]—as separate from the medical phenomenon of impaired hearing. Deaf cultural identity is characterized by distinct social mores, history, and language. James Kyle and Bernice Woll's definition of Deafhood serves to illustrate its particular character: 'it involves a shared language [sign language]…it involves social interaction and politics…all of these interrelate and interact with attitudes towards other Deaf people'.[7]

The Silencing of the 'Deaf-Mute' in Biblical Studies

Silencing like muting, is used in cultural anthropology to denote the process by which certain marginal groups, on account of race, gender, social stratification, or perceived disability, are not represented in ethnographic records due to suppression by another dominant group's ideology. Cheris Kramarae, writing particularly on the muting of women, for example, states that 'the language of a particular culture does not serve all its speakers equally, for not all speakers contribute in an equal fashion to its formulation'.[8] The metaphor of silence and muteness is of course especially apropos to the present task. Here I will show a variety of ways in which the 'deaf-mute's' agency and communication strategies have completely been eclipsed by audio-centric agendas which picture the man as incapable of communication, wholly dependent on others, and link his condition with intellectual incapacity and the demonic.

Mary Ann Beavis in her recent commentary on Mark notes how Mark 7: 31–7 has 'received very little scholarly attention in journal articles, perhaps because of its similarity to the healing of the blind man in 8: 22–6'.[9] Both stories are often subsumed into a single discussion in biblical commentaries, united by their similar narrative structures and the very tactile and magical techniques of treatment used by Jesus in both instances. In effect both recipients of the therapies are totally silenced in such analyses, they function, as Lewis rightly states, merely as 'objects to demonstrate the power of Jesus'.[10] Many equate the physical deafness with spiritual ineptitude[11] and others have linked the location of the healing, Gentile territory, to be 'symbolic of the future mission in which Gentile ears would be opened to hear the gospel and tongues loosed to praise God for the salvation wrought in Jesus'.[12] Thus both the man's condition and location mark him out as 'other', and, as is common in disability characterizations, he becomes a crutch in the story to illustrate the fulfilment of prophecy and fruits of messianic healing.[13]

At the opening of our story the 'deafmute' is not given a personal name, but rather introduced solely by his condition (*kwfon kai mogilalon*). Brought to Jesus, he is considered by commentators to be submissive and totally reliant on the directions of others. Whilst as Bas van Iersel notes, deafness would not necessarily have impeded the man's ability to travel around,[14] the fact that he does not approach Jesus autonomously encourages commentators to put him into a similar category as the blind and paralytic who are likewise managed and moved by those around them.[15] The 'deaf-mute' is further silenced by negative intellectual attributes he is presumed to demonstrate. Many commentators note that *kwfos*, usually translated 'deaf', can also denote 'mute' in Greek.[16] 'Mute' can implicitly harbour a malign association between the inability to articulate clearly and an inability to think clearly, forcing one to be vulnerable and powerless.[17] Gundry, for example, forthrightly states:

> The Greek word translated 'mute' means 'speaking with difficulty', that is, with *inarticulate grunts, and, of course, deafness caused muteness. Having never heard, he never learned to talk.* The people's imploring Jesus stresses the *helpless plight* of the deaf mute.[18]

Of course ancient elite, literary sources, for whom dextrous ability in reading, writing, rhetoric, and oral delivery were central, frequently made disparaging associations between deafness and an inability to articulate oneself clearly. Martha Edwards in her provocatively titled piece 'Deaf and Dumb in Ancient Greece' (for in her words that 'obsolete expression [deaf and dumb] is an apt description of the way in which a deaf person was perceived in ancient Greece',[19] namely as one of 'diminished worth'[20]) cites the example of Midas who turned deaf on account of his foolishness and wore asses ears to demonstrate his idiocy.[21] Whilst Edwards is keen to stress that there were likely differences between elite and non-elite views on the associations and implications of speech and acumen, it is almost impossible to read history from below on such points, thus 'it is the literate elite on whom we must rely for almost all our information about deafness'.[22]

Aristotle famously stated that 'all persons who are deaf from birth (*kwfoi ek genetes*) are dumb (*eneoi*) as well: though they can utter a sort of voice, they cannot talk'.[23] (Note the division between sound and words made here.) The pseudo-Aristotelian *Problemata* goes further when it makes a physiological link between loss of hearing and loss of speech: 'For men become deaf (*kwfoi*) and dumb (*eneoi*) at the same time, and diseases of the ear change into diseases of the lung. So when men scratch the ear, they cough at the same time.'[24] Exploring the association of deafness and muteness in Graeco-Roman Antiquity, Christian Laes has noted an ancient tendency to 'privilege muteness over deafness'. [25] He cites Herodotus' tale of Croesus' two sons, 'one of whom was wholly undone for he was deaf', and Croesus' cruel admission that on account of this he in effect only has one son, 'for that other, since his hearing is lost to him, I count as no son of mine'. However, when Sardis falls it is this same son who delivers his first verbal utterance, a cry to the soldier about to kill his father, 'Man, do not kill Croesus!'[26] Laes notes that whilst 'deafness' looms large in Herodotus' story, in its various receptions by Nicolaus of Damascus, Cicero, and Valerius Maximus deafness is hardly mentioned and the thrust of the story becomes the son's inability/ability to speak, this in Laes's opinion is due to the fact that in the ancient world the incapacity to converse had the most serious bearing on one's ability to function in collective, social, and political life.[27] Ancient commentators were therefore 'biased by the impairment which had the more important consequences in an oral culture'.[28]

It is interesting in this light that frequently biblical commentators on this story tend to focus pre-eminently on deafness as the most serious impairment and muteness seems to be treated as secondary, or as a mere corollary of deafness. Yong, for example, supposes that 'deafness was often understood by the ancients more in terms of intellectual rather than sensory impairment, deaf persons were assumed incapable of bearing legal responsibility and [were as such] politically marginalised'.[29] It is of course often noted that Mark adds the rare term *mogilalon* (lit. having difficulty with speech or mute)[30] in his character description, which many exegetes see as a direct echoing of Isaiah 35: 6 in the Septuagint rendering, and this perhaps encourages them to disassociate the two phenomenon.[31] The perceived cause of the character's condition also plays a part in 'muting' his agency and identity. The fact that part of the cure for his 'muteness' is narrated as a tongue's freedom from bondage (*desmos*) (lit. translates bond, chain, imprisonment, prison) encourages commentators to understand the source of the condition to be demonic. Robert Bratcher claims that the mechanism of spitting was often used by exorcists in delivering a subject from the ravages of an evil spirit.[32] Similarly, Morna Hooker, probing her cosmic conflict theme in the gospel, vividly pictures this character bounded by Satan.[33] Others have linked the condition to the man's sin: Marie Noonan Sabine for instance writes, 'the Aramaic phrase *ephphatha* literally means "be released" which links to Jesus' saying to the paralytic that his sins are released (2.5)'.[34] Others have connected Jesus' exhalation and gesture in v. 34 to an invocation of God's power over evil spirits. Robert Stein, corroborating this viewpoint notes that 'a later reference in Mark in which Jesus tells his disciples that a demon that caused muteness (Mk 9: 25) could only be cast out by prayer (Mk 9: 29) gives additional support to this interpretation'.[35] In all these estimations, the 'deaf-mute's' condition therefore slips from the 'ear' and 'mouth' alone to swamp his whole being in evil. Illustrating this colonization of the demonic, William Lane writes 'the act of healing itself was accomplished with the word of liberation addressed not to the defective auditory organs but to the man as a whole person: "Be Opened."'[36] He goes on to state that for Mark the bondage was also likely to demonstrate the social shackling which muteness imposed on him, disabling full participation in social and political relations.[37] Perhaps the most arresting muting of the character comes at the end of the story, when even though the narrator tells us the man 'was speaking plainly' (*elalei orthws*, v. 35), he is given no direct speech in the narrative whatsoever and the ambiguous ending could be read that the people, not including the formerly 'deaf-mute' man, cry out the refrain of praise (v. 36). Ironically, even when healed, the 'deaf-mute' is still verbally and ideologically, silenced within the narrative.

All the above features serve to crush, deaden, silence, and mute alternative conceptions of the 'deaf-mute's' characterization. Even those exegetes who seem to show at points more consciousness of the 'deaf-mute's' biography still often exhibit normalizing agendas in their analyses or paternal readings of Jesus' tactics in communicating with him. For example, Ben Witherington avers that the man's hearing impairment was not congenital, as the man is said to have 'spoken plainly' following the healing, indicating he had acquired speech prior to losing his hearing.[38] However, Witherington makes no comment whatsoever on how this character may have been engaged in communication in the mean time. Others have been keen to point out that the gestures involved in Jesus' exchange are to facilitate a more sensitive interaction given the man's condition.[39] Frequently such viewpoints are, however, still tinged with condescension and audiocentric sentiments which centre on Jesus' generous accommodation to gestural communication which is viewed as a poor relative to speech. Clayton Robinson's declaration, that 'healing came through touch as they requested, but in the process Jesus creatively met the man at the point of his faith and cured him of his deficiencies',[40] is symptomatic of such viewpoints. In short, it is indisputable that the character of the 'deaf-mute' has been silenced by hearing/verbal agendas of commentators, who have eclipsed the man's identity completely and laden him with negative assumptions which have furthered his stigmatization. Even at the climax of the story, rather than any sustained reflection on the transformed position of the healed individual being given, commentators still seem to assume his marginality (he has no voice, others declare what has been done for him). In common with many caricatures of disability within literature here, as Susan Gregory notes, the 'deaf-mute' is not so much a real person who happens to be deaf but rather a deaf character who on the whole seems not to be a real person.[41] He stands as a static buttress in the plot to exhibit the restoration of wholeness and the dawn of the Kingdom of God.

If multiple features do sustain the ideological muting of the 'deaf-mute' and promote the cult of the hearing as normal, then any method of recovery will need to access 'the social-symbolic world of persons with disabilities, such that the disabling framework of the normal becomes questionable'.[42] What remains to be seen is how, if at all, it is possible to 'sound out' the 'deaf-mute's' own performance strategies and refigure both his and Jesus' interaction with a more prominent Deaf consciousness. Engagement with Deaf world arts and performance seems one promising prompt to start this conversation.[43]

Deaf World Arts: Subverting Audism and Cultivating a 'Third Ear'

Audism is an ideological stance which values hearing and spoken language over other forms of communication and meaning. The hearing world has, at various junctures, sought to normalize the Deaf, whether it be through oralist education, the insertion of cochlear implants, or other such assimilations to the hearing world. In Tony Booth's terms, 'the purpose of normalization is seen not only as giving deaf and partially deaf young people access to the hearing world but also as *making them more acceptable to it*'[44] Reacting against such oppressive strategies, Harlan Lane, from a Deaf-advocacy perspective, believes that the Deaf community should be understood as an ethnic group with a rich history, tradition, and language. For, in Lane's opinion, 'like all members of other ethnic minorities, Deaf people are generally not disturbed by their identity, despite the need to struggle for their rights. Culturally Deaf people have always thought and think today that being Deaf is a perfectly good way to be, as good as hearing, perhaps better.'[45] Paddy Ladd likewise sees the 'culture concept' as central in movements of resistance and change. In his opinion, 'culture is the key held in common with other colonized peoples and linguistic minorities. Political and economic power may or may not be the driving forces behind language oppression. But both the key and the lock in which it turns is culture'.[46] Conceiving of the Deaf as a cultural minority, akin to an ethnic group, has also allowed interpreters to utilize insights from postcolonial theory to reflect on oppression suffered under hearing imperialism. Lewis reveals that historical instances of the disempowerment of the Deaf (particularly in reference to their own language) are analogous to political colonization defined as 'a process of physical subjugation, imprisonment of an alien language...and the regulation of education on behalf of colonial goals'.[47] Davis has also drawn comparisons between racial stigmatization and Deaf stigmatization as outsiders, for in his view 'if an *ethnos* is defined as a culturally similar group sharing a common language...then the Deaf conceivably fit that category'.[48]

Deaf world artists have been particularly active not only in exposing and challenging the imperialism of audism but also producing a discourse which attempts to rehabilitate the perspective of the muted/silent Deaf minority. Susan Burch for example, explains how audiocentric views often understand deafness as 'the inability to perceive sound' and, like the commentators on our passage, view 'deafness as a communicative as well as physical disability'.[49] Such perspectives unhelpfully sustain binary oppositions between 'hearing/Deaf' when,

in reality, the borders between the two are much more fluid. In rejecting erroneous dualisms and objectifying stereotypes of Deaf culture,
Burch sets about initiating a dialogue between Deaf and hearing
contexts by outlining the communicative potential of poetry, itself
a genre which has traditionally been assumed to only occupy hearing, verbal, or written space. Deaf poetry, delivered in sign language
combining hand shapes, bodily, and facial articulations, and drawing
on dramatic and mime traditions, asserts a certain destabilizing of the
poetic genre. In Burch's words:

ASL [American Sign Language] poetry subverts both the hearing and written paradigms normally associated with poetry. Signers and viewers of ASL
poetry become the majority; the hearing audience become the minority. The
discomfiture of this position, unusual in itself for the hearing, is intensified
by the non-written and non-oral nature of ASL poetry and by the use of a
language most hearing do not understand. This reversal of roles and this new
kind of poetry become powerful challenges to old traditions and misconcep-
tions, to normal concepts of poetry and to the role of the audience. Poetry is
no longer abstract; in ASL it is a physical presence that cannot be avoided.[50]

Kanta Kochhar-Lindgren, in her exploration of other types of Deaf
Performance (drama, mime, installation art, etc.), similarly reflects on
dissension from audio-centric norms. She proposes the cultivation of a
'third ear' which she defines as 'a method of hybrid listening' in showing how Deaf artists pull apart the hegemony of hearing and initiate a
different soundscape in which the Deaf/hearing dualisms are disrupted
and multiple 'sound waves' resonate and converse with one another.[51]
Listening with the 'third ear' has important hermeneutical implications, for it shifts attention from the explicit subject matter of the piece
and focuses instead on its communicative and expressive repertoire. As
such, audiences start to 'sense' a performance in alternative ways: 'the
silences, the gaps between image and sound, the incongruities between
movement and text, dissonant intercessions of noise and gesture and
the positions of the performing bodies that speak to us'.[52] By using
different media the borders of the language communities become permeable and the audiences themselves (comprised of both hearing and
Deaf) are transformed from passive 'spectators' to active 'spec-actors',
participants and performers in the piece. Deaf performance thus refigures the traditional hearing–Deaf hierarchy, by compelling the hearing

world to acknowledge the legitimacy and equality of other modes of communication. Signed communication in particular is visually orientated, must be done face to face, and therefore the audience, as much as the actors and dramatists, become caught up in the performance.[53]

With the sensitivities of a 'third ear', I am going to creatively juxtapose two Deaf performances with our story of the 'deaf-mute'. In common with Deaf cultural arts, outlined above, the focus in this interpretation will not be on the explicit content of the story (which brings certain relief as it ameliorates to some degree the uncomfortable status of the story as a healing narrative which is frequently viewed as symptomatic of an audio-centric 'normalization' agenda from a Deaf perspective) but rather the media of communication variously adopted, adapted, corroborated, or questioned within the story. Wayne Morris has recently challenged the utility of biblical texts from a Deaf perspective, given that 'for Deaf people, words—spoken or written—are thought to be a peculiarly hearing phenomenon'.[54] Because sign languages' primary media are visual and spatial, sounds and texts are not part of their communicative repertoire. Morris also notes that metaphors, as understood by hearing cultures, literally 'fall on d/Deaf ears' within the Deaf community. In Morris's words, they are 'linguistic characteristics…peculiar to hearing people'.[55] This caveat notwithstanding, one can still approach a text with a Deaf-sensitive hermeneutical framework, for interpreting with sign and gesture is not entirely anachronistic with regard to ancient literature. Christian Laes, for example, notes that gestural communication for Deaf-mutes was known in antiquity. Citing Augustine's *De Magistro* and other sources he notes how finger counting, rhetorical performances, and 'mute' trade with foreigners of a different tongue all had recourse to gestural media in their communication.[56] Edwards likewise notes that 'a Greek would not have differentiated between gestured communication and true sign language, or cared much, probably, that there was a difference'.[57] The participation of the audience who would have originally been subject to the performed oral delivery of the story will also be kept in mind throughout. Brenda Joe Brueggemann relates how disability performances challenge autonomy and reorder relationships between actor, spectator, and subject as separate and rather conceive of these as cooperative and collective.[58] This certainly will be attested in part, here.

Aaron Williamson's 'Phantom Shifts'

In 1999 the British Deaf performance artist, Aaron Williamson, produced a work titled 'Phantom Shifts' which comprised a sequence of expressive contemplations on the authority of the ear and a disruption of the neat equation between the sound of a voice and hearing. Williamson lost his hearing in his twenties and much of his artwork has been devoted to exposing the socially constructed nature of both Deaf and hearing ever since. In the first 'act' called 'Breath', Williamson carried a large ceramic ear on his back to a soundtrack of his own strained breathing as he bore the ear's physical weight. At certain points the soundtrack cut out, leaving the [hearing] audience in silence and violating the link between the images and the sounds they were witnessing. Williamson ended this opening scene on the ground, literally buried under the weight of the enormous sculpted ear. He was clothed in white and to the audience his body and the plaster ear were virtually indistinguishable. Kochhar-Lindgren notes that the spectacle before the audience reverberated in multiple ways: the ear is an ideological burden for Williamson, weighing him down socially and politically. He also makes the organ of the ear very visible and by carrying the ear on his back it is exiled from its more usual place in the corporeal order. All these elements force the audience to question: 'what happens if we start to line the ear up with different parts of the body? Is there, perhaps, somewhere else the ear belongs? What if the whole body is an ear?'[59]

In many ways the 'deaf-mute' at the opening of our story can likewise be imaged as saddled with an ear which completely bears him down. He is totally dependent on others (Mark 7: 32), such is the weight of his affliction. Moreover, his identity, like Williamson's, is made completely indistinguishable from his condition. In Gundry's words, 'the whole man is concentrated in his ears'.[60] Edwards accordingly witnesses that, 'Because deafness and muteness were intertwined, models of mouth or complete heads are just as likely as ears to have represented deafness. But the ear was, certainly, the most obvious charge of hearing, listening, and understanding, and this is why it was important to have the ear of the god from whom one sought a favour'.[61] The people accordingly urge Jesus to 'lay his hands' on the man, a well-known motif in biblical traditions, variously functioning as 'a symbol of blessing, power, the communication of authority and benediction…and healing'.[62] However, Jesus' actions do not follow their expected plans.

Jesus' removal of the man from public space and view (Mark 7: 33) signifies a move away from hearing culture and a context in which hearing and meaning are perceived as unified. Both Jesus and the 'deaf-mute' embody an alternative charged performance in which other sensory dimensions beyond hearing and words become all important. Such a move also encourages the audience to enter a reordered sensorium in which the ear does not take pre-eminence and the 'deaf-mute' can start at last to remove the audio-centric mill-stone which doggedly inhibits his character and social intercourse. They rather encounter a vivid visual scene in which hearing and words seem peripheral and to a certain extent, redundant. Indeed those cultures that communicate without words often put far greater emphasis on visual perception. Illustrating this, George Veditz speaks of the Deaf as 'first, last and for all time a people of the eye'.[63]

In his second 'act' titled 'Wave' Williamson covered over the sculpted ear with a cloth to symbolize the erroneous link between deafness and stupidity—so-called 'cloth-ear'. Williamson again used deep breathing as a sound to accompany his lifting of the material in a wave-like motion. For the audience, the wave could symbolize breath, or sound-waves, however for Williamson as a Deaf performer it is assumed that the 'gesture is about the separation of breath from sound, of sound from sense. The ear is less an extension of the body than a prosthesis toward which the body aspires.'[64] Others have noted that 'Wave' may be providing a pointed commentary on the fact that voices and sounds often 'pass over' ears without meaning. More provocatively, Williamson may well have wanted to exhibit the ear as an inert, passive, moveable object when confronted with visual and tactile sensory data. Again the audience is prompted to ask 'What plaster ear can hear image? Who hears image? How do we hear the image of sound? Since the sequence is repeated a number of times, in approximately the same way, the section can be interpreted to indicate the need to repeat the phrase in order to get the point across: reception may or may not occur'.[65] To close the performance, Williamson utters the sound 'Ha': 'the most expressive and primal of sounds, deployed equally in laughter and crying',[66] before once again lowering the cloth over the sculpted ear. In Kochhar-Lindgren's opinion the scene completely regroups the sensorium and associated 'functions' of the sensory organs:

Everything about this scene is embodied, materialized, kinesthetic, and visual. Though we may not be able to hear the 'ha', the visibility of the taking of a breath, the swing of the arms as the breath passes through Williamson's body and transmits into the rippling of the cloth, the distance between Williamson and the ear, and the final roll of the cloth over the ear gives us the palpable experience, translated, of hearing differently (metaphorized and materialized). Here we hear through the body, as Williamson suggests, by carrying the ear into the installation space on his back.[67]

As Jesus touches the man's ears, spits, and looks to heaven and groans (Mark 7: 34) we find an equivalence of themes with Williamson's 'breath'. This scene too moves beyond referential 'wordiness' and exhibits a far more rasping collective of sounds from the body and a visual spectacle which is both arresting and provocative. Fingers are pushed into bodily orifices, saliva is coughed and spewed. The fact that Jesus' only utterance '*Ephphatha*' (Mark 7: 34) is itself a 'foreign' term in need of translation by the author[68] also plays a part in distancing the audience from a simple equivalence between words and meaning. Delivered orally, without immediate translation, as in the written text, such a term would literally 'pass over' a native ear. Indeed Mark's translation has been seen by some as a deliberate ploy to 'remove any quality of esoteric strangeness from them, and thus the translations neutralize any magical power that the foreign words might have',[69] in short a normalization of a volatile act. *Ephphatha* gutturally delivered thus produces physiological and ideological 'sound-waves' which rumble and vibrate dramatically in movement from one body to another. Moreover it is this basic sound which is used when looking up to heaven to invoke the divine's attention. Elsewhere in the narrative the divine is dramatically revealed through the renting asunder of the heavens and visionary signs like the dove at the baptism (Mark 1: 10) the transfiguration vision (Mark 9: 2–7), and the violent ripping of the temple curtain (Mark 15: 38). God is present in both sounds and visions reverberating through the body in Mark's world.[70] Such elements also question the hearing (with sound)/Deaf (without sound) binary. Carol Padden and Tom Humphries expose this fallacy when they state that the audio-centric supposition that 'sound plays no part in their [Deaf] world...are deeply distorted. The truth is that many Deaf people know a great deal about sound, and that sound itself—not just its absence—plays a central role in their lives.'[71] Michele Friedner and Stefan Helmreich similarly show how Deaf-world can 'penetrate' hearing contexts and vice versa. Deep vibrations, bass rumbles, and breath which cross distances and are experienced by both hearing and Deaf can question what they term 'the ear centrism of Sound studies' and the assumption that Deaf people sense through sight alone.[72] Like Williamson's performance, Jesus' action too refigures hearing not just as a reception of words and voice but rather as a visual and spatial practice in which communication is 'seen' and sounds come from deep within the body in a foreign tongue. In so doing he challenges in his performance the shackling of discourses which question neat equivalences between hearing, spoken words, and knowledge.

Both Williams and Mark 7: 31–7 also play with the interplay between sound, vision, image, and gesture and make their respective audiences active participants in the performances of the work. Whilst, in narrative terms, Jesus and the 'deaf-mute's' exchange is done in private on the margins of the hearing world, it is embodied by Mark's audiences in a public reception of the gospel, and in turn reorients their maps of meaning. It is not insignificant in this respect that the 'deaf-mute' remains without direct speech even at the end of the story when the narrator reports that he could 'speak plainly' (Mark 7: 35). This feature could be read subversively, not as a muting of the character, but rather a protest against audio-centric norms. One way to disrupt the hegemony of hearing is silence. Developing this trajectory, the deaf-mute could be remodelled as a resistant character who defies what Stanley Hauerwas has termed the 'tyranny of normality'.[73] Such musings produce counter-memories or hidden transcripts which crumble the hegemonic through envisioning alternative narrations. Davis likewise, from a Deaf perspective, has noted the violations through silence that can be affected within narratives. In his words, 'deafness in effect is a reminder of the "hearingness" of narrative. It is the aporetic black hole that leads to a new kind of deconstruction of narrativity.'[74] Communication for Mark is felt within the body, it is not just cerebral. Inarticulate sound has a power and energy independent from mere reference.

Kochhar-Lindgren appropriates Stuart Hall's concept of 'emergent ethnicities' to Williamson's work to show how he decentres hearing. This focuses on the claim that one has to articulate one's own experience in order for one's 'emergent identity' to develop. In that way others, also, when faced with these emergent powers will be enabled to 'hear differently, more richly', and in Kochhar-Lindgren's terms will accordingly 'be oriented in new ways toward contemporary questions of the hybrid production of meaning and come to know, through practice, what it means to listen with the third ear'.[75] In this sense the fact that the 'deaf-mute', while recorded by the narrator as 'speaking plainly', does not directly speak is significant. Oral deliveries of gospel narratives involved the performer taking on the personalities of the respective characters. The performer, therefore never voices the 'deaf-mute' at all. This character persists as a model of bodily communication rather than oral communication. In contrast it is the people who zealously proclaim (Mark 7: 36) what they witness and in direct speech voice the fulfilment of prophecy (Mark 7: 37). Most importantly it is the audiences of both Williamson and Mark's performances who have also been developing a 'third ear' (sensitivity to other channels of communication) through the exchanges they witness. Just like Williamson's audience, we presume Mark's too can start to co-perform in a world in which the hearing/Deaf binary is both challenged and questioned.

Peter Cook and Kenny Lerner's 'I Am Ordered Now to Talk'

'I Am Ordered Now to Talk' is part of *Flying Words*, a collaboration between a Deaf poet (Peter Cook) and hearing poet-interpreter (Kenny Lerner). Their partnership involves signed communication (usually by Cook) and piecemeal voiced translation (usually by Lerner). Cook normally remains the central visual focus and in this respect it is his medium of sign which surpasses the phonetic voice. Whilst the coupling of a hearing translator and a Deaf artist is in Davidson's words 'problematic to say the least' for Deaf nationalists (in some way akin to the problematic focus of Mark's story, namely the 'healing' of a 'deaf-mute'), nevertheless for these two it is 'a way of extending gestural potentiality of ASL into what we might call an "imminent critique" of audist ideology'.[76] This is given particular focus by the fact that Lerner's translation rarely renders the signs wholesale. The hearing audience is always left wanting.

In the piece 'I Am Ordered Now to Talk' the native media respective to each (speech and sign) are swapped quite purposefully as Cook initiates a satirical look at the differences between oralist teaching (through lip reading and speech) and manual learning (through sign). One of the most explicit ideological clashes between signed and spoken languages has occurred in the promotion of oralism within educational practice, with oralism defined as 'an ideology that privileges spoken (and written) languages over signed ones, often denying the validity or linguistic nature of signing altogether'.[77] Cook remembers with horror the therapies he endured at school which tried to coerce him to speak. Cook, as the Deaf performer accordingly verbalizes, while Lerner, the hearing performer, signs—both thus perform alienation from their mother-tongue. One of the most significant factors uniting Deaf culture is of course the use of sign language. Harlan Lane speaks of 'the mother tongue' as an 'aspect of the soul of a people' and a visible mark of ethnicity within a specific culture. Accordingly, 'a language not based on sound is the primary element that sharply demarcates the Deaf-World from the engulfing hearing society'.[78] The respective media by which spoken and signed languages are communicated are very different. The former is based on sounds and words, the latter on three-dimensional uses of hand and body movements and facial expressions. Another defining feature of sign-language use is of course occupying a minority status within a hearing culture. Ladd states, 'sign language users know that they cannot find "home" within a majority society until the day when that society is able to use their language'. They must endure the daily struggle of coexistence 'alongside majority culture members who do not understand them'.[79] Deaf clubs and schools are accordingly often pictured as safe houses in which sign language is the norm and in which there is a 'general disassociation from speech'.[80]

When 'I Am Ordered Now to Talk' is staged a copy of a written 'script' is given to the audience prior to the performance. This too disorientates communication for 'hearers' may well search the script to decipher Cook's words, but in so doing consequently miss the dramatic visuals which are the centre of the piece. Cook's vocals are to a hearing audience stilted and awkward, whilst Lerner's signs to the Deaf are rigid and overstated. As a result, the communication channels of the delivery reinforce the poem's ferocious condemnation of education which does not respect one's own language. Cook's awkward and cumbersome delivery of the constant refrain 'you-must-now-talk' gets more and more frenzied as the performance progresses. Cook's 'speaking' of course brazenly manifests the oppressive audist ideology he was subject to, whilst Lerner's silence and exaggerated signs powerfully demonstrates embodied language. Both performers transgressively exhibit the media they adopt. Hearers are with due reason told to 'feel paranoid' at the outset of the performance.

In Mark 7: 31–7 we likewise witness two characters on a stage, where each in turn adopts a language which is foreign to them. Jesus performs gestures and signs which are considered by some to echo 'pagan'/'magical' practices with saliva, indeed Howard Kee proposes that this may be more irregular if it breaches purity laws, spitting potentially being connected with shaming (Num. 12: 14),[81] touching body parts, and employing strange words. He 'speaks' an uncharacteristically, for him, gestural and 'foreign' language that others feel a certain distance from and embarrassment with, indeed Mark translates the *ephphatha* and Luke and Matthew omit this story and its 'alien' therapies altogether. The 'deaf-mute' though silent throughout is reported to 'speak plainly', though as mentioned above, he never delivers any direct speech in the narrative whatsoever.[82] Both seem to inhabit languages which are unfamiliar to them. This scene, too, makes a hearing audience 'paranoid'. Communication is not just purely verbal and temporal, but also spatial and embodied. The character's interchange prompts the audience to question who belongs and who is excluded by the respective media used. What does communication look like when it crosses two linguistic and cultural borders? Why should hearing/verbal media be ubiquitous? Why should those communicating with their body in healings be muted and silenced?

The other main parallel that can be drawn with Cook and Lerner's poetic performance and the story of the 'deaf-mute' is that both 'illustrate a fruitful mixture of sign and sound contributing to a critical as well as aesthetic performance'.[83] Moreover, the hearing audience is assaulted into experiencing 'otherness' in its witnessing of Jesus' spitting, touching, groaning, and employment of alien terminology. This 'otherness' unveils in some small way the sense of alienation and struggle, as well as the endurance of projected foreignness and danger, that the character of the 'deaf-mute' must have forcibly tolerated every day of his life: 'the difficulty of understanding and being understood, the feeling of being considered dumb, the sense of being unheard and being invisible'.[84]

Sounding Out a 'Deaf-Mute'

In his 'White Noise' installation (1992) Joseph Grigely, a Deaf artist, covered an oval room with a cacophony of notes and disparate pieces of paper. One could not read them in a linear fashion, they were haphazardly displayed. This graphically illustrated for Grigely what Susannah Mintz has since termed 'the problem of fluency'. This is caused not by the inability of Grigely to hear, but rather 'his interlocutor's inability to sign'. The indiscriminate slips of paper are emblematic of the irritations involved in communication across bodily differences.[85]

Mark 7: 31–7 likewise pictures 'the problem of fluency' figured by different media and differently abled bodies. By juxtaposing the story of the 'deaf-mute' with Deaf World Arts, those interpretations which 'mute' and belie a paternal coercion of the character into a hearing-verbal world have been questioned. For as Petra Kuppers realizes, 'the very act of being positioned/positioning themselves' is working against the view of the disabled person as merely passive, 'incarcerated by an overpowering body', 'tragic victim' of a 'pre-discursive physicality'.[86]

The alternative 'Deaf world' resonances with the story unveil a dynamic exchange between two characters, Jesus and the 'deaf-mute', in which audio-centric channels of communication are variously questioned and challenged. For Deaf performance is not a 'body of literature' as much as 'a literature of the body',[87] unveiling vision, touch, space as it comments on 'official' and 'unofficial' channels of communication. Jesus' tactile actions, inaudible sounds, and use of foreign terms, coupled with the 'deaf-mute's' resistant silence, initiate a space where meaning does not equate solely to verbal language. Whilst of course there can be no simple or naive equivalence drawn between sign and gesture, nevertheless from a Deaf cultural perspective the exhibition of bodily means of communication which appeals to visual and tactile 'hearers' beyond the 'ears' is crucial.

Whilst some commentators have patronizingly noted that Jesus uses gestures and signs to accommodate the 'deaf-mute' or even conceive of the true miracle being Jesus merely 'noticing' him as a person,[88] the interpretation proposed here is far more radical. Both characters are involved in a display which questions a hearing/Deaf binary and alienates the hearing audience by making them occupy, if only for a short while, a disorientating, frustrating, and alien space, which in part embodies the 'deaf-mute's' daily lot. Deaf performances are not just artistic but also activist in their quest for liberation. Understood in this way, the sounding out of the 'deaf-mute's' story powerfully reminds us that actions and silences at times, can speak far louder than words.

4

The Stench of Untouchability: Sensory Tactics of a Leper, Legion, and Leaky Woman

At first 'sight' it may seem strange to feature a leper (Mark 1: 40–5/ Matt. 8: 1–4/Luke 5: 12–15), Legion (Mark 5: 1–20/Luke 8: 26–39), and leaky woman[1] (Mark 5: 25–34/Matt. 9: 20–2/Luke 8: 43–7) in a book focused on sensory disabilities, for none have self-evident physiological impairments of sensory organs. However, all three characters are subject to corporeal sanctions on account of ideologies surrounding their respective conditions: skin disease, demon possession, and disordered bleeding. These characters could of course physically touch and feel other people or objects (they were not 'touch-unable'[2]), but social and religious sensibilities vigilantly controlled and regulated their haptic encounters for fear of the impurity and ritual defilement they posed to those around them (they were 'not-touch-able'[3]).

Haptic stigmatization which results from these characters being viewed as unclean and impure according to priestly purity regulations has frequently been highlighted by biblical commentators. Here however, following Yasumasa Sekine's recent ethnographic work, I want to draw a distinction between 'purity/impurity' systems that are codified in religious texts and the actual employment of such codes and related phenomena in daily interactions across social levels. Sekine uses the terminology of 'pollution' (as opposed to impurity) when talking about these everyday social exchanges to heighten sensitivities to their dynamic and flexible nature. He shows how at times untouchables not only experience 'pollution' negatively in discrimination, but can also at times use it creatively and subversively to achieve particular social goals.

I also submit that the leper, Legion, and leaking woman's sensory disablement was not only manifested in the censoring of haptic encounters but would also have been associated with olfactory dimensions. Rejection on account of real and perceived 'odours' would have frequently evoked disgust and revulsion in others. Even though smell is not explicitly featured in the portrayals within our texts, nonetheless the 'stench' (both physical and symbolic) of their bodily conditions would have been more than obvious in the first century. The ancient world was one in which odours, both aromatic and putrid, brought to mind a subject's status and condition and accordingly impacted on all social encounters, variously evoking either positive ideological associations with wholeness and vitality or negative associations with disjuncture and mortality. The leper, Legion, and leaky woman as will be seen, predominantly called to mind foul attributes associated with the latter.

With this in mind, I employ assorted insights from ethnographies of 'untouchable'[4] groups in India and the various sensory tactics which are available to such individuals, to read alongside our gospel characters. Ethnographers have revealed how persons can challenge or manipulate their status, for 'pollution' is not an objectified state but rather one which can be productively directed. They also reveal how foul ideological smells can themselves be used as sensory 'weapons of the weak'[5] in challenging the maps of meaning which exclude and marginalize them. This has significant repercussions for our understandings of the untouchable characters in our stories. Whilst many biblical commentators have highlighted Jesus' transcending of purity laws in his encounters with the leper, Legion, and leaky woman,[6] how far Jesus actually disrupts the elite purity/impurity system is debatable. Cecelia Wassen in her review of Qumran purity texts alongside the gospel healing stories recently submitted that 'most Jewish listeners or readers would not assume that Jesus [irreversibly] contracted ritual impurity'.[7] Commenting specifically on the leaky woman's healing, Wassen argues that 'nothing in the story indicates that Jesus either rejected purity laws, or that he was anxious about becoming ritually impure through the woman's touch'.[8] Similarly in reference to the leper's healing, James Crossley strongly asserts that Jesus does not negate the system. He writes, 'it cannot be emphasised enough: becoming impure does not necessarily equal opposition to Torah. If Jesus became impure…he could become pure again by one means or another if he so wished.'[9] Indeed, the command to the leper to go and show himself to the priest would seem to witness to 'Jesus' obedience to law'.[10]

Here likewise, I will argue that Jesus' actions are not an abrogation of purity laws, for even when touching 'untouchables', his purity status could be reinstated through appropriate means. Rather it is the untouchables themselves who constructively manipulate conventions surrounding their 'polluted' conditions and make political points through their bodily performances. It is worth noting that Jesus does not directly approach the leper, Legion, or leaky woman, but rather the initiative for each contact is audaciously taken by the characters themselves. These dissident approaches should give us a hint that these characters may be exhibiting similar sensory tactics to those 'untouchables' in other contexts who strategically influence the very structures that mark them out as dangerous and repress, impede, and 'disable' their social interactions. For ironically, as Sundar Sarukkai notes in her phenomenological study of such relations, ultimately the real site of 'untouchability' is not those whom religious codes label as 'impure', but rather those others who on account of such regulations refuse to touch such as these.[11]

The Leper, Legion, and Leaky Woman as 'Untouchables'

Ethnographic records on untouchables in India frequently draw on Louis Dumont's seminal work *Homo Hierarchicus: The Caste System and its Implications*[12] to plot purity and pollution as the main symbolic binary underlining caste; this schema, Dumont contended, was governed by the vision of the Brahmins and had strict ramifications for the lot of the out-castes. For Dumont, 'superiority and superior purity are identical: it is in this sense that, ideologically, distinction of purity is the foundation of status'.[13] Stigmatized status through blood was demonstrated through the polluting occupations 'untouchables' were forced to carry out, including collection of human excrement and handling of corpses and skins of dead animals. Jewish 'maps' of purity and pollution have strong resonances with Dumont's analyses. Jerome Neyrey, in his review of concepts of purity and pollution in biblical traditions,[14] for example, draws on Mary Douglas's seminal work, *Purity and Danger*,[15] to note how often persons, objects, and places were designated as 'unclean'. The maps of purity largely set down in the priestly writings, rendered cleanliness and purity as states fit for worship, whilst dirt and impurity were carefully distanced from such sacred activities. In these law codes, purity was symbolic of not only an individual body but the wholeness of the community and in turn constituted the desired 'norm'. Dirt as 'matter out of place' (whether that was people or things) posed a risk of defilement to the whole order and was accordingly rendered taboo. The entire system plotted 'relations of order to disorder, being to non-being, form to formlessness, life to death'.[16] Whilst purity was often symbolic of life, dirt was more often symbolic of death. Corpses and diseased bodies were therefore seen as particularly potent sites of danger.

All three of our characters, as many commentators have frequently submitted, share to some degree elements of a state of 'impurity' and correlated association with mortality. Whilst many recognize that the leprosy referred to in the New Testament was likely to encompass a variety of skin complaints and not necessarily equate with what modern medicine understands by Hansen's disease,[17] nevertheless the condition itself was symbolic of death: 'socially the leper was the equivalent of a corpse (Josephus *Ant* 3.11.3)'.[18] Similarly Legion was physically and figuratively equated with death: his space was a cemetery—an unclean place from which, in David deSilva's words, 'he would have been contracting corpse defilement continuously'.[19] The leaky woman's condition is likewise caught up in the symbolic of mortality within the narrative. Commentators make frequent reference to the juxtaposition of Jairus' daughter's healing and the leaky woman's. Both women are associated with the number twelve, the age of maturity for the young girl and the length of the leakage from the woman. Moreover, each character is confronted with their own demise: 'the woman with the slow encroachment of death anticipates the healing of the girl who actually experienced death'.[20]

Similar social experiences of untouchables in India as outlined by Dumont and his followers, and those rendered impure in Jewish traditions, can also be traced. Both groups were often relegated to marginal spaces, away from populated areas where others risked ritual defilement and from those places hallowed as 'pure' (temples, etc.).[21] Untouchables frequently heralded their arrival in a city by striking wood so that others could avoid them, for 'the Dharmasutras make it clear that direct or indirect contact with [untouchables] can cause pollution. Pollution would occur if [untouchables] are touched, conversed with or even looked upon. Rites of purification become mandatory after such pollution.'[22] Similarly, Levitical tradition states that the leper was likely perceived as not only capable of polluting holy places and 'the camp'[23] but also the 'mundane sphere[s] of persons, objects and premises (Lev 14: 36; 46–47)'.[24] A leper's interactions in populated areas were necessarily controlled; indeed customary practice was, like the untouchable, to visually perform their status as proscribed in Leviticus as a warning for others: 'The person who has the leprous disease shall wear torn clothes and let the hair of his head be dishevelled and he shall cover his upper lip and cry out, "Unclean, unclean"' (Lev. 13: 45–6).[25] Likewise, Legion's banishment to live in isolation among the tombs and unclean animals has also been seen as a symptom of his social expulsion. Demon possession was itself disabling and his nakedness in open space has been recognized by some as emblematic of his impurity, for being without clothes 'was unclean outside of one's home'.[26] Whilst the leaky woman is portrayed within a large group of people, her condition is frequently assumed to hold ramifications for her social movements. Indeed some commentators link her character with the leper, for in the words of Susan Haber, 'both have conditions that induce a severe form of impurity, both are made well through physical contact with Jesus that is miraculous and both are subsequently advised to undergo the appropriate purification rituals which are technical in nature'.[27] All three characters, through skin disease, corpse defilement, demon possession, and disordered bleeding, are rendered as 'impure' and 'out of place' in their communities, two key related social issues which are typical of 'states of bodily rejection'.[28]

Whilst this neat categorization of both Indian and Jewish traditions under the binary classification of purity/impurity may be heuristically useful, it has not been without its detractors in both contexts. Dumont's theories have been subject to extensive critique in anthropology. Anupama Rao, for example, questions Dumont's assumption that the purity ideology of the dominant castes shaped the entire scaffolding of Indian social hierarchy. In Rao's opinion Dumont mistakenly equated 'power with the power of the upper castes',[29] thus ignoring the potential influence of others lower in the system. Gerald Berreman similarly notes how Dumont's analysis relied heavily on the vision of purity outlined in Brahminical tracts, but was at the same time seemingly ignorant of the shortfall between literary texts which set out 'the high caste ideal of what the caste system of Hindu India ought to be like according to those who value it positively'[30] and the actual performances of the system across all social levels in daily exchanges. The purity/impurity binary bore little resemblance to the lives of many Indians or 'to the feeble reflections of those lives that have made their way into the ethnographical, biographical and novelistic literature'.[31] By overlooking the actual lived experiences of the 'untouchables', Dumont was also largely unaware of the agency and resistance they posed to the polluting, demeaning statuses attributed to them.[32]

Similarly, in biblical studies, Jonathan Klawans has argued that the 'ritual' impurity set out in priestly texts has often been used erroneously by biblical scholars to pattern social stratification. Impurity has frequently and uncritically been subsumed with sin and low social status, and, similar to Dumont's analyses, an overinflated sense that 'Pharisaic temple elite asserted power over others'[33] in all day-to-day interactions. Klawans is at pains to stress that ritual impurity affected all people of all statuses in different degrees in different situations. Thus, as in India, status categorization as 'impure' is not totally absolute, but always relative.[34] Untouchables live with probably the most extreme and regular form of classification as 'impure', for others 'defilement can be turned back into purity by cleansing, which is achieved through purification rituals'.[35] As Richard Davis notes, theories such as Dumont's which focus not on individuality but rather a social whole, are not aware of individuals 'whose own bodily substance codes are repeatedly transformed through material transfers and transactions'; in his opinion, 'society is the outcome of ongoing transforming interactions rather than of an overbearing ideological whole'.[36] So, whilst the association of 'untouchability' with certain individuals' whole identity (like the leper, Legion, and leaky woman) is perhaps not surprising given that touch of all the senses is dispersed across one's whole body, touch should also remind us of one's material presence in the world. People, no matter what their status, have bodies which have the potential to perform, direct, and influence other's labelling of them as 'impure' or 'untouchable'. For, in Elizabeth Harvey's words, 'touch evokes at once agency and receptivity, authority and reciprocity, pleasure and pain, sensual indulgence and epistemological certainty'.[37]

This insight has been given particular substance by Sekine, in his recent ethnography of untouchables in a Tamil village. He purposefully set out to question Dumont's purity/impurity binary, which he, along with critics cited above, saw as a 'top down' and 'centripetal' force, alien to the life experiences and self-identity of the untouchables themselves. For heuristic purposes Sekine posits 'impurity' (an elite, high-caste, and oppressive label) as distinct from 'pollution' (a more fluid designation). He submits:

> In the 'pure–impure' ideology, polluted phenomena are only seen as objects of repression and rejection as 'impure'. I argue that in reality, the very marginal nature of pollution makes it a creative space (a space with hidden potential for decentralization) where it is possible to radically change one's own sense of order through encounters with others…in order to clearly depict this creative nature of pollution, which maintains the basis of the lives of the villagers, it was necessary to distinguish it as 'pollution' from 'impurity' which is an unequivocally negative concept.[38]

Pollution, in Sekine's view, is a notion in continual flux. A concept 'used to indicate a chaotic situation that destroys conventional order'.[39] He sees that there are two responses to such chaotic moments: first, it can be *rejected* as 'impurity' or alternatively, it can be *shared* as 'pollution'. In unpacking the latter notion, Sekine offers the example of mourners, who on entering a house with a corpse 'share' the pollution of death. This sharing of pollution is itself an innovative moment which 'converts the pollution of death into vitality for the future of the people left behind'.[40] Charting similar instances in the day-to-day interactions of the people he observed, Sekine avers that pollution frequently functions as a survival tactic of the untouchable and should not be viewed as an equivalent of the overwhelmingly negative label of 'impurity' with which they are frequently branded. Just like the house of the corpse is figured as an inventive space of pollution, Sekine sees that the untouchable's social position on the fringes of society provides a 'creative locus where social boundaries are dissolved' and 'social discrimination is vanished'.[41] Sekine sees pollution as metaphorically linked with the 'liminality of death'.[42] Thus when confronted with polluting events (birth, death, bleeding, disease) others may well partake in pollution and as such mobilize a subversive power from the margins.[43] Before going on to explore the potential agency of our characters within this sort of system, it is worth stopping for a while to probe another hitherto largely ignored sensory stigmatization to which they would almost certainly have also been subject, namely, the olfactory.

The Stench of Untouchability

Rejection through smell has been identified cross-culturally as a particularly potent way to 'corporealize dislike'[44] and to subjugate and distance 'the other' in specific situations.[45] Gale Largey and Rod Watson, in their 'Sociology of Odors', maintain that 'odors, whether real or alleged, are often used as a basis for conferring a moral identity upon an individual or a group'.[46] The feelings of disgust surrounding smell are part of the mechanics by which the 'pure' are ideologically distanced from the 'polluted'.[47] This attribute of smell, in Theodor Adorno's and Max Horkheimer's opinion, gives its toxic provocation of revulsion and horror.[48] Thus when smells are transposed to the political realm, 'subjects are viscerally experienced as biological "danger signs which make the hair stand on end and the heart to stop beating."'[49]

In the Indian context, untouchables often toil on foul-smelling animal hides, collect and dispose of rotting corpses and stinking excrement. But this 'secular filth',[50] in Julia Kristeva's words, becomes 'impurity' when inscribed with moral and religious dimensions.[51] 'Smelly' occupations etch their 'reeking' social status on the actors and uphold their disconnection from the others. In Susan Miller's words:

As long as there are 'untouchables' to whom we can point and say 'They are the ones who dwell in squalor, dispose of excrement and disinfect areas of disease and contamination' then we can rest assured we are not such people. We may then reinforce our sense of separation by feeling disgust over what the untouchables do and who they are.[52]

Similarly, in the ancient world, olfactory systems frequently organized identities for, in Jerry Toner's words, 'a Roman was what he or she smelled'.[53] Susan Ashbrook also notes how 'mortality was associated with stench, for all things subject to decay (change or corruption) were thought to emit a putrid smell'.[54] How apt then, as established above, that the leper, Legion, and leaking woman are all associated with mortality in their characterizations. Others similarly note how odours, evoking as they do physically and emotionally powerful responses, were key elements in the evaluation of different people and groups in antiquity and pinpointing their 'proper place in the social order'.[55] The poor and diseased particularly, in elite sources, were thought of as 'dung heaps'. In the words of Jerry Toner, 'the filth of the city was transposed on to the crowd: they became the *faex populi*—the shit of the people'.[56]

In biblical traditions likewise, just as God's nose inhaled the pleasing odours of sacrifices and prayers of the righteous (Gen. 8: 21; Exod. 29: 18; Num. 28: 6) so foul smells were often associated with repugnance to others (2 Sam. 10: 6) and indicative of morally abhorrent actions and dispositions. Prophetic texts feature the divine chastisement of Israel as making 'the stench of your camp go up into your nostrils' (Amos 4: 10) and 2 Maccabees pictures the demise of the evil Antiochus Epiphanes in arresting olfactory terms: he was 'swarmed with worms', 'his flesh rotted away', and 'because of the stench the whole army felt revulsion at his decay' (2 Macc. 9: 9–10). In the end the narrative reveals that Antiochus Epiphanes himself cannot stand his own fetid odour (2 Macc. 9: 12).

Of course the stories of the leper, Legion, and leaking woman make no direct comment on odours surrounding their conditions. This is perhaps not surprising given the fact, as William Ian Miller observes, that the lexicon of smell in most languages is very narrow and frequently makes 'an adjective of the thing that smells'[57] (faeces smell like faeces, flowers smell like flowers). Could it be therefore that the conditions of leprous skin, demonic possession, and disordered female bleeding may have conjured up such strong olfactory associations for the original authors and receivers of the gospel stories that these conditions did not need explicit comment? Their mere mention would have 'odorized' these characters and evoked disgust or fear in others. After all, it was common knowledge that smell was an incredibly important tool in the ancient world for detecting disease.[58]

A leper's association with death was no doubt due to the mass of skin conditions which produced rotting, decaying flesh. Luke 5: 12–15 characterizes him as 'a man full of leprosy', presumably to underline the total invasion of the chronic disease. Theophrastus, in the fourth century BCE, gives a sense of the 'disgust' evoked by an uncivilized 'squalid leprous character' who goes around 'leprous, covered with ulcers' and 'sores and wounds'; moreover, 'he is hairy as a bear, his teeth are black and decayed; so that he is altogether an unapproachable and most unsavoury personage'.[59] Legion likewise is characterized as uncivilized through his nakedness and the sores and bruises he has inflicted on himself with stones (Mark 5: 5).[60] His association with tombs also evokes his 'putrefied' state. Ideologically, Rikki Watts convincingly links the narrative to Isaiah 65: 1–7[61] in which the idolatrous worshippers are also subject to olfactory imaging: they 'sit inside tombs, and spend the night in secret places, who eat swine's flesh, with broth of abominable things in their vessels'.[62] It is also not insignificant in this regard that Yahweh is characterized by Isaiah as rejecting the people and their practices by olfactory symbolism: 'These are a smoke in my nostrils, a fire that burns all day long' (Isa. 65: 5).[63] Even the references to swine on the hillside which have frequently been seen to mark the territory as 'Gentile' and 'unclean' for Jews could also be understood by olfactory means. Whether or not a wholly convincing characterization, pigs, according to Plutarch, were avoided by Jews because the pig's belly was frequently marked by flaky outbreaks and filthy habits (including rolling in urine and eating excrement) which in turn affected the quality of their meat.[64]

The leaky woman's complaint can likewise be understood as odorous.[65] Common understandings in ancient physiology conceived of the male form as dry as opposed to the oozing, damp, leakiness of the female.[66] Female bleeding, even in healthy women, came to repulsively 'reek'. Ezekiel 36: 17 for example draws parallels between the house of Israel's defilement and 'the uncleanness of a woman in her menstrual period'. Elsewhere female bleeding is also used to signify evil and malevolence.[67] Classen submits how to a large degree even elite, high-status 'healthy' women in antiquity were often perceived as offensively smelly. She cites Lucretius' estimation that even 'beautiful women…reek of noisome smells in private'.[68] The practice of perfuming brides she accordingly sees as a 'normalising' process 'in which naturally foul, disruptive women were symbolically turned into sweet, obedient helpmates'.[69] Shane Butler in his work on Lucretius offers a particularly interesting discussion on smell and the medical treatment of gynaecological complaints in the ancient world. These are of course particularly important given that our leaky woman is portrayed as having spent all her money over the years on medical treatment without success. Lucretius pictures a man's behaviour at the door of his lover by saying that, if he could have had 'just one whiff…he would scramble for an excuse to leave'. Butler notes how various scholars have tried to imagine what the source of this whiff would be: perfume? natural secretions? However, Butler concludes that it is indicative of 'fumigation' an ancient practice in which vapours—including burnt sulphur, urine, dung, and wool—were inserted into the vagina.[70] Thus the lover could literally 'smell' the treatment of her diseased parts. Whilst this is unlikely to have informed Mark Moore and John Weece's creative actualization of the leaky woman, it does evoke a new dimension to their statement that 'her odor would be an olfactory reminder of her uncleanness: as she approaches Jesus from behind the other peasants get a whiff and step aside'.[71]

It has been established that both haptic and olfactory discrimination hail certain individuals as 'untouchable'. Moreover, in such formulations it is often the perspective of the labeller which is predominant rather than the perspective of the individual designated as such. Rao yearns for scholarship on Indian untouchables to 'take us away from an epistemology of caste toward the existential life worlds of caste subalterns',[72] to listen to their stories and to chart their actions and exchanges. Such performance-based interpretations have the ability to refigure 'untouchables' by exhibiting their strategic agency in negotiating the 'pollution' to which they are subject and resisting the 'stench' of the conditions with which they are saddled. When subaltern consciousness is given due acknowledgement, these haptic and olfactory stigmatizations are revealed not as objectified and static, but at times, flexible, negotiable, and unstable. A similar plea should be issued in biblical studies, to engage the character beyond the label—leper; demoniac; leaking woman—despite our sparse evidence we can still interpret their bodily performances alongside their narrated identities.

Stinking Humiliation: The Sensory Tactics of the Leper

The bodily gestures of the leper in all three Synoptic accounts have some interesting features which could be configured as sensory tactics. First, in light of the Levitical codes outlined previously, no specific warning is given about the leper's approach to others. He does not shout 'unclean, unclean' but rather is presented as within crowds (Matt. 8: 1) and boldly coming straight up to Jesus (Mark 1: 40; Luke 5: 12). Second, the leper performs a humiliating and degrading advance, 'begging and kneeling' (Mark 1: 40; Matt. 8: 8) and most evocatively in Luke, literally 'falling (*peswn*) on his face on the ground', Luke 5: 12). In a Hebrew Bible context, this behaviour marks the leper out as a worshipper, one who recognizes the divine. His gesture is the appropriate debasement of humanity in such contexts, but notably a form the leper would not be able to exhibit in the mainstream because he would be kept away from the temple. The term *piptw* could even be read more strongly as self-annihilation as this word can also denote one's self-ruin or destruction. Third, in all three accounts, the leper's question is rhetorically framed to put the onus on Jesus: 'if you choose you can make me clean' (Mark 1: 40; Matt. 8: 2; Luke 5: 12). There is no egotistical 'I' in the untouchable's request. The question delivered in public demands an immediate response.

Ashis Nandy, in his ethnography of the political psychology of humiliation by untouchables, notes that individuals who adopt degrading gestural appeals to others often do so, 'not because they are reconciled to their lot but because they consider it legitimate manipulative behaviour when confronting the powerful: they think it is a small price to pay, to neutralize or contain the dominant in a fluid politics of hierarchies and to gain privileged access to power'.[73] Interesting in this respect is that, whilst most manuscripts depict Jesus as 'moved with compassion' (*splagxnistheis*) at the leper's approach and plea, some other manuscripts picture Jesus as 'angry' (*orgistheis*), a term which is also used to denote the rage of the snubbed host in Luke 12: 41 who experiences public shame.[74] Given that the latter jars with more typical theological and cultural preferences, maybe it actually has a stronger claim to be the original. Certainly if the leper's approach and question evoked anger in Jesus it would indicate that his tactics had provoked a strong reaction in the one he wished to influence. Graham Twelftree also accepts Jesus' anger as the earlier reading, and goes on to give a number of possible reasons for this emotive response, including: 'ritual agitation or pneumatic excitement that a miracle worker might experience in reacting to situations of distress' or 'righteous anger' at the demonic power of the disease which so cruelly 'disfigured one of God's creatures' or anger at the very purity/impurity sanctions to which the poor leprous man was subject.[75] Discounting all these readings, Twelftree favours the suggestion that Jesus may actually have been angry at the leper for the breach of law he poses. This is a really interesting angle and transforms this incident, in Sekine's terms, from 'impurity' to 'pollution'. The leper effectively puts Jesus into a corner and asks whether Jesus will 'eliminate' him on grounds of impurity, or share his 'pollution' in order for a creative transformation of both their positions to be initiated.

Other ethnographic studies of 'Dalit' groups—'ex-untouchable communities'—who 'define themselves first as Dalit (oppressed) rather than as untouchable'[76] to purposefully convey a political and social consciousness reveal how individuals can, whilst acknowledging their current degradation, also reposition, contest, and reinscribe their identities from their marginal locations. Rao describes these political moves, not as a transcending of purity conventions, but rather 'corporeal politics premised on the continued salience of embodied difference'.[77] Dalit power rests paradoxically on their historical weakness. They seek release through their embodied stigma, not in spite of it. Odour itself becomes a prominent signifier of 'pollution' for Dalits and is, in Sekine's terms, also used as a tool through which these individuals can force others to 'share' their status. Classen likewise recognizes the unique ability of odour to 'transcend class boundaries' and 'disintegrate' maps of exclusion. For, in her words: 'The foul other can invade one....The very ability of odour to break down barriers, which renders it so dangerous in one regard, also makes it, however, a powerful force of integration...a shared smell can give the partakers a strong we feeling, while an interchange of personal or other odours between individuals and groups, such as takes place in many forms of greetings, can serve as a basis for the recognition and mediation of mutual differences.'[78] This certainly seems to be corroborated here not only in the leper's audacious approach to Jesus, but also his pollution, which quite literally gets up his healer's nose!

Elsewhere foul odours also produce anger in biblical traditions. Amos 4: 10 for example, pictures offence at the putrid smell of excrement and corpses. Could Jesus likewise be reacting not only to the stench of the leprous skin but the impudent and conniving strategies of the leper? An 'inflamed' or 'snorting' nose is often indicative of extreme irritation and fury, as in the raging nostrils of Elihu, one of Job's friends (Job 32: 2–3), and God's 'inflamed nose' which snorts that Zedekiah and the people will be handed over to King Nebuchadnezzar for abuse and rejection (Jer. 21: 4–7).[79] But what could have provoked such a response in Jesus? It would seem that the leper's request ironically parodies Jesus' 'untouchable' status, for he and others like him, bound by fears of ritual defilement, actually are reticent to touch others. This seems to be an instance then in which a subaltern openly contests the purity/impurity maps of his culture. Like Dalits who 'use coded language to caricature the pretension of the lordly, and build a critique of caste-injustices',[80] here the leper goads Jesus to respond to his provocative self-humiliation and stench, by sharing his 'pollution'. By putting his hand out to touch the leper and deliver the response 'I do choose, be made clean' (Mark 1: 41; Matt. 8: 3; Luke 5: 13) Jesus does as the leper wishes. Whether or not this act confers physical healing or not[81] it does certainly stand as a symbol of the effect that 'weapons of the weak' can have in garnering attention, manipulating the perceived 'pollution', and deconstructing the 'untouchability' which surrounds both themselves and those who will not touch them. The same act of touch has different implications for both Jesus and the leper. Speaking of the Indian context Sundar Sarukkai writes: 'In the case of the former [the pure], it could be associated with psychological feelings of revulsion, power, rejection and so on whereas in the latter [the Dalit] it is associated with feelings of humiliation, shame and so on.'[82] Both responses, as have been seen, are evident in the leper narrative. Sarrukai goes on to talk about the sensory organ of touch, the skin, as itself an evocative boundary marker between life and death. To 'close your skin' is, in his opinion, to 'close off contact with the world'. When this happens, you in some way symbolize mortality: 'thus, it is the partial death/decay of the subject who practises untouchability that is the first consequence of practising untouchability. This happens not just because practising untouchability is morally wrong but because the person is denying himself a part of his ability, his capacity to engage with his own sense. In not touching others, he is not able to touch himself.'[83] The leper demonstrates, through his body, gestures, and probing question, the paradoxes of his oppressed condition; moreover, he coerces Jesus into likewise demonstrating the paradoxes of his own un-touch-ability.

The story concludes by stating that the leprosy leaves the man and Jesus orders the leper, or in Mark's version 'harshly criticises' him (Mark 1: 43), to say nothing to anyone about what has happened but go and present himself before a priest 'as a testimony to them' (Mark 1: 44; Matt. 8: 4; Luke 5: 14). Jesus thus still pays lip service to religious purity conventions, whilst at the same time sharing the odour and touch of one whose condition deemed him 'polluted'. Jesus and the gospel recipients however, have learnt important lessons from the leper's performance: namely, the system that sustains untouchability inevitably cuts off individuals of all statuses from one another. Un-touch-ability of the 'pure' it would seem has as much symbolic resonance of death and mortality as a debilitating skin condition which rots and putrefies flesh.

Dirty Protest and Naked Ambition: The Sensory Tactics of Legion

Legion is introduced in our texts as a multiple personality that is fragmented and self-destructive. Many postcolonial critics have read his name as 'double-voiced', referring to Rome's military occupation of the land. As a result, many interpreters have seen the main point of the story as the actual exorcism performed by Jesus, when the evil spirits are sent into nearby swine and fall defeated into the abyss. In Halvor Moxnes's words, 'the exorcism represented a form of power "from below" that was a challenge to established authorities'.[84] In such readings, the exorcism presents a powerful resistance to imperialism and prophetically announces empire's certain and violent end.

Could it be though that the actual narration of the character of Legion, so briefly skipped over by many commentators, prior to his 'normalisation' as 'clothed and in his right mind' (Mark 5: 15; Luke 8: 35), constitutes the real heart of the tactical sensory resistance within the story? Namely, Legion's shackled, naked, bruised, dirty, and disordered body (Mark 5: 4–5; Luke 8: 27, 29) provocatively performs his brokenness and in turn serves as a powerful remonstration against his social marginality.[85] Possession of course has long been recognized by anthropologists as an arena in which the subjugated can perform and mimic the effects of oppressive regimes on their bodies.[86] Legion's shackling (ironically by the people themselves) perhaps demonstrates their own implicit compliance with the shackles of the portrayed religious mainstream, not to mention the imperial regime and associated resistance to freedom. A similar point has been made by Richard Horsley who writes, 'their chaining him and restraining his violence out among the tombs, had been a way of establishing *modus vivendi* with the Roman imperial power that had invaded and disrupted their lives'.[87] Legion thus makes the physical and sensory brutalities of the system, to which all are subject, vividly apparent to those around him.

Legion's embodied performance incorporates powerful somatic tools of political demonstration. As Barbara Sutton submits, 'the body (clothed or unclothed) is the tool of protest *par excellence*. Most political protest is enacted through the body—from marches, to political theatre, to the chaining of the body to a tree or building. The body is a key vehicle of protest. The body also serves as a symbol, a text that conveys political meanings.'[88] Many such protests have involved, like Legion, the subject's nakedness, to paradoxically demonstrate their subversive power in weakness; for as Brett Lunceford states, 'human beings are at their most vulnerable when naked, but, when engaged in protest, are also strangely powerful'.[89] In biblical traditions too, the naked body stands as a provocative distortion of the desired norm which was an appropriately clothed body (Gen. 2: 25; 3: 6–7). The model bodies of priests were to be covered and putting on particular items of clothing often demonstrated a change in status (Gen. 41: 42), while ripping or removing clothes could denote mourning or a loss of pride. The naked body particularly held subversive suggestions of 'exposure, shame and illegitimacy'.[90] Legion's naked body is also scarred through self-mutilation: 'bruising himself with stones'

(Mark 5: 5). Jewish law specifically outlawed self-cutting, wounding, or marking one's own flesh (Lev. 19: 28) (save of course for the legitimating cut of circumcision) for the 'normative body' was to be redolent of life; in contrast the disordered, dirty body exhibited within itself corpse-like features.[91] Legion's damaged body even resides in tombs such is its cadaver parallelism. Interestingly, slashing flesh was part of the ritual repertoire for the dead and divination which was outlawed by the 'official' priestly religion which sought to maintain a monopoly on accessing divine knowledge.

Adeline Masquelier notes that dirt is often equated with nakedness in such contexts. For in her words, 'dirt' is 'a visible index of difference' and like nudity has a 'capacity to inscribe stigma to human bodies': 'to be "dirty" in such instances, is to be "naked" and vice versa'.[92] Both conditions are ultimately symbolic of alterity and deviance. Legion is in effect a dissident 'disrober'. His name is Legion, but he is not 'dressed' in the apparel of Roman power, but rather the nakedness of victimhood, a mutilated subject of that power. Legion is also implicitly depicted as stinking of the tombs he inhabits and covered in self-inflicted sores and bruises. Untouchables have variously staged similar 'dirty' protests to publically exhibit the stench of their subjugated identities. The *Deccan Herald* in 2010 reported a Dalit protest at Savanur station in which night soil collectors covered their whole bodies with human excrement and stayed out all day in the sun, to protest against a commercial complex being built on their homes and water connections being cut off from their village.[93] In effect their bodies were transformed into stinking symbols not only of protest against the development plans, but also their own humiliating occupations and social lives. The 'stench' of their daily existence was forcibly and physically shared through noxious odour with all the people in that place. Masquelier submits that, because odour and dirt have often been used as a basis to rationalize social segregation and oppression of the 'impure' by the 'pure', odour, dirt, and nakedness accordingly become in her words 'surprisingly powerful weapons when deployed by the "unwashed" against the "washed."'[94]

If Legion's state prior to the exorcism is read as a political demonstration typical of sensory tactics of the weak, then what are we to make of the transformation which follows the exorcism, in which Legion is tamed, clothed, and pictured 'in his right mind'? Laura Donaldson, in her subversive interpretations of exorcism stories in the gospels offers some interesting pointers. She sees that, in many instances, possession as a state holds 'ghostly' reminders of indigenous experiences which are trampled and negated by the imperial power which 'civilises' such 'barbaric' behaviour. In reference to Legion's exorcism she sees Jesus effectively 'domesticate' and 'neutralize' his disorderliness, with the ultimate result being 'the confinement of this potentially subversive state, to the ordinary (one might say "hegemonic" world)'.[95] In this perspective the exorcism actually defuses Legion of his tactical power which could unmask the people's complicit cooperation with the imperial regime.

If we do see the heart of the protest being Legion's possessed body, rather than his exorcised, normalized self, then another interesting sensory element which can be brought into play is the use of foul odour in exorcism. Tobit 8: 1–3, for example, features the stench of burning fish liver repelling a demon 'that he fled to the remotest parts of Egypt'. Similarly, Josephus narrates how Eleazer used a ring with strong-smelling roots (proscribed by Solomon) in it to exorcize a demon via the nasal cavity of the possessed (*Ant.* 7: 46–9). Could it be that Legion's liminality, his stench of death, actually has the potential to release the people (literally exorcize them) of their naive compliance with the imperial powers? Indeed, while performing his 'dirty protest', Legion also functions as a prophet of the tyranny others will undergo: Jesus, like Legion, will ultimately be brutalized and killed by Roman power.

Legion, like the leper, when read as a figure who utilizes sensory tactics to unveil social oppression and abuse, becomes another example of the jarring coupling of subversive power and vulnerability, so characteristic of untouchable resistance. His nude, self-mutilated, stinking form graphically exhibits his, and others', physical oppression. In his 'possessed' state he literally 'exorcizes' people of empty acquiescence to the imperial power. In his 'normalized' state, he is rendered politically ineffective. Indeed, the 'polluted' condition he dramatically performs when possessed (naked, tortured, beaten) is ironically 'eliminated' by Jesus. Ultimately, however, the pollution is later 'shared' by both characters in the narrative as Jesus himself is flogged, stripped, bruised, and executed.

Seeping Bodies: The Leaky Woman's Sensory Tactics

As outlined previously, many interpretations of the leaky woman's story underline Jesus' healing power and his subsequent appellation of 'Daughter' which indicates her reintegration into social life. In the words of one commentator, 'the woman becomes pure…physical health and ritual purity are imparted'.[96] However this healing, probably more than any other in the gospels, underlines the subversive agency of the woman herself. The cure is not accomplished as such by Jesus, but rather the woman's manipulation of the divine power that works through him. It is her inner voice that we hear narrated as she creeps up behind him in the multitude: 'If I but touch his clothes, I will be made well' (Mark 5: 28).

Furthermore, as argued above, Jesus should not be celebrated as a model of 'righteous disobedience'[97] through his transgression of 'purity' codes. Rather, the woman's actions themselves initiate contact. The medium of touch is of course never a one-way endeavour: someone reaches out to touch someone else who is accordingly touched. Touch can variously exhibit superiority or subordination, reverence or insolence, the offering or removal of a status, sanctification or desecration. To decipher the meaning of the touch, as Gabriele Alex submits, one needs to consider among other elements, 'who touches whom, in which context and [with] which parts of the body'.[98] Many biblical interpreters have rendered the leaky woman's touch as one of a social pariah. However, some recent critics have detected a latent anti-Semitism at play in such readings for Levitical codes only proscribed untouchability for bleeding women in particular social contexts which are not represented here. In F. Scott Spencer's opinion, 'none of these limitations have any relevance to the woman's case. She's by the sea of Galilee, nowhere near the temple, she seems to have no husband [who she would be proscribed not to have sexual relations with due to her condition], and is not trying to have sex with Jesus. She's walking outside in public, not lying or sitting on her bed or chair and certainly not carrying them with her.'[99] While this may be generally true, the narrative does still seem to show an internalized sense of 'pollution' on the part of the woman. She creeps around surreptitiously and anonymously in the crowd and does not want to draw attention to herself or her plight. Her covert approach would seem to indicate a tacit acceptance of some sort of social marginality based on her disordered bleeding.

It is perhaps not insignificant that, whilst the crowd hastens and helps in the healing of the elite Jairus' daughter, this leaky woman who is poor (for she has spent all she has on therapies to no avail) is ironically isolated among the masses, the crowd if anything hinders her approach to Jesus. This 'segregation' in a multitude in itself reveals the inconsistencies endemic to exclusion based on perceived pollution or disorder. Just as the leaky woman feels alone in the crowd, so in India 'institutional space and…colonial urbanity exacerbated the experience of the caste body by highlighting the irrationality of the caste system'.[100] Gopal Baba Valangkar, a Dalit activist, interestingly challenged civic exclusion by using a model of a menstruating woman who is shy of her husband and going out in public as a result of internalized shame and self-revulsion. He noted that, without two ends of the continuum, the 'fortunate pure' and the 'stigmatised polluted', there would be no 'public' from which to shy. Building on Valangkar's insights, Rao similarly stated that 'the organisation of the world through the phenomenology of touch and smell enabled an extension of stigma from biological bodies to the metaphorical collective of the body politic'.[101] This interchange between the social body and the actual interchanges and interaction of flesh and blood bodies, whilst socially debilitating, did also however hold within it potential avenues for political change.

If the site of the woman's sensory tactics is not overtly an act of 'impure' touch, how should we understand it? Jesus' own reaction offers some interesting clues. Spencer avers that there is an 'edge of irritation, even of personal insult' reflected in Jesus' response: 'Who touched my clothes?' (Mark 5: 30). Indeed he renders this question as an indignant 'Who dare take my power without asking?'[102] Returning to the idea that the woman's prior treatments for her condition were 'polluting' and odorous, maybe this gives some rationale behind Jesus' strange question of who 'specifically' touched him among the masses. Smell is his primary sensory alert to her imminence. However even a rancid odour does not really account for the offence she seems to have provoked and the humiliating public exposure of her that Jesus goes on to perform. The narrative reveals of course that the woman covertly extorts physically rehabilitating energy from Jesus. Her touching of his garment 'triggers a potent discharge from his body to hers; his dynamic flow into her body remedies her defective flow'.[103] Indeed this could be read quite erotically, she is sucking his power from him while he is not looking. Recent feminist and disability readings of this passage have made something of this. Candida Moss, for example, sees the story purposefully reversing the usual channels of healing in the ancient world, in which an ill, weak, and leaky body would be fused and dried. Here, however, Jesus jarringly takes on characteristics of the porosity of the woman; he too wildly leaks substances, albeit power, not blood.[104] Similar tropes of shared 'seeping substance' have interestingly undergirded Dalit protests as well, where shared identity between all people is an underlining theme. In Gopal Guru's words, 'as pathological investigation would reveal, every organic body—human or animal—consists of organic refuse...bodies become objects of ridicule depending on their capacity to emit the filth in a controlled way'.[105] At the leaky woman's demand, Jesus' body starts, like hers, to involuntarily leak. It will also leak blood at the crucifixion. Jesus thus exhibits the woman's plight, for as Susan Wendell submits: 'the failure to control the body is one of the most powerful symbolic meanings of disability'.[106] Such moments are essential in establishing a connection between organic bodies. Indeed the entire narrative neatly dovetails with the sentiments expressed by an untouchable woman in an ethnography focused on the potential democratization of all somatic experiences: 'Nothing will happen until they see that our bodies are made of the same clay as theirs. We both are equally pure [or] equally impure.'[107] In this respect, Jesus' address to her as 'daughter' takes on a different resonance, rather than inclusion or paternal care, this familial relationship underlines the acknowledgement of parallel experiences within their bodies, and also similar to the interaction with the leper, a certain 'un-touch-ability' related to each.

Untouchability and Sensory Tactics

I have submitted here that the leper, Legion, and leaky woman can be creatively read alongside ethnographic studies of 'untouchables' and their respective sensory tactics. Our characters have often been flatly labelled as impure according to religious codes and are correspondingly frequently associated with mortality and death. Following Sakine, however, I contended that the everyday embodiment of these 'religious' codes can be somewhat different. I adopted his heuristic classification of 'impurity' as an elimination of a person or thing considered as 'dirt, out of place' and contrastingly 'pollution' as a more fluid concept which could be creatively directed and shared by those on the social margins to initiate change and even dissolution of social boundaries. In exploring 'pollution' as it was experienced in an embodied state, I also probed olfactory stigmatization (based on real or imagined odours) related to specific conditions, moral positions, and social identities.

I then went on to refigure the leper as a character who ironically unveils the 'untouchability' of religious elite, here imaged in the characterization of Jesus who is given the option to touch and share the pollution of the leper in a creative moment. Legion likewise was pictured as an individual who in his possessed state inscribed the political and social oppression of empire onto his body. His naked, dirty protest was a potent and evocative unveiling to the people of their own compliance with the Roman imperial machine. The leaky woman, whilst to some degree embodying an internalized sense of shame concerning her condition, at one and the same time is singled out because of her audacious approach which results in a demonstration of the seepage of all bodies. She thus dissolves, like Dalit protesters, the false ontological differences between polluted and pure flesh.

All three characters are ironically empowered by their 'pollution'. For whilst on account of their various conditions they are subject to haptic and olfactory discrimination, and variously hailed as the social dead, 'walking carrion',[108] invoking repulsion in others, their conditions also ironically arm them with sensory tactics which can at times function as 'poisoned weapons'.[109] Ultimately they are shown to possess the explosive ability to spread nervous disquiet among those people and systems that would alienate the 'stench' of their untouchable bodies.

Sense, Seizures, and Illness Narratives: The Case of an 'Epileptic'/'Demon-Possessed' Boy

The story of Lia Lee, a child of Hmong refugees from Laos who was born in California in 1982, and the condition which found her in the cross-fire between Western medicine and her indigenous culture, has become legendary in medical anthropology and cross-cultural studies of illness.[1] To her American doctors, Lia Lee presented classic symptoms of severe epilepsy, though to her family she was caught by a malevolent spirit which made her fall down (*quag dab peg*). Miscommunication and misapprehension on both sides due to language issues, different conceptions of time, and vastly different therapies (prescription drugs and invasive brain procedures versus consultations with shamans, ritual washings, and pig sacrifices) saw Lia's condition worsening, until at 4 years old she experienced a massive seizure accompanied by sepsis and shock that left her comatose. She was returned to her family for what was thought to be short-term palliative care. Remarkably, there she remained for twenty-six years, until on 31 August 2012, at the age of 30 years old, she passed peacefully away. The ethnography which propelled Lia Lee's story to fame, Anne Fadiman's, *The Spirit Catches you and you Fall Down: A Hmong Child, her American Doctors and the Collision of Two Cultures* (1997) arrestingly concludes 'that her life was ruined by cross-cultural misunderstanding'.[2]

Janelle Taylor's review article on Fadiman's ethnography, whilst acknowledging its poignancy, power, and emotional potency—hence the title of her piece, 'The *Story* Catches you and you Fall Down: Tragedy, Ethnography and Cultural Competence'[3]—nonetheless critically questions the collision course set up by the simplistic binary opposition between medical science and Hmong indigenous culture and their respective 'explanatory' models of illness. Tapping into recent social-scientific debates into the enacted, performed, and fluid nature of culture, Taylor submits that:

'Culture' is not a 'thing' somewhere 'out there', that books are 'about'. It is a process of making meaning, making social relations, making the world we inhabit, in which all of us are engaged—when we read and teach, or when we diagnose and treat, no less than when we embroider *nyas* or conduct sacrifices.[4]

What Fadiman interprets as Lia's parents displaying a central 'Hmong cultural trait', namely unwillingness to recoil under those exerting power over them, for domination and assimilation to super-powers such as China and in this case America are strongly resisted by this minority group, Taylor sees as a gross homogenization of culture. In Taylor's words, 'Hmong culture appears as an unchangeable and unstoppable entity, bound to crash into whatever gets into its path'.[5] Likewise, the depiction of the doctors and medical team in the ethnography is also in Taylor's view marked by an unremitting and exaggerated inflexibility. Taylor, for example, documents an alternative medical testimony which openly admits that Lia Lee's final seizure may have been caused by a bacterial infection which her lowered immune system, due to prescription drugs, made her more susceptible to, rather than any confusion or reluctance from her parents to cooperate with medics. In light of such hiatuses, in Taylor's words,

If what we make of a book such as *The Spirit Catches You* is a set of stereotypes about what 'they' think, or a bunch of rules about how to deal with 'them', like so many specialized tools to be stashed in a briefcase and trotted out each time one of 'them' shows up, then we will certainly fail to keep alive the empathetic curiosity that allows one to be thoughtfully alert to difference...cultural competence [is when] we take them not as solid clumps of congealed truth, but as goads to curiosity, invitations to make meaning, moments in the ongoing process that is culture.[6]

Despite these shortcomings, Taylor also sees extraordinary 'possi-bilities' within Feldman's ethnography, namely a 'summoning [of Lia Lee] back to life' through narrative retelling, itself a rather staggering phrase in this context. Whilst Lia Lee occupied a liminal space fol-lowing her seizure, hovering between life and death in a coma, like shamanic cures that work through stories, Feldman's ethnography too has the potential to produce a 'trance-like state in which invisible and mute souls show themselves and speak'. [7] For Taylor, 'there is quite a perfect fit between shamanism as a *subject* of storytelling and storytelling as a *form* of shamanism'.[8] Taylor thus sees the crafting of the ethnography, the characters, and the receivers intersubjectively involved in the narration of an otherwise inert and voiceless Lia Lee:

> Like shamans, they [ethnographers; storytellers; other characters] are called to their work by being themselves 'afflicted' and 'possessed' by stories…When Fadiman concludes *The Spirit Catches You* with the words recited by *txiv neeb* whom Faou and Nao Kao had hired to call back Lia's soul, the reader feels the power of the incantation through the power of storytelling. Lia can be brought back; medical failure can be overcome, if not by the physician in what we usually call real life, at least by a shamanic storyteller in the powerfully real experience of reading.[9]

This opening vignette has some resonance with the comments made by a student in a module on 'Disability and the Bible' that violently railed against what he saw as two different, but equally 'disabling', interpretive models in biblical studies surrounding the boy with seizures (Mark 9: 14–29; Matt. 17: 14–20; Luke 9: 37–43). The first Western 'medicalizing' model either simplistically 'diagnosed' the boy in light of what Western neuro-science understood as 'epilepsy' or saw the seizure as symptomatic of a psychiatric problem. Though the student thought at least the former diagnosis quite plausible, such readings in his opinion diluted the social implications of the condi-tion (employment opportunities, limiting of social activities); it also 'domesticated' and 'tamed' the seizure and robbed it of its otherness. This model also seemed to him to limit the effects of the condition to an individual or nuclear family rather than considering a wider communal network. Most devastatingly, it silenced the voices of those who, in other cross-cultural contexts, occupied a world-view in which such conditions were still associated with malevolent spirits.

The second 'spirit-possession' model, while taking 'possession' and its social effects more seriously, often categorically equated the seizures with a totalizing social 'stigma'. In such readings no devices or localized strategies of resistance were engaged whatsoever. The possessed boy was painted as passive and pitiable who, like a helpless insect, was caught in the spider's web of discrediting and disabling social attitudes. The student went on to tell us that he saw these two respective 'illness' models as extreme poles on a continuum he himself inhabited. Within his particular (non-Western) cultural tradition his 'epilepsy', though now closely controlled with Western medicine's prescription drugs, still posed shame on account of deep-seated cultural beliefs surrounding malevolent origins of such conditions and the potential chaos or misfortune they risked posing to others. Not only were such beliefs prospectively devastating for him and his own marriage prospects, but also his wider family. For this reason, no one beyond his intimate kin knew about his seizures for their visibility had been carefully and strategically managed throughout his life and were purposefully hidden from the wider community. Rather than an insect caught, he and his family it seems had themselves spun subversive storied webs to reimagine their own identities. We, in the class that day, were the first witnesses to his story, and I was particularly intrigued by the potential his, and Lia Lee's, specifically styled narrative disclosures could have for refiguring the interpretation of the boy with seizures in the gospels.

In the context of this book's theme, sensory disabilities, here 'making sense' is central. This faculty is often assumed to be a conscious and cognitively normative process. One is said to be the epitome of 'common sense' when acting intentionally, rationally, and with wise counsel; conversely, when seemingly unconscious or 'out of one's senses', aggressive attempts to 'bring to one's senses' are put into effect. When normative theories of consciousness or awareness are sustained those who are presumed to feel or think differently from what is regarded as 'typical' in respective cultural contexts are often outlawed as deviant or abnormal. Moreover, sensory faculties are often seen to act differently in such situations, either being repressed or conversely experienced in hyper-sensitized forms. Auras (precursors to seizures) have for example been seen to manifest themselves primarily through sensory channels: 'touch, sound or sight hallucinations' are common as are the detection of 'strong, often unpleasant, smells or tastes'.[10] One's whole identity and sense-making ability seems to be embodied in such associations. It is also worthwhile noting, at the outset, the marked absence of consideration of experiential or consciousness differences in disability studies itself. A number of theorists have bemoaned this imbalance, some even seeing disability studies as a discipline only tooled to deal with the physical.[11] Illustrating this discrepancy, Stuart Murray for example notes how in Mitchell and Snyder's magnum opus, *Narrative Prosthesis,* there are more index references to 'Nazism' than to 'cognitive';[12] furthermore, there is no entry for 'seizures' or 'epilepsy' whatsoever. Anne Louise Chappell sees the marginalization of these areas as akin to 'suggesting that the analyses of society offered by feminism are applicable only to white women'.[13] Engaging experiences of those variously castigated as 'other' in seizure states seems one important response to this glaring omission.

In light of the above, in this chapter I will offer some illustrations of biblical commentators who have utilized either a Western medical model or conversely a 'spirit possession' model as the sole framework for interpreting the boy's story. Limitations on both sides will be identified. I will then go on to introduce the work of those who have sought to bring narrative and story to bear on representations of illness in different cultural settings. This sort of work enables interpreters to move beyond both the modern medical analyses which situate seizures solely 'in the body' and conversely homogenizing cultural analyses that categorically label them as 'stigmatizing' on account of negative associations. Rather hybridity and pluralism are the hallmarks of illness narratives for all conditions are 'present in a life'.[14] In this light one can start to see where models, in particular ancient medical treatises on seizures and folk beliefs surrounding spirits, potentially coalesce as well as conflict, and can start to take seriously the strategic and interpretive managing of seizures not only through monitoring of visibility or 'instrumental telling and disclosure'[15] (as employed by my student) but also a variety of other means, particularly those centred on narration and performance.

I will, following Bryan Good's work on ethnographic and narratological surveys of stories which 'reconstitute life worlds unmade'[16] by seizures, attempt to show that narratives are not just the preserve of the person experiencing seizures or their close kin, but rather are inherently intersubjective, involving a more extensive populace. In light of the stories collected by Good and other associated ethnographic evidence of seizures which were 'dialogically constructed, told often by interwoven conversations of several persons' stories whose referents were often the experiences of persons other than narrators',[17] so the narrow focus on the boy and father in understandings of the gospel traditions should be revised. I propose here to explore the intersubjective performances of the seizure by the surrounding crowds, disciples, and Jesus in the accounts. In this way, not only will the contextual dynamics of seizures within distinct situations be taken more seriously, but also the deliberate staging, mixing, and fusion of narrations endemic to the accounts will be brought into clearer view. Moreover, through teasingly juxtaposing diverse ethnographic evidence with the traditions in the gospels I hope to show how, 'shamanically' through story, this voiceless character can in some respects be encouraged to speak.

A final word by way of introduction, the term 'seizure' is specifically chosen to title this chapter, as it speaks intelligibly within medical, psychiatric, and spirit-possession constructions. For epilepsy as a term can constitute a 'medicalization' of particular seizures; it also functions coherently within the orbit of spirit possession, for it is etymologically derived from *epilepsia* the Greek for being 'seized, attacked, or overcome'.

Diagnosis and Exegesis: The Boy with Seizures

The story and experiences of the boy with seizures (Mark 9: 17–29; Matt. 17: 14–20; Luke 9: 37–43) have, like many other healings in the gospels, frequently been swiftly bypassed by more theologically orientated interests of commentators: the disciples' fallibility, faithlessness, and Jesus' dramatic acts of healing. John Donahue and Daniel Harrington's commentary on Mark's account is emblematic of such a diversion when they state that the major interest of the passage is not the seizure but rather 'the theological theme of faith' and 'the power of Jesus as healer'.[18] Similarly W. D. Davies and Dale Allison in effect depict the boy as nothing more than means for Matthew to demonstrate 'the authority of Jesus' and the establishment of the broader theological point that 'faith enables [and] lack of the same cripples'.[19] Eugene Boring and Fred Craddock likewise, in figuring the Lucan version, contend that the Markan source is compressed to 'concentrate on Jesus' action [which] results in praise of God'.[20] The boy and his seizure once again slip largely unnoticed from view.

What little comment is given to the boy and his condition by commentators is often achieved by way of 'diagnosis': 'the identification of the nature of an illness or other problem by examination of the symptoms'.[21] Diagnosing the dead is a problematic business, yet the urge to identify and ascribe a label to historical and literary characters even from antiquity is for many irresistible. Diagnoses of course matter for 'what we call a thing determines much about how we respond to it'.[22] The boy with seizures, probably more than any other character, illustrates both divisions and slippages between diagnostic analyses; for seizures have been explicated for as long as they have been apparent. Moreover they have been the focus of a variety of ideas surrounding cures and therapies which correspond to the 'heterogeneity of cultures and places'[23] in which they take place. Steven Schachter and Lisa Andermann accordingly groups beliefs about seizures into four general categories: 'diseases of the brain', 'contagious diseases', 'bewitchment or possession', and 'punishments for sin'.[24] A brain disorder most closely matches modern Western biomedical constructions. Contagion, bewitchment, possession, and retribution for misdeeds have most relevance to contexts which commonly view such phenomena as originating from the spirit world or demons.

The boy in the gospel stories has frequently been identified by Western translators and commentators in terms of the first model as 'epileptic'.[25] John Wilkinson, for example, notes that whilst 'the evangelists do not give us exact medical descriptions of the convulsion such as we might find in a modern text-book of neurology, and we have no right to expect this from them, even so the detail given and the words used give us a very vivid picture of the seizures and leave us in doubt that this boy suffered from the major form of epilepsy or *le grand mal* of the French neurologists'.[26] John Meier similarly states that 'needless to say *we moderns* recognise the problem as epilepsy',[27] albeit with the proviso that the evangelists and characters in the story would have seen the origins of the boy's complaint as 'demonic' characteristic of a 'pre-scientific' or 'pre-enlightenment worldview'.

The terms used to denote phenomena and bodily sensations are of course the 'linguistic means through which illness acquires a social existence'.[28] Thus the tendency to collapse the language of Mark's 'mute spirit' (*pneuma alalon*, Mark 9: 17), Luke's 'spirit who takes him' (*pneuma lambanei auton*, Luke 9: 39), and Matthew's 'moonstruck' (*seleniazetai*, Matt. 17: 14) into modern 'epilepsy' is somewhat simplistic. As John Pilch contends, such interpretations belie a certain 'mediocentrism' which he sees as a dubious 'species of ethnocentrism that chooses to view texts about sickness and healing from the ancient Middle East in a Western biomedical perspective'.[29] Such fixed categorizations also seem distant from the diversity of seizure types which Western medicine itself constructs, indeed C. P. Panayiotopoulos's recent clinician's guide talks throughout of a diversity of 'epilepsies' to indicate the vast array of 'syndromes and diseases' with a 'multitude of different manifestations and causes'[30] encapsulated by this broad term. Perhaps the dominant weakness however of so easily equating an ancient and culturally distant literary character's seizures within a Western medicalizing framework is that the 'healing' is conceived primarily as 'disciplining' of the disorder; moreover its cause is located firmly in an individual body with little attention being paid to a wider community. The identity of the 'patient' and the social marginalization they experience is to a certain extent dissolved and circumvented in such constructions. This tendency is the grounding of one of the fiercest criticisms of Western medical models in general, namely the 'colonisation' of the body implicit in such diagnoses.[31] The agency and personhood of the individual experiencing seizures are totally eclipsed as they are perceived as oft-times inanimate 'problems' in need of 'fixing'. Oliver Sacks gave voice to this weakness when he stated:

There is no subject in a narrow case history; modern case histories allude to a subject in cursory phrases which could well apply to a rat as a human being. To restore the human subject at the centre, the suffering, afflicted, fighting, human subject, we must deepen a case history to a narrative or tale; only then do we have a 'who' as well as a 'what', a real person, a patient, in relation to disease, in relation to the physical.[32]

Commentators that take a Western medicalized framework as the primary means to interpret the boy's seizures all too frequently pass over the 'boy' himself and rather see his identity solely in terms of the disease. Rory Foster's 'objectification' of the boy is a case in point: 'deaf and dumb, violently epileptic...*the child seemed to offer an insuperable obstacle* to the man's search for help, especially after the failure of the apostles'.[33] In short, the 'condition', rather than a person with the condition, is the focus of 'healing', 'cure', and 'normalisation' and Jesus impressively and instantaneously brings this about.

Responding perhaps in part to the need to 'story' particular characters, other contemporary Western commentators have recently offered alternative 'diagnoses' for the boy's condition, including somatoform disorders, which whilst producing powerful physical effects, including disruption of motor and sensory functions, are symptomatic of psychologically stressed states. James Keir Howard, for example, notes that the boy's symptoms could, rather than epilepsy, actually point to 'conversion disorder' which itself would be more acquiescent to the therapies offered by Jesus.[34] Donald Capp's controversial Freudian psychological reading of the boy's complaint as self-directed aggression expressed symbolically through seizure adopts a similar view. Capp proposes that psychological conflicts the boy experienced included 'base and evil wishes towards his parents'.[35] Capp accordingly reads falling into fire and water as self-destructive acts symptomatic of 'the displacement of the desire to inflict punishment on someone else, quite possibly his mother'[36] due to her harsh disciplinarian treatment. Muteness, grinding of teeth, and foaming at the mouth all centred on the 'organ of verbal aggression' are also seen as symbolic screams at an overbearing father:

In fact name-calling, insults and slurs were common....Symptoms of falling down rolling and rigidity would reflect the impulse to engage in physical aggression against his father....Thus these symptoms suggest that both the desire—and the containment of this desire—to attack his father physically with the intent to do serious bodily harm.[37]

Capp considers that Jesus' ultimate 'lifting up' of the boy by the hand at the end of the Markan version of the story (Mark 9: 27) and so often read as figurative of Jesus' own raising from the dead at the resurrection, rather demonstrates a 'father-like performance' similar to those employed by young men who, when a father had been killed in war or was absent for some other reason, had to become surrogate parents to younger siblings: 'In this regard, Jesus became, for the moment at least, the boy's surrogate father, the protective father he never had'[38] and also 'acted as his own Father's [God's] surrogate'.[39] Capp concludes that the category of epilepsy should be extended to include all manner of 'seizings, fits, or sudden changes in mood appearance or behaviour' for what unites such instances is that the person at the centre of them is perceived by others to be disordered:

Regardless of the medical, psychiatric, or religious term that is used to identify persons who suffer from seizures, the common observation is that the person appears to be 'out of control' as though one is being 'controlled' by an external agency outside oneself.…We don't know that there was something in the voice, the touch and the very demeanour of Jesus that enabled him to put these 'base and evil wishes' behind him and to take control of his life … *The demon-possessed boy is us, and the man to whom his father took him—the man whose power to cure was due to his faith in himself—is in our neighbourhood too.*[40]

The shortcomings of Western psychologizing approaches are once again the narrow focus on a nuclear kin unit, the boy had problems with his own father and mother, but few implications of his condition to a wider populace are ever mentioned. Moreover, the 'domesticating' of seizures, of which my student spoke, is implicit in Capp's statement that 'we' (modern Western readers) in sharing psychological stress, also potentially share symptoms of seizures. For someone who lives with these experiences day in day out, however, the disruption they cause seems to be disparagingly dismissed in such universalizing interpretations.

A second dominant model found in modern commentaries is to assign the seizure in 'emic' terms to spirit possession, given that these categories seem to be the main operative system by which the evangelists and characters in the story understand the phenomena. Owsei Temkin in his magisterial treatment of 'the falling sickness' in history relates that 'the gospel itself, where Jesus was reported to have driven the demon out of the epileptic boy makes the acceptance of a purely physical theory impossible'.[41] He paints a world in which Schachter's and Anderman's other three categories of seizures, 'contagious disease', 'punishment for sin', and 'bewitchment and possession' are prevalent;

and the 'dread of sinister power lurking behind the possessed'[42] had dire consequences not only for the victim and their kin in terms of social stigma, but also posed a threat to the wider community they inhabited.

All three evangelists talk in terms of spirits underlying the condition. Mark identifies the spirit as the cause of the boy's inability to speak and hear (Mark 9: 25) and in common with his interest in displaying cosmic conflict, is seen by many to be part of an 'ongoing battle [within the gospel] against the forces of evil'.[43] Twelftree remarks that 'mute spirits were considered particularly difficult to exorcise'[44] thus the statement at the close of the passage that 'this kind' (*touto to genos*) can only come out through prayer (Mark 9: 29) refers to 'this kind of demon', namely a 'particularly vicious…desperate character'.[45] The vivid visual spectacle of the seizure narrated by Mark also no doubt, as Joel Marcus submits, contributed to the demonological interpretation of the seizure, for 'the sufferer's loss of control of themselves…conveyed being victims of an attack from the outside'.[46] In the narration leading up to Jesus' exorcism of the demon, Mark and Luke both call it an unclean spirit (*tw pneumatic tw akathartw*, Mark 9: 25; Luke 9: 42) to denote its potential for contamination and contagion. Indeed, spitting at an individual possessed by such a power was a common occurrence to ward off the threat of demonic corruption of others.[47]

In Matthew's version of the story we encounter the boy being described as *seleniazetai* (Matt. 17: 15). Whilst many translations render this term 'epileptic' it is better translated as 'moonstruck'. Those commentators forwarding a possession model often contemplate the associative evil power of the moon and Selene, the moon goddess.[48] J. Ross observes that 'moonstruck' could also denote insanity, which was commonly thought to be influenced by lunar cycles at the time.[49] Ann Jacoby, Dee Snape, and Gus Baker similarly submit that 'seizures were often considered bad omens…epilepsy [was frequently seen] as a form of madness, and the notion of people as "lunatic" held widespread currency'.[50] Plutarch for example records the importance of the moon on sensory disorders when he reported that:

Nurses are exceedingly careful to avoid exposing young children to the moon, for, being full of moisture like green wood they are thrown into spasms and convulsions. And we see that those who have gone asleep in the light of the moon are hardly able to rise again, like men with senses stunned or doped, for the moisture poured through them by the moon makes their bodies heavy.[51]

Carter extends the reference of the seizure to a wider colonized populace when he links this image with imperial propaganda which denoted 'the moon-blessed success of Rome' but which was jarringly experienced as a 'destructive effect on people's lives'.[52] For him the main point of the narration is that 'the moon/demon/goddess threatens the boy's life in destructive acts'.[53] Carter also goes on to explore the social stigma such a condition would have not only on the boy but also his family. Speaking of the desperate approach of the father in the narrative he writes:

The man's social and economic circumstances, both present and future are serious. A demon-possessed son probably means social ostracism for the family as others keep their distance. A son who cannot work cannot contribute to the family support or continue the family line of work, whether a small business or land. And since a child is its parents' old age policy, their outlook is bleak. The man is desperate.[54]

In the 'possession' model, the story has also often been reframed as a parable of social collapse in which possession is the main signifier, as for example was the case for the patristic authors who used seizures as 'a tool for constructing communal identities and policing group boundaries'[55] and articulating 'that which is to be avoided', those categorized as 'other', infidels, or disobedient and who do 'not belong to the Christian community'.[56]

Taking an 'emic' model of 'spirit' or moon possession as the primary heuristic framework from which to interpret the boy's seizure therefore does go some way to moving beyond an individualizing of the seizure in a diseased body as conceptualized by modern Western analyses, and reflects on social implications of the condition. However, often the seizure in this framework, as my student pointed out, is equally at risk of bypassing the characters themselves, for they are swamped by negative associations: at best they are helpless, hopeless, and passive, and at worst, degenerate, disordered, and demonized. Once more the stories or potential agency of the individuals involved are eclipsed.

Capp's conclusion that the difference between 'we moderns', the evangelists, and characters populating the story, 'is not that we believe the boy was suffering from epilepsy and they believed he was demon-possessed. Rather the difference is that we believe…that the symptoms had a natural cause while they believed that the cause was an evil spirit who had taken residence inside the boy',[57] seems too simplistic in this light. Just like Lia Lee's story, it is not the collision of two illness models which is the fate of the boy, but rather losing the person who is denied any capacity to 'proactively define and redefine their own body' and 'to recapture and reappropriate'[58] it. One wonders what sort of story could 'lift up' this boy not only from the ground as Mark's Jesus does, but also 'lift up' an alternative voice against fixed illness models which rob his story of its vibrant complexity.

Medical Anthropology and Storytelling

In the realm of medical anthropology, people tell stories not only to document symptoms or feelings but also to make sense of the somatic and cultural experiences they, or others related to them, are subject to. Arthur Kleinmann, one of the central figures in the reflection on illness narratives in anthropology, states that 'for patients [and those related to them] to tell stories about their illnesses is a way to create meaning and cope with their particular experiences'.[59] In such tellings the identity of the narrator, what form the story takes, and what elements are highlighted are never 'innocent' or 'neutral', for as Gaylene Becker notes, 'narrative is always political'.[60] Moreover they are distinct episodes and not monolithic, for they purposefully draw on diverse elements and understandings within a culture. Thus, as James Wilce contends, 'studying discourse (language in its fullness) and medicine together brings us to encounter culture as discursively constituted'.[61]

It is interesting that much social-scientific work on the experience of conditions such as seizures had until recently often used thematic bases for comparison. Joseph Schneider and Peter Conrad, for example, identify common subjects such as family life, seizure experience, stigma, and the management of information and treatments to unite such stories.[62] Such thematic impulses have to a certain extent been common in the biblical interpretations surveyed thus far. However, others have noted that such thematic analyses are detached from narrative and 'the artfulness of storytelling'.[63] For 'the whats' are not 'simply produced and reproduced in narrative episodes',[64] rather they are always situational, contingent, and purposefully presented in social activities. The storyteller brings together elements on the 'horizons of meaning' to create 'patterns or narrative linkages that serve to convey a constructed meaning to the audience'.[65] Good's ethnographic and narratological survey of seizure stories in Turkey is a good example of such tactics. He observed how some of those studied named their condition as 'fainting' which is culturally linked with trauma, as opposed to 'epilepsy' which is more often associated with madness.[66] This is illustrative of the fact that narrators draw on a number of contextually fitting idioms. Moreover, it serves to warn ethnographers of the hazards involved in monolithically 'diagnosing' persons with physiological, neurological, psychological, or spiritual conditions.

Good's study also highlights the fact that the stories he witnessed in Turkey were focused on the 'predicament' of illness, namely the anguish, origin, and pursuit of therapy. These narratives were, by their very nature, open-ended, indeterminate, and what Good calls 'subjunctivising': open to alternative retellings and endings in the future.[67] Particularly when seeking therapy, conditions were specifically and subtly negotiated, both drawing on accepted and recognizable forms but also interrupting, challenging, or refiguring elements of the condition during the conversation. He reveals that the 'network of meanings' of seizures drawn upon in these retellings incorporated 'traumatic experiences of fright, shock, and loss…attacks by jinns [spirits] and being struck by bad glance or evil eye'.[68]

Good's study also corroborates Kleinmann's thesis that, 'the plotlines, core metaphors, and rhetorical devices that structure the illness narrative are drawn from cultural and personal models for arranging experience in meaningful ways and for effectively communicating those meanings'.[69] His work also reminds us that, even though different contexts may have standard words to denote a particular condition, nonetheless, such appellations should never be used to irreversibly encase a seizure occurrence. For as Veena Das and Ranendra Das contend, 'there are no hermetically sealed cultures within which illness is experienced, diagnosis is made and therapies are sought'.[70] Taking hybridity and plurality seriously within illness narratives sensitizes one to the fact that, whilst seemingly embodying one type of discourse, at the same time a story may 'challenge another's version of reality'.[71]

By engaging a 'meaning-centred model', clashes of the sort described in Lia Lee's story and those that mark both Western medicalizing and spirit-possession readings of the boy in the gospels are to a certain extent ameliorated. Rather than a sole focus on diagnosis, one can actually 'help rewrite a story of sickness into a story of healing'.[72] This does not mean the physical or social understanding of healing which Jesus is presumed to accomplish at the end of the story in each gospel, but rather, what Taylor termed 'shamanic' raising-up of a muted life story. Shamans, in the words of Mircea Eliade, 'stimulate and free the imagination, demolish the barriers between dream and present reality, open windows upon worlds inhabited by gods, the dead and spirits',[73] and thus offer opportunities to creatively juxtapose traditions and experiences in order to refigure those flattened and silenced by existing configurations.

Refiguring the Story of the Boy with Seizures: Chaos and Quest

If we take Arthur Frank's thesis seriously, that 'wounded storytellers' tell narratives through their own and other's bodies,[74] then we can legitimately approach our gospel traditions concerning the boy with seizures as a dense illness account, told and enacted through the diverse voices and forms of characters populating the narrative. Taking the 'hows' as well as the 'whats' of a story seriously inevitably makes one look at particularities rather than homogenizing universals. Moreover, it allows one to recognize not only concord but also dynamism and dissonance in exchanges, for illness narratives cross-fertilize, manœuvre, and transform according to their respective tellers and receivers. Recognizing how interlocutors do things with stories transforms these tales from media of accepted knowledge to ideologically composite and weighted tales.[75] In this vein, rather than being a treatise on faith or a demonstration of Jesus' extraordinary power to heal, this tradition purposefully interpreted as an illness narrative puts the identity and experience of the boy at the centre of the drama and in some ways therefore also serves to mitigate the objectification and depersonalization of his character so inherent in the constructions surveyed thus far.

In all three accounts, the boy's story is immediately preceded by the transfiguration, an event which itself has been read by many as a 'trance-like state' in which Jesus and the disciples are caught up in a visionary experience redolent of shamanic alternative states of consciousness.[76] Mark's account in particular makes the connecting link between Jesus' transformed state and his appearance to the crowds as he approaches them. Namely they are said to be 'overcome with awe' (*exethambethesan,* Mark 9: 15) at the sight of him and run forward to greet him (Mark 9: 15). Many commentators find parallels in Jesus' changed appearance and descent from a mountain with Moses' shining face in Exodus after 'he has been talking with God' (Exod. 34: 30). William Placher accordingly remarks, 'does something of the radiance of the transfiguration remain?',[77] and A. E. Harvey submits, 'Mark may have been thinking of a reflection of glory still visible on Jesus' face some hours after the event and producing awe in all those who saw him'.[78] However, *exethambethesan* can also be rendered more strongly as surprised, alarmed, or distressed. Gundry captures the potent strength and force of the term when he contends: 'here we read the compound form having the perfective—*ek*—which elsewhere will connote awe so extreme as to cause emotional distress, bodily tremors and psychological bewilderment'.[79] It is not incidental that the same root is also used to denote the pole-axing fear of Jesus faced with his own imminent death (Mark 14: 34) and, at the end of the gospel, the women's bewildered fright at the sight of a young man dressed in white at the tomb (Mark 16: 5). Thus reactions to Jesus' transfiguration could be said in some way to evoke parallel responses to seizures, for 'an altered state of consciousness or altered perceptions leads to difference in one's subjective experience of the world' and as a result such individuals have 'often been marginalised in their societies'.[80]

The use of the term *exethambethesan* also brings to mind the fact that ancient authors noted strong sensory and emotional prompts prior to 'seizures'. Hippocrates in the fourth century BCE, in *On the Sacred Disease*, contended that environmental factors including sudden changes in temperature, the exposure of the head to the sun, and, interestingly in light of the above, weeping and terror could frequently initiate such phenomena.[81] In his *Medical Definitions* in the second century CE, Galen similarly identified sensory 'auras' which preceded seizures [82] and Aretaeus of Cappadocia, in the first century CE, listed hallucinations, foul odours, light, and trembling as symptomatic of such episodes.[83] Could it be, then, that the crowd seized by terror, awe, and bewilderment are themselves also constructed to some degree with seizure signifiers, thus ameliorating at the outset the notion that these characteristics are solely to be found in this story in the boy's own convulsive body?

The narrative continues in Mark's account with Jesus asking 'What are you arguing about with them?' (Mark 9: 16). Presumably a question addressed to the disciples about the scribes, however it is a member of the crowd who responds, a father of a boy with seizures. The father becomes the voice-piece of an extended catalogue of the boy's symptoms in the respective accounts and thus constitutes an important thread in the illness construction. Anthropologists have long noted how storytellers monitor and specifically engineer their accounts in reference to the anticipated responses of others, often subtly reframing their performances to achieve particular goals. In Mark's account the father addresses Jesus as 'Teacher' and tells him of his son who, due to a spirit, is unable to speak; the spirit also 'dashes him down; and he foams and grinds his teeth and becomes rigid' (or withered, scorched, or dried, thus denoting the life-threatening nature of the condition) (Mark 9: 17). In Luke's version, the pathos is intensified as the status of the boy as an only child is underlined: 'Teacher, I beg you to look at my son; he is my only child. Suddenly a spirit seizes him and all at once he shrieks; it convulses him until he foams at the mouth; it mauls him and will scarcely leave him' (Luke 9: 39). In Matthew's story the father's address is almost a worshipful lament, with him kneeling before Jesus crying, 'Lord have mercy on my son, for he is moonstruck and he suffers terribly; he often falls into the fire and often into the water' (Matt. 17: 14–15).

Whilst all three accounts testify to spiritual origins of the malady, nevertheless the actual narration of the symptoms, as Eric Sorenson has convincingly shown, have striking parallels with those outlined in the medical Hippocratic corpus, including speechlessness, foaming at the mouth, the body becoming stiff, falling, and convulsing.[84] He also notes however, that the origin of the phenomena in the Synoptic gospels must be seen as demonic possession rather than a 'medical' or material reason, for:

Though the symptoms of possession might lend themselves to medical definition and treatment the synoptic gospels distinguish them from such by attributing to them spiritual agencies subject to non-medical methods of exorcism. On the one hand, the author of the [Hippocractic] treatise is eager to point out the need for interpreting the disease in material rather than in spiritual terms, and to prescribe for it a material treatment. On the other hand the synoptics describe the illness in terms of spiritual possession, cured when the spirit departs from the body. Again interpretation dictates the methods of treatment.[85]

However, this is perhaps too easily dismissing the verbatim echoing of the terms of the medical treatise in the father's speech. Hippocrates' *On the Sacred Disease* purposefully plotted the struggle between scientific and more magical interpretations and insisted that epilepsy was not more sacred or divine than other diseases, indeed its origins could be traced to dysfunctions in the brain including melting which led to an excessive phlegmatic constitution, also hereditary causes or conditions in the womb.[86] Could it be that the father's dialogue intentionally weaves elements of both discourses together, in order to maximize his chances of effecting a 'cure' from Jesus in whichever form? After all, we presume he has already made a failed 'pitch' to the disciples, who have been unable to help the child.

Annette Weissenrieder in her study of the Lukan account is more open to the transformation of traditions when she forwards the thesis that 'the author of the Gospel of Luke is qualifying a "folk medical" interpretation which presumes the presence of a demon as an illness-producing phenomenon—in favour of a medical interpretation of this illness'.[87] She notes that, whilst Mark's account of the boy's treatment is narrated in terms of the exorcism of a mute spirit, 'in Luke's account the language of "healing" (9: 42) is more central'.[88] She proposes that in Luke's account the boy's condition was likely conceived as '"epileptic phenomena" brought about by phlegm'.[89] Antigone Samellas, in his review of such conditions, reveals that it was believed that under the pressure of 'black bile' and 'phlegm' 'the entire nervous system was affected by the disease. Whenever there was sudden overheating of the brain shouting and shrieking' ensued. Moreover, such conditions often 'exhibited many of the symptoms of melancholy'.[90] Whether Weissenrieder's neat transformation of a folk model in Mark to a medical model in Luke can be sustained, however, is questionable.

Indeed the more direct echoing of the Hippocratic corpus is featured in Mark (rather than Luke), and claiming that Mark's account should be seen as a straight exorcism, as opposed to Luke's healing, also seems to overlook the fact that 'spirits' are endemic to each. Jesus' question in Mark regarding how long the boy has had seizures (Mark 9: 21) could also, rather than being read as an opportunity for the evangelist to demonstrate the severity of the demonic possession—'the difficulty if not impossibity of the cases confirmed from the response that the boy has been this way from childhood'[91]—can also function coherently in medical frameworks. Hippocrates believed that cases in which the disease were apparent in childhood (as is the case with the boy in our story) tended to have more serious and devastating effects and were much harder to treat than those cases which had manifested themselves later in life.[92] In situations of crisis, it is not unknown for stories to draw on commonly held symptoms, or turns of phrase, for the enormity of the condition 'overwhelms' the teller and little biographical information is given, to use Deborah Kirklin's terminology, 'authentic narrative is displaced by medical narrative'.[93] An alternative reading could be that the father spoke in 'medical' terminology to try and dilute the stigma that surrounded the son's condition if it was thought to originate from an evil spirit. In this light, the dissonance with which the father speaks should be purposefully retained, rather than simplified into a unitary model. Neat divisions between the medical, magical, and spiritual are hard to sustain, for often illness narratives purposefully evoke a 'double consciousness'—the capacity to 'simultaneously accommodate mutually exclusive ideas'.[94] For as Samellas notes, in antiquity the alienated

> resorted to medical experts as much as to magicians and priests. Those in despair visited renowned physicians, took drugs, prayed, wore amulets, confessed their problem to a friend, or to a spiritual guide....Confidence in rational medicine did not preclude recourse to supernatural remedies.[95]

The bold and open disclosure of the son's story by the father should also not be dismissed lightly. Ethnographic evidence time and again notes that one of the most widespread familial rejoinders to stigma is the control of visibility of the condition, or discerning and anticipatory disclosure for particular strategic purposes, which can include the procurement of therapy.[96] The father does not shy away from the details in describing his son's plight in a public space for the latter purpose. However, in ascribing such graphic evocations of the condition, the father may at the same time, whether intentionally or unconsciously, be acting not only as an advocate but also what Graham Scambler and Anthony Hopkins identify as a 'stigma coach',[97] schooling their kin to feel ashamed and apprehensive and unable to see anything other than negative implications of the condition. The father's plea in all cases underscores the desperate repercussions of the condition for the whole family—'have pity on *us* and help *us*' (Mark 9: 22); 'have mercy' (Matt. 17:15); 'I beg you to look at my son, he is *my only child*' (Luke 9: 38)—and the fatal consequences it holds. The son is the vehicle of perpetuated fertility for the whole household (Gen. 22). The embodied nature of his symptoms shows the body's social 'dysfunction' for the household, as well as physical deviancy. This might also account for the 'scorched' and dry imagery, as a motif of impotence and sterility. Both Mark and Matthew also mention the mortal danger of fire and water (Mark 9: 22; Matt. 17: 15) which no doubt would have 'marked' the body of the boy. Louise Jilek-Aall, in her ethnographic review of work on seizures in Tanzania, similarly comments on the burns which covered the skin and marked those, even when not in seizure states, as 'other' within community and kin networks:

Here, [seizure sufferers] came with limbs deformed from burn scars and others with horrible fresh wounds from burns often reaching to the bone or covering large segments of the body....They were malnourished, dishevelled, and depressed they kept their head lowered and their eyes fixed on the floor. It took some courage to clean and treat their burn wounds, festering and buzzing with flies. I observed that other people retreated from these wretched ones even family members showed little sympathy and spoke with harsh language to them.[98]

Jilek-Aall also notes how 'few close family members dared to rescue a convulsing person from burning in a fire or from drowning in a river'[99] because of the fear that a spirit would be transferred to them. Could this in any way also be a part of the 'stigmatizing' rationale by both kin and community in the gospel tradition? Peter Bolt's study of death in Mark's Gospel notes that ancient magic often made use of 'epileptic' boys as mediums, and spells were 'often associated with lamp and water divination'.[100] Moreover, Graeco-Roman receivers of the gospels would also be all too aware of the mortal danger of mediums:

Lamp and bowl divination aimed at bringing *daimon* into the presence of a medium. In order to do so if the boy sat staring at water or into fire, the opportunity for destroying him was immediately at hand once the *daimon* was conjured. If a session involving these boys went wrong, it is not too extraordinary to imagine them being cast into the two 'tools of the trade' in order to damage or kill them.[101]

Whether through the stereotyped narration of material symptoms, the inculcation of negative attributes from the boy to a whole family, or by the public exhibition of the marked body of the seizure sufferer, it would seem true that it is not just 'outsiders' who objectify such characters, but also their close kin. Such implicit stigma inscription becomes even more serious when such ascriptions are implicitly mediated in supposedly therapy-seeking stories.

Jesus' retort following the narration of the condition by the father, and the revelation that the disciples failed to successfully treat the boy, is powerful and indignant: 'You faithless and perverse generation how much longer must I be among you? How much longer must I put up with you?' (Mark 9: 19; Matt. 17: 17; Luke 9: 41). Commentators have questioned to whom the response is actually directed. Jeannine Brown, locates the focus on those who have failed to provide a cure for the boy, namely the disciples: 'Since Jesus' words are a direct response to the report concerning the disciple's inability to heal the boy it is difficult to argue that the disciples are not at least included in "the faithless generation".'[102] Robert Tannehill, in relation to the Lukan account, similarly is keen to put the disciples firmly in the frame as the main subjects of the retort: 'Since Luke's story gives no attention to the faith of the father and since this reproach immediately follows reference to the disciples, Jesus seems to regard the disciples as the prime example of a "faithless and perverse generation".'[103] David Turner in contrast sees the retort primarily addressed at a crowd who 'expect miracles from him but do not grasp his identity and mission'.[104] However, given as Harrington comments, the direct parallels with Moses' rejection of the people in Deuteronomy 32: 5 as 'a perverse and crooked generation', it seems more persuasive to see the refutation being addressed to not only the disciples, but also the crowds and the father who collectively have played a part in the construction of what Frank terms 'a chaos narrative'[105] concerning the boy.

Chaos narratives for Frank are told when 'restitution' narratives (cure and normalization) seem almost hopeless. Chaotic illness stories are entrenched in the calamity of the disorder and struggle to shift beyond that phase.[106] They embody the dramatic 'abyss of illness as it spreads chaos in the normal ordering of life'.[107] Such stories are marked by choking, dark, and destructive elements (as have characterized the boy's story thus far) and are frequently scattered with what Frank calls 'narrative wreckage',[108] including failed attempts to bring healing, so much so that life is conceived as fragmented, contingent, and out of control. Jesus in his abrupt command to 'Bring him [the boy] to me' (Mark 9: 19; Matt. 17: 17; Luke 9: 41) sets in motion a counter-story to the chaotic narratives witnessed hitherto, namely what Frank terms a quest narrative. These stories 'search for meaning, patterns, regularities' and 'in a sense represent alternative ways of being ill, or even alternative ways of being well'.[109] By facing conditions 'head on', those caught up in quest stories come not to be physically cured, but rather transformed into those 'who know more about the self and life and return to share insights with others'.[110]

The 'quest' narrative here involves the physical presence of the 'boy' himself. Whilst the character of the boy in all three synoptic accounts is passive and silent, he does, if only briefly, occupy explicit 'bodily' space. In Matthew's version of the story, following Jesus' command to 'Bring him here to me' (Matt. 17: 17), we are told that 'Jesus rebuked the demon, and it came out of him, and the boy was cured instantly' (Matt. 17: 18). In Luke's version also, the actual dramatic performance of the boy is limited. Once again his condition is narrated through the words of his father and following Jesus' command to bring the boy to him (Luke 9: 41) the narrator tells us that 'the demon dashed him to the ground in convulsions' but that, following Jesus' rebuke, 'the healed boy is given back to his father' (Luke 9: 43). Mark's account gives the boy the most developed physical presence in the performance when he states that, at the sight of Jesus, the boy is thrown 'into convulsions, and he fell on the ground and rolled about, foaming at the mouth' (Mark 9: 14). Whilst as Samellas contends, 'mental illness was a painful and humiliating experience' and as 'the author of the Hippocractic treatise, *On the Sacred Disease* observed fled from the people, for they were ashamed of themselves',[111] here the boy's performance is before others (including the gospel recipients) who are curiously drawn to the spectacle, rather than fearfully retreating away from it.

Furthermore, in Mark's account, the tragedy of the boy is underlined by the loss of his voice. Jesus rebukes the spirit and identifies its most serious impairment of the boy as impeding speech and hearing: 'You spirit that keeps this boy from *speaking and hearing*, I command you come out of him' (Mark 9: 25). Deafness and an inability to speak, as argued previously in this book, 'meant isolation from human communication'[112] and thus had dire political and social implications in the ancient world. Perhaps not insignificantly, the character does not ever directly speak in the narrative (to affirm a cure), but through him we are privy to an alternative to the debilitating chaos stories which surround him and begin at last to hear a more affirming voice which could speak of a more 'democratise[d] human experience'.[113]

Frank notes that, unlike restitution narratives which dominate Western medicine centred on a straight 'curing' of a disease, quest narratives often do not include 'cures' but rather draw their power from an ability to evoke alternative meanings for conditions. In this light it is perhaps not insignificant that, as the spirit leaves the boy, we are told 'the boy was like a corpse' (Mark 9: 26). Such images have more in common with what was known of post-seizure states, rather than a definitive cessation of seizures. Susan Reynolds in her ethnography of seizures in East Africa notes that the Swahili term 'Kifafa', literally meaning 'little death', is frequently used to speak about a post-seizure state in which 'falling, jerking of the limbs, foaming at the mouth…[are] followed by sleep and confusion'.[114] Wilkinson makes a similar claim in his materialist reading of this tradition that, 'like an epileptic in a postictal state the boy is left limp and seemingly lifeless'.[115] The boy does not demonstrate a physical cure explicitly within the narrative. He does not speak, he just stands up (Mark 9: 27). John Dominic Crossan and John Pilch have both drawn distinctions between a physical cure of a biomedical 'disease' and the 'healing' of the social stigma surrounding an illness.[116] Whether such straight binary divisions are sustainable is an open question, but certainly, by taking dimensions of the 'quest' narrative genre seriously, one does see 'illness is more than just the absence of health, because healing is more than simple restoration of physical well-being'.[117]

Whilst much has been made on a theological level of the imagery of 'lifting up' as a parallel to resurrection—or as William Lane puts it, 'the healing points beyond itself to the resurrection [when] Satan's power can be definitively broken'[118]—Meier's devilish question 'Where in this or other gospel miracle stories are we given assurances the relapses did not occur at a later date?'[119] is perhaps not wildly inappropriate here. Rather than witnessing the definitive 'cessation of seizures' or the 'normalization' of this character in a cure, perhaps we are witnessing what could be termed a subversive 'lifting up' of the wider community themselves.

In Mark's narrative, even before Jesus' exorcistic words are uttered, we are told that 'a crowd came running together' (*episuntrexei*, Mark 9: 25) or, to translate this more deliberately, as 'closing rapidly in on', 'magnetically drawn to', or 'seized by', the seizure spectacle. The cocktail of crowds and seizures was frequently seen as dangerous and chaotic in the ancient world. Often a seizure was held to be a 'bad omen' not only for those who witnessed them, but for the whole social order.[120] As a result Sabine Lucas tells how in ancient Rome whole assemblies were dispersed when a seizure happened.[121] Indeed 'epilepsy' was often termed the *morbus comitialis* (the disease of the people's assembly) for this very reason and was 'based on the custom at the time of breaking off popular assemblies (*comitiae*) such as elections'[122] due to such events. Here, however, far from being dispersed, the crowd themselves seem strangely 'seized' and drawn to the event. Whilst as Samellas has recently shown, non-voluntary movements in seizures were often seen as a 'loss of reason', 'self-estrangement', 'a state of blindness', and symptomatic of 'cognitive alienation, evident in the illusions and hallucinations of the afflicted',[123] here the compulsion of the crowds towards the seizure in this narrative is a reversal of their portentous power. Or to use Frank's terminology, a chaos narrative is here being transformed into a quest.

In Luke, the story ends with everyone being 'astounded at the greatness of God' (Luke 9: 43). In Mark and Matthew the final word is given to Jesus who, responding to questions asked in private by the disciples about their inability to help the boy, responds respectively with 'this kind can only come out through prayer' (Mark 9: 28) and the saying about faith the size of a mustard seed which will move mountains (Matt. 17: 20). In neither case is a straightforward answer given. Many see Mark's Jesus' response as odd, as he himself is not featured as praying within the exorcism and Matthew's account speaks only proverbially of faith, rather than a particular failure which happened in this case. Perhaps what is most striking is that the 'the defining boundaries of normality' so usually 'demarcated by abnormality'[124] are here reversed. The disciples themselves by asking Jesus in private arrestingly seem to employ the strategic management of their selves which was known to be so common to those with seizures. Rather than being defiantly visible before others in weakness, and ultimately 'standing up' within the community as the boy had done, they strategically manage and conceal their 'disabilities' from others. Their 'faith' is as a result rendered ineffective.

By ideologically 'leaking' seizure traits into the narrative about the boy, the story itself, as Jeanette Stirling notes of other such characterizations in world literature, 'subverts the notion that the epileptic is reliably and exclusively defined by these properties'.[125] Furthermore the fact that this story and its characters are to a certain extent fragmented, disjointed, have double consciousness, and at times border on the ecstatic, 'all function as part of a spectrum of [seizure] signifiers' which belie a strategy to purposefully 'destabilise socio-medical links between the epileptic and social disorder'.[126]

Sense, Seizures, and Illness Narratives

Seizures are perhaps one of the most suited phenomena for crafting illness narratives, for the dramatic nature of their symptoms affects a wide array of persons' experience of the 'here and now'.[127] Moreover, due to their nature, first-person descriptions are scant, and other models (medical, cultural, folk) become the pre-eminent means of 'diagnosing', 'narrativizing', and 'understanding' such experiences. Within this chapter I have attempted to illustrate how particular uses of 'Western medical' or 'spirit-possession' models can 'lose' the story of the person at the centre of them. Illness impacts on relationships, lives, and societies just as much as bodies and minds and stories are one means by which these can be transformed from passive and pitiable victims to active and admirable meaning-makers, or to use the evocative analogy of Nora Jones, stories are the means by which the sick can 'colonize new land [including the lands and shores of the "well"] to move beyond liminality and to remap the world'.[128]

Conceiving of the boy's story as an illness narrative involved identifying a number of different discursive threads within it: a story of medicine as well as folk therapies; a story of paternalism and stigma as well as fatherhood and advocacy; a story of communal repulsion as well as embrace; a story of difference marked by seizures of one body and a story of solidarity with seizures in a collective body. It was at once a chaos narrative but also a quest: 'meeting suffering head on' and 'seek[ing] to use it'[129] for particular ends. Moreover, it was a story of multiple voices, for wounded quest storytellers never find a voice alone. In Frank's words:

The self-story is never just a self-story, but becomes self/other story. In telling such a story, the three issues of voice, memory, and responsibility emerge. Finding a voice becomes the problem of taking responsibility for memory. Different quest stories all express this voice-memory-responsibility. The self-story becomes ethical practice.[130]

The triumph of the boy in this light comes not in finding a 'physical' voice, for he never explicitly speaks in the narrative, but rather, like Taylor's estimation of Lia Lee's shamanic 'lifting up' through storytelling, finding his wounded story in others and in turn posing a transformative example to follow. Ultimately, ironic as it may seem, sense can become known through seizure.

Conclusion: 'Sensory-Disabled' Characters Refiguring God

'If you are "severely normal" and only want to think and move between the limits of validated knowledge there is still time to push this book from your table'.[1] Thus states Theo Peters in his challenging 'Foreword' to Olga Bogdashina's 2010 volume, *Autism and the Edges of the Known World*. Unfortunately for you, my reader, if you are still with me, and have not just read the contents page then sneakily skipped over the main body of the text (like most commentators hastily skip over 'disabled' bodies) it is probably too late to push this book away, or use it as a support for an uneven table (like disabled characters who conveniently prop up grand plots and schemas in literature). However, if you have read it through, and I sincerely hope you have, you must surely be starting to 'sense' that 'severe normality' and 'abledness' is in itself, at times, 'disabling'.

I opened this book with a discussion of the 'disabilities' of the biblical studies discipline. Predominantly this is a sight-centric and textocentric pursuit in which 'socially located' or 'advocacy' hermeneutics and their diverse methodologies are pitted as radically 'other' from dominant historical-critical interests. Moreover, an Aristotelian hierarchy of the senses is still largely presumed as normative. Birch has seen this as an impairment of the discipline and has urged exegetes to explore ways in which a disability consciousness, including alternative sensory patterns, can become central parts of the exegetical task. This does not entail a mere 'accommodation' of such perspectives or even 'inclusion' of them into a disciplinary similitude; rather difference and diversity must themselves be constitutive, for variation in human capacity is itself part of the human condition and *all* human bodies. Taking this rallying call seriously, in this book I have attempted to initiate various refigurations of 'sensory-disabled' characters within the gospels, with reference to disability studies, sensory anthropology, and associated ethnographic evidence. I have also sought to recover these characters' strategic agencies so often lost in both biblical texts and their interpretations, behind stigmatizing labels and associations.

Here, in conclusion, I want to show how the 'sensory-disabled' characters surveyed can each challenge and refigure dominant conceptions of the 'normal' in both biblical traditions and scholarly analyses at a more fundamental level. Fiona Campbell's recent work on using 'disability' to expose the construction and safeguarding of 'ableism' is particularly provocative in this respect. She shifts prevailing frameworks to posit 'ableness' in relation to 'disability', akin to positing 'whiteness' in relation to 'race' and 'masculinity' in relation to 'gender'. Of course in biblical traditions 'normativity' and 'ableness' is, as discussed in Chapter 1, frequently patterned through the character of God. Unlike inanimate idols that are characterized by sensory 'inability', God is fully sensory-abled and moreover is conceived as the originator of sense experience. Thus as Avrahami submits, 'sensory experience as knowledge and understanding is linked to the idea the [*sic*] God is giver of life. Most important from the theological perspective, however, is that once sensory experience is damaged, it implies lack of divine support.'[2] In the biblical traditions and scholarly commentaries surveyed Jesus, as God's representative and medium, is also frequently seen to effect 'healings' which 'enable' and 'normalize' those who are perceived to suffer sensory lack or loss. In juxtaposing the sensory-disabled characters surveyed with the characterizations of God and Jesus however, perhaps in Campbell's terms we will start to approach a position where 'all bodies and mentalities' can be considered 'within the parameters of nature/culture'[3] and 'shift our gaze [note the sighted imagery] and concentrate on what the study of disability tells us about the production, operation and maintenance [of its constructed binary opposite] ableism'.[4]

Challenging the Binary: Ability and Disability

For the most part, dominant discourses constitute what is normal and those perceived as deviations from that norm are accordingly rendered disabled. Lennard Davis goes further in underlining the interdependence of concepts of normalcy and disability when he states:

Disability is not an object—a woman with a cane—but a social process that intimately involves everyone who has a body and lives in the world of the senses. Just as the conceptualisation of race, class and gender shapes the lives of those who are not black, poor or female, so the conception of disability regulates the bodies of those who are 'normal'. In fact, the very concept of normalcy by which most people (by definition) shape their existence is in fact tied inexorably to the concept of disability, or rather the concept of disability is a function of a concept of normalcy. Normalcy and disability are part of the same system.[5]

Paul Harper has argued that changing the phrasing of the debate may help in exposing the oppressive logic lurking behind the binary division of abled/disabled. He proposes that 'dis-able-ism' may be a linguistic way in which the binary can be collapsed and exposed as a system of 'discriminatory or abusive conduct towards people based upon their physical, [sensory] or cognitive abilities'.[6]

Campbell also has set out to decentre the cultural project of 'ableism' which in her opinion is rehearsed, performed, and ultimately habitualized so it appears as the 'given' naturalized order of things. A 'system of compulsory ablebodiedness' in her opinion 'repeatedly demands that people with disability embody for others an affirmative answer to the unspoken question: "Yes, but in the end wouldn't you rather be more like me?"'[7] For Campbell the positing of a normative concept (such as displayed in an 'abled' God or messiah or a fecund, male, circumcised Jew who is able to offer sacrifice at the temple) implicitly institutes what she terms a 'concept of difference'[8] for, in the face of such dominant ideologies, divergence is tantamount to deviance. However, it is also true that within such contexts disability can serve as a subversive and deconstructive reminder of the inherent uncontainability and dynamism of all flesh and blood bodies. Campbell thus urges theorists to read disabled bodies in a positive, and what she purposefully terms 'anti-social' light, for they function as forceful sites of resistance to dominating ideologies and nurture what Foucault terms 'the implantation of perversions'.[9] Campbell's thesis effectively asks scholars to refigure research questions so that disability functions as a dissident 'norm'.

Thus, what does blindness tell us about sight? What does deafness tell us about hearing? What does untouchability tell us about touch? And what does being 'out of one's senses' tell us about 'being in them'?

'Sensory-Disabled' Characters Refigured

In many ways this book has attempted to tackle the questions that Campbell considers central in any decentring of 'ableism'; for it has taken the strategies, identities, and experiences of those considered as 'disabled' to centre stage. In so doing it has also moved beyond one-dimensional characterizations of both the 'disabled' and Jesus and God so frequently propagated in both biblical texts and commentaries. The former are often seen to be weighted down with negative burdens of their condition and are fragmented and disordered, and the latter in marked contrast are rendered entirely positively, redolent with full abilities and wholeness. In the interpretations proposed here the binary of abled and disabled is buckled and all characters emerge more roundly exhibiting multifarious traits.

In Chapter 2, the widespread metaphorical trope which linked 'blindness' with misunderstanding and social rejection, in contrast to 'sightedness' which denoted comprehension and salvation, was shown not only to have been applied within biblical discourses but also functioned in indirect characterizations in narratives. The man at Bethsaida (Mark 8: 22–6), Bartimaeus (Mark 10: 46–52), and the man born blind (John 9: 1–34) were perceived as illustrating dimensions of sighted characters, particular Peter, the disciples, and the Jewish leaders. Moreover these textual traits were frequently uncritically perpetuated in the readings of modern scholarship. Through the disability consciousness of Deshen and Kleege, however, the epistemological dominance of the physical 'eye' as the purveyor of knowledge was subverted. The importance of touch in restructuring social relationships (and dissolving social hierarchies between healer and healed) also sound and kinaesthesia enabled the recovery of these characters not just as inert beneficiaries of divine cure or simplistic foils for other characters, but rather potent agents who, in diverse ways, 'revealed' knowledge and instructed other sighted characters they encountered. This was powerfully demonstrated in

Jesus' question to the blind man at Bethsaida: 'tell me [though you are blind] what *you see*' (Mark 8: 23).

Chapter 3 refigured the exchange between the 'deaf-mute' and Jesus in Mark 7: 31–7 as an example of Deaf world arts in which the 'normalization' of the character into a hearing-verbal world was questioned and queered through listening with a hybrid 'third ear'. Audio-centric channels of communication were reordered and vision, touch, space, vibration, and inaudibility of speech were exhibited. Jesus adopted 'communication' foreign to himself and the deaf-mute was silent even after the text assumed a 'healing' had been accomplished. Ultimately the performance underscored the point that 'sense' does not equate exclusively with hearing and spoken words, a strident transformation of the normative call of Jesus that one must '*hear* the word and accept it and bear fruit' (Mark 4: 20).

Chapter 4 took as its subjects a leper (Mark 1: 40–5/Matt. 8: 1–4/ Luke 5: 12–15), Legion (Mark 5: 1–20/Luke 8: 26–39), and leaky woman (Mark 5: 25–34/Matt. 9: 20–2/Luke 8: 43–7); all characters who religious systems had marked out as 'not-touch-able' on account of their perceived impurity and threats of disorder. Whilst 'impurity' frequently associated such characters with stench and death, 'pollution' here conceived as a more fluid notion demonstrated how moments of creativity which redrew the 'normative' boundaries of the religious elite could be initiated by untouchables. Utilizing insights from ethnographies of untouchable communities in India each of these characters were seen to be armed, through their physical and ideological stench, with powerful weapons against the normative codes which sought to censure and reject them. The leper jarringly reversed 'untouchability' to reveal how it made the religious elite, imaged here in Jesus, themselves 'untouchable'. Jesus when prompted however opts to share the polluted space of the leper in an inventive moment. Legion was 'exposed' to launch a bare and filthy protest against collusion with imperial powers. Jesus' exorcism ultimately normalized this character and rendered him politically ineffective. It in turn perhaps prompted the receiver of the gospel to question the strength of Jesus' opposition to empire, or indeed expose his tacit compliance with the powers that be. The leaky woman in turn exhibited through her audacious approach, which leads to Jesus' involuntary bodily seepage, the false binary between 'disability' and 'ability', for all bodies occupy a continuum of control and uncontrollability, boundaries and outflows.

Chapter 5 reconceived the story of the boy with seizures (Mark 9: 14–29; Matt. 17: 14–20; Luke 9: 37–43) who is supposed to be 'out of his senses' and posing a threat to community stability, as a complex and multifaceted illness narrative. Both the 'Western medical' and 'spirit-possession' models were respectively seen to elude the story of the person at the centre of them. By refiguring the narrative as an illness tale based on seizure, both chaos and quest elements were revealed. Quest narratives do not evoke a cure but rather propose alternative meanings for conditions. It was argued that seizure signifiers were leaked onto other characters in the narrative, including the crowd and Jesus, to challenge the notion that only 'disabled' epileptics or demon-possessed are the exclusive receptacles of such phenomena. More crucially this, and the other narratives surveyed, showed how boundaries of 'abnormality' are codified by 'normality' and when such divisions are reversed, deconstructed, or rejected, the whole structure of 'abled' and 'disabled' itself caves in.

Refiguring Jesus and God

Disability theology, in marked contrast to the use of disability models in biblical studies, has often achieved what Adrian Thatcher has termed 'a memorable solidarity between the being of God and the being of disabled people'.[10] This reaches its zenith in the picture of 'God crucified' for 'vulnerable bodies find their spiritual home in the crucified body of Christ'.[11] Nancy Eiesland's metaphor of the 'Disabled God' is perhaps the most prominent of such attempts in which Christ's tortured corpse becomes the basis for emotive metaphorical images such as 'God as survivor' and 'broken', as illustrated in the scarred resurrection flesh which Thomas is invited to touch in John 20. In Eiesland's words:

The resurrected Jesus Christ in presenting impaired hands and feet and side to be touched by frightened friends alters the taboo of physical avoidance of disability and calls for followers to reconsider their connection and equality at the point of Christ's physical impairment. Christ's disfigured side bears witness to the existence of hidden disabilities as well.[12]

Whilst Eiesland's thesis recognizes the importance of radical embodiment at the heart of the gospel's construction of God, nonetheless by equating a tortured corpse with disability the 'hegemonic imaginary' of ableism still dominates. Touchstones between divinity and disability are found in suffering and death rather than embodied life. What each of the sensory-disabled characters in this book has shown, however, is that Jesus in his earthly ministry is himself restricted in communication, knowledge, and by normative assumptions; moreover he shares bodily experiences of leakage, pollution, and the like.

Deborah Creamer's notion of a 'God with limits' seems to provide a better fit with the sort of characterizations which have been proposed here. She is careful to point out that a god with limits is not one conceived from 'limited-ness', i.e. 'a blind god who cannot see, a deaf god cannot hear', but rather one that shares limits of the human condition. This, in Creamer's opinion, speaks to a postmodern conception of culture in which 'partiality of knowledge and fluid borders and boundaries' are key hallmarks. In Creamer's words, 'a notion of God that includes limits is consonant with these contemporary understandings of finitude, and even with experiences of decay and death. [More crucially]…this sort of reworking means disability is not less than complete, or that diversity is necessarily disorderly, perilous or hazardous'.[13]

Limits, in Creamer's view, give rise to three characteristics which are 'ably' demonstrated by the sensory-disabled characters reviewed in this book: perseverance (battling to achieve goals and access), strength (developing alternative strategies), and creativity (adapting to limits and capitalizing on them). A 'limits God' for Creamer illustrates 'a divine preference for diversity'[14] and offers a far more democratic conception than a 'supra-able' or 'severely normal' deity who 'stands' and 'looks out' (for such a god can of course always walk and see) strictly guarding boundaries of difference. In her words:

In an age of war, terrorism, economic injustice and environmental risk, a recognition and theological affirmation of limits seems more responsible than apathy and omnipotent control and offers a perspective that can lead to hopeful possibilities of perseverance strength, creativity, and honest engagement with the self and the other'[15]

Ultimately disability studies which offer knee-jerk reactions to patterns which 'other' them without providing a cultural consciousness model in the end are destined to be trapped within an able/disabled binary. However, by proposing a model of culture as hybrid in which diversity is not only embraced but is itself constitutive, one can literally refigure not only characters and deities but more importantly cultural practices and norms. The 'sensory-disabled' characters surveyed in this book have, I think, a central part to play in such a project, for they function as, what Susan Peters terms, 'hybrid border crossers' who in their respective performances 'blur cultural, political or disability borders in order to adapt to different symbolic and material constructions of the world'.[16] In short, they defiantly unpick, violate, and transcend hegemonic maps of difference.

This book has daringly reconceived these 'sensory-disabled' characters' 'sensational lives'—for 'everyone lives a sensational life…it's just that "sensational" means something different for each person'[17]—and in so doing, encouraged them to overcome the debilitating silencing of their stigma. Their stories should not however, be seen as mere historical curiosities through which the living can sense the dead. Rather, the refigurations proposed here have themselves a part to play in refiguring wider disciplines, research methodologies, ethics, and social systems which currently sustain strict divisions of 'ability' and 'disability' in the contemporary world. It is only when these wider dynamics are transformed that we can begin to suppose that 'sense' will ultimately overcome 'stigma'.

| *Notes*

INTRODUCTION

1. A word on definitions: 'sensory disability' (dis|abil|ity) (a social category) is often distinguished from 'sensory impairment' (a physiological category). *The Oxford English Dictionary* defines 'disability' as 'a disadvantage or handicap, especially one imposed or recognized by the law'. 'Impairment' in contrast, is defined as 'the state or fact of being impaired, especially in a specified faculty'. Whilst largely opting to use the language of 'sensory disability' throughout this book to encapsulate its socially constructed nature, I am also not unaware that scholars in disability studies have recently cautioned that impairment itself is not just a 'natural category'. Rather, impairment is only made manifest in contexts in which being 'abled' means not having a certain physical characteristic, thus it shares key elements with 'disability' (see Russell Shuttleworth and Devva Kasnitz, 'The Cultural Context of Disability', in Gary Albrecht (ed) *Encyclopedia of Disability* (Thousand Oaks, Calif.: Sage, 2005), 94–106.

2. G. Thomas Couser, *Signifying Bodies: Disability in Contemporary Life Writing* (Ann Arbor, Mich.: University of Michigan Press, 2009), 9.

3. Nancy Eiesland, *The Disabled God: Toward a Liberatory Theology of Disability* (Nashville, Tenn.: Abingdon Press, 1994), 70.

4. Robert McRuer and Michael Berube, *Crip Theory: Cultural Signs of Queerness and Disability* (Albany, NY: New York University Press, 2006), 1.

5. David Mitchell and Sharon Snyder, *Narrative Prosthesis: Disability and the Dependencies of Discourse* (Ann Arbor, Mich.: University of Michigan Press, 2000), 56.

6. Erving Goffman, *Stigma: Notes on the Management of a Spoiled Identity* (Englewood Cliffs, NJ: Prentice-Hall, 1963), 3.

7. Thomas Reynolds, *Vulnerable Communion: A Theology of Disability and Hospitality* (Grand Rapids, Mich.: Brazos Press, 2008), 63.

8. Dennis D. Waskul, Phillip Vannini, and Janelle Wilson, 'The Aroma of Recollection: Olfaction, Nostalgia, and the Shaping of the Sensuous Self', *SenSoc* 4 (2009), 12.

9. Petra Kuppers, *Disability and Contemporary Performance: Bodies on the Edge* (London: Routledge, 2004), 8.

10. Carrie Sandahl and Philip Auslander, 'Introduction', in Carrie Sandahl and Philip Auslander (eds), *Bodies in Commotion: Disability and Performance* (Ann Arbor, Mich.: University of Michigan Press, 2005), 2.

11. Sandahl and Auslander, 'Introduction', 3.

12. Sandahl and Auslander, 'Introduction', 10.

13. Sandahl and Auslander, 'Introduction', 3.

14. Lennard Davis, 'Introduction', in Lennard Davis (ed.), *The Disability Studies Reader* (New York: Routledge, 1997), 1.

15. Hector Avalos, Sarah Melcher, and Jeremy Schipper, 'Introduction', in Hector Avalos, Sarah Melcher, and Jeremy Schipper (eds), *This Abled Body: Rethinking Disabilities in Biblical Studies* (Atlanta, Ga.: Society of Biblical Literature, 2007), 1–2.

16. Christopher Newell, 'Disabled Theologies and the Journeys of Liberation to Where our Names Appear', *FemTh* 15/3: 324.

17. Jeremy Schipper, *Disability and Isaiah's Suffering Servant* (Oxford: Oxford University Press, 2011), 16.

18. Gill Green, *The End of Stigma? Changes in Social Experience of Long-Term Illness* (Oxford: Routledge, 2009), 1.

19. Mark Osteen (ed.), *Autism and Representation* (New York: Routledge, 2008), 8.

20. This was marked in the introduction of the first issue of a pioneer journal in this area, *SenSoc*, founded in 2006.

21. David Howes, *Sensual Relations: Engaging the Senses in Culture and Social Theory* (Ann Arbor, Mich.: University of Michigan Press, 2003), p. xi.

22. Constance Classen, 'Foundations for an Anthropology of the Senses', *ISSJ* 49 (1997), 402.

23. *Oxford English Dictionary*, available online at <http://www.oed.com>.

24. Elizabeth Keating and R. Neill Hadder, 'Sensory Impairment', *ARA* 39 (2010), 115–29.

25. See David Howes and Constance Classen, 'Doing Sensory Anthropology'. Available online at <http://www.sensorystudies.org/sensorial-investigations-2/doing-sensory-anthropology>.

26. See Nora Ellen Grace, *Everyone Here Spoke Sign-Language: Hereditary Deafness on Martha's Vineyard* (Cambridge, Mass.: Harvard University Press, 1985).

27. This goes some way to explaining the consequent absence of reference to some standard historical-critical readings of the texts featured in this book. I am purposefully drawing on an alternative body of literature to refigure these characters.

28. Avalos *et al.*, 'Introduction', 4–5.

CHAPTER 1

1. Katherine Thompson, 'Library Rules: No Loud Yells, No Bad Smells'. Available online at <http://www.newser.com/story/56021/library-rules-no-loud-yells-no-bad-smells.html>.
2. *Oxford English Dictionary*. 'Perception' likewise has dual meanings: 'Perception as the reception of information through the sense organs' and perception as 'mental insight or a sense made of a range of sensory information with memories and expectations'. Paul Roadway, *Sensuous Geographies: Body, Sense and Place* (London: Routledge 1994), 10.
3. George Roeder, 'Coming to our Senses', *JAmHist* 81 (1994), 1112.
4. Roeder does note that histories from the margins—feminism, African-American histories—have however, increasingly contributed to more interest in other sensory experiences within sectors of his profession. See Roeder, 'Coming to our Senses', 1116.
5. Mark Smith, *Sensing the Past: Seeing, Hearing, Smelling, Tasting and Touching in History* (Berkeley-Los Angeles, Calif.: University of California Press, 2007), 19.
6. Robert Jütte, *A History of the Senses: From Antiquity to Cyberspace* (Cambridge: Polity Press, 2005), 1.
7. Dorothy Lee, 'The Gospel of John and the Five Senses', *JBL* 129 (2010), 115–27.
8. Isaac Kalimi, 'Human and Musical Sounds and their Hearing Elsewhere as a Literary Device in the Biblical Narratives', *VT* 60 (2010), 569.
9. Dominika Kurek-Chomycz, 'Spreading the Sweet Scent of the Gospel as the Cult of the Wise: Sapiential Background of Paul's Olfactory Metaphor in 2 Cor 2: 14–16', in Christian Eberhart (ed.), *Ritual and Metaphor: Sacrifice in the Bible* (Atlanta, Ga.: Society of Biblical Literature, 2011).
10. Dominika Kurek-Chomycz, 'The Fragrance of her Perfume: The Significance of Sense Imagery in John's Account of the Anointing in Bethany', *NovT* 52 (2010), 334–54.
11. 'Kinaesthesia', *Oxford English Dictionary*.
12. Steven Weitzman, 'Sensory Reform in Deuteronomy', in David Brakke, Michael Satlow, and Steven Weitzman (eds), *Religion and the Self in Antiquity* (Bloomington, Ind.: Indiana University Press, 2005), 124.
13. Weitzman, 'Sensory Reform', 124.
14. Weitzman, 'Sensory Reform', 125.
15. Weitzman, 'Sensory Reform', 132.

16. Ian Ritchie, 'The Nose Knows: Bodily Knowing in Isaiah 11: 3', *JSOT* 87 (2000), 59–73.

17. Meier Malul, *Knowledge, Control and Sex. Studies in Biblical Thought, Culture, and Worldview* (Tel Aviv-Jaffa: Archaeological Center Publication, 2002), 313.

18. Malul, *Knowledge, Control and Sex*, 313.

19. See Hector Avalos, 'Introducing Sensory Criticism in Biblical Studies: Audiocentricity and Visiocentricity', in Avalos *et al.* (eds), *This Abled Body*, 31–46.

20. Louise Lawrence, 'Exploring the Sense-Scape of the Gospel of Mark', *JSNT* 33 (2011), 387–397.

21. Lawrence, 'Exploring the Sense-Scape', 387–397.

22. Yael Avrahami, *The Senses of Scripture: Sensory Perception in the Hebrew Bible* (London: T. & T. Clark, 2012).

23. Having taken classes with Paul Stoller, a sensory anthropologist, Avrahami is sensitive to organizational and relational aspects of the sensorium in the Hebrew Bible, though very seldom engages with actual ethnographies.

24. Avrahami, *Senses of Scripture*, 2.

25. Avrahami, *Senses of Scripture*, 190. On this theme see also Saul Olyan, 'The Ascription of Physical Disability as a Stigmatizing Strategy in Biblical Iconic Polemics', *JHS* 9: 1–15. Available online at <http://www.jhsonline.org/Articles/article_116.pdf>.

26. Avrahami, *Senses of Scripture*, 274.

27. Avrahami, *Senses of Scripture*, 62.

28. Avrahami, *Senses of Scripture*, 72.

29. Avrahami, *Senses of Scripture*, 183.

30. Avrahami, *Senses of Scripture*, 195.

31. Avrahami, *Senses of Scripture*, 206–7.

32. Avrahami, *Senses of Scripture*, 202.

33. Avrahami, *Senses of Scripture*, 221.

34. Ritchie, 'The Nose Knows', 72–3.

35. In Clifford Geertz's terms, the world is a text: 'The culture of a people is an ensemble of texts…which the anthropologist strains to read over the shoulders of those to whom they properly belong'. Clifford Geertz, *The Interpretation of Cultures* (New York: Basic Books, 1973), 452.

36. Paul Stoller, *Sensuous Scholarship* (Philadelphia: University of Pennsylvania Press, 1997). See also Sarah Pink who sees the ethnographer as an emplaced researcher. Sarah Pink, *Doing Sensory Ethnography* (London: Sage 2009), 43.

37. My emphasis. Dwight Conquergood, 'Performance Studies, Interventions and Radical Research', *Drama Review*, 46 (2002), 151.

38. Conquergood, 'Performance Studies', 146.

39. Conquergood, 'Performance Studies', 147.

40. David Howes, *Sensual Relations: Engaging the Senses in Culture and Social Theory* (Ann Arbor, Mich.: University of Michigan Press, 2003), p. xii.

41. David Howes, 'Controlling Textuality: A Call for a Return to the Senses', *Anthropologica*, 32 (1990), 58.

42. David Howes discussed in Richard Carp, 'Hearing, Smelling, Tasting, Feeling, Seeing: The Role of the Arts in Making Sense Out of the Academy', *Issues in Integrative Studies*, 13 (1995), 25–36. Available online at <http://libres.uncg.edu/ir/asu/f/Carp_Richard_1995_Hearing.pdf>.

43. Stoller, *Sensuous Scholarship*, 6.

44. Stoller, *Sensuous Scholarship*, p. xv.

45. Bruce Malina, *The New Testament World: Insights from Cultural Anthropology*, 3rd edn (Louisville, Ky.: Westminster John Knox, [1981] 2001); Bruce Malina and Richard Rohrbaugh, *Social-Science Commentary on the Gospel of John* (Minneapolis, Minn.: Fortress Press, 1998); Bruce Malina and Richard Rohrbaugh, *Social-Science Commentary on the Synoptic Gospels*, 2nd edn (Minneapolis, Minn.: Fortress Press, 2003). For an extensive critique of the use of the honour and shame model in New Testament Studies see Louise Lawrence, *An Ethnography of the Gospel of Matthew* (Tübingen: Mohr Siebeck, 2003).

46. Saul Olyan, *Disability in the Hebrew Bible: Interpreting Mental and Physical Differences* (Cambridge: Cambridge University Press, 2008), 5.

47. Olyan, *Disability*, 5.

48. Avrahami, *Senses of Scripture*, 215.

49. Carol Fontaine, 'Roundtable Discussion', in Alice Bach (ed.), *Women in the Hebrew Bible: A Reader* (New York: Routledge, 1999), 439.

50. Bruce Malina, *Windows on the World of Jesus: Time Travel to Ancient Judea* (Louisville, Ky.: Westminster John Knox Press, 1993), 80.

51. My emphasis. Julian Pitt Rivers, 'Honour and Social Status', in John G. Peristiany (ed.), *Honour and Shame: The Values of Mediterranean Society* (Chicago: University of Chicago Press, 1965), 47.

52. Michael Herzfeld, 'The Horns of the Mediterraneanist Dilemma', *AmEthn* 11 (1984), 439–54.

53. Arjun Appadurai, 'Introduction: Commodities and the Politics of Value', in Arjun Appadurai (ed.), *The Social Life of Things: Commodities in Cultural Perspective* (Cambridge: Cambridge University Press, 1986), 3–63.

54. João de Pina-Cabral, 'The Mediterranean as a Category of Regional Comparison: A Critical View', *CA* 30 (1989), 399–406.

55. James Crossley, *Jesus in an Age of Terror: Scholarly Projects for a New American Century* (London: Equinox, 2008), 112.

56. Evthymios Papataxiarchis, 'Dealing with Disadvantage: Culture and the Gendered Self in the Politics of Locality', in Christian Bromberger and Dionigi Albera (eds), *L'Anthropologie et la Méditerranné: Unité, diversité et perspectives* (Paris: Éditions de la Maison des Sciences de l'Homme, 2001), 179–211.

57. Lila Abu Lughod, *Veiled Sentiments* (Berkeley-Los Angeles, Calif.: University of California Press, 2000).

58. Nadia Seremetakis, *The Last Word Women, Death and Divination in Inner Mani* (Chicago: University of Chicago Press, 1991), 118.

59. Seremetakis, *Last Word*, 120.

60. Seremetakis, *Last Word*, 121. See also Saul Olyan, *Biblical Mourning: Ritual and Social Dimensions* (Oxford: Oxford University Press, 2004), 4.

61. 'A mutual engagement should fully encourage and legitimate the anthropological study of disability. Anthropology and medical anthropology can no longer marginalize disabled people in their research.' Devva Kasnitz and Russell Shuttleworth, 'Semiotics and Dis/Ability: Interrogating Categories of Difference', in Linda J. Rogers and Beth Swadener (eds), *Anthropology and Disability* (Albany, NY: State University of New York Press, 2001), 32.

62. Shlomo Deshen, *Blind People: The Private and Public Life of Sightless Israelis* (Albany, NY: State University of New York Press, 1992), 37.

63. Roger Just, 'On the Ontological Status of Honour', in Joy Hendry and C. W. Watson (eds), *An Anthropology of Indirect Communication* (London and New York: Routledge, 2001), 34.

64. Nadia Seremetakis, *The Senses Still: Memory and Perception as Material Culture in Modernity* (Boulder, Colo.: Westview, 1994), 6.

65. Gary Palmer and William Jankowiak posit an alternative model of 'culture as performance' to try and reclaim embodied and physical experiences, including the sensory. Gary B. Palmer and William R. Jankowiak, 'Performance and Imagination: Toward an Anthropology of the Spectacular and the Mundane', *CultAnth* 11 (1996), 253.

66. Conquergood, 'Performance Studies', 149.

67. Michael Herzfeld, *Anthropology: Theoretical Practice in Culture and Society* (Oxford: Blackwell Publishers, 2001), 240.

68. 'In the very long view, the shift from orality to literacy accordingly, most famously to Walter Ong and Marshall McLuhan—gradually transformed people from engaged speakers and listeners into silent scanners of written words, isolated readers in the linear world of texts...words became printed objects more than breathed speech, things to be seen rather than voices to be heard'. See Leigh Eric Schmidt, 'Hearing Loss', in Michael Bull and Les Back (eds), *The Auditory Culture Reader* (Oxford: Berg, 2003), 42.

69. See Whitney Shiner, *Proclaiming the Gospel: First-Century Performance of Mark* (Harrisburg, Pa.: Trinity Press International, 2003).

70. David Rhoads, 'Performance Criticism: An Emerging Methodology in Biblical Studies'. Available online at <http://www.sbl-site.org/assets/pdfs/Rhoads_Performance.pdf.

71. Meir Bar-Ilan, 'Illiteracy in the Land of Israel in the first centuries C.E'. Available online at <http://faculty.biu.ac.il/~barilm/illitera.html>.

72. Rhoads, 'Performance Criticism'.

73. Rhoads, 'Performance Criticism'.

74. Paul Rodway documents a similar 'sensuous move' in geographical theories of perception where the senses are shown to be crucial pointers in theories of environment: 'the context of perception, played a vital role in structuring stimulation received by the senses—reflected, echoed, disseminated'. Rodaway, *Sensuous Geographies*, p. ix.

75. Elisabeth Schüssler Fiorenza, *Democratizing Biblical Studies: Toward an Emancipatory Educational Space* (Louisville, Ky.: Westminster John Knox Press, 2009), 94.

76. Dale Martin, *Pedagogy of the Bible: An Analysis and Proposal* (Louisville, Ky.: Westminster/John Knox, 2008); Fiorenza, *Democratizing;* Elisabeth Schüssler Fiorenza and Kent Harold Richards (eds), *Transforming Graduate Biblical Education: Ethos and Discipline* (Atlanta, Ga.: Society of Biblical Literature, 2010); Stephen Moore and Yvonne Sherwood, *The Invention of the Biblical Scholar: A Critical Manifesto* (Minneapolis, Minn.: Augsburg Fortress, 2011).

77. Bruce Birch, 'Impairment as a Condition in Biblical Scholarship', in Avalos *et al.*, *This Abled Body*, 187.

78. Elisabeth Schüssler Fiorenza and Kent Harold Richards, 'Introduction', in Fiorenza and Richards, *Transforming*, 4.

79. Martin, *Pedagogy*, 3.

80. Moore and Sherwood, *Invention*, 101–2.

81. Moore and Sherwood, *Invention*, 9.

82. I speak as one who has had the great pleasure of visiting these amazing islets in the North Atlantic and as a former flatmate of a delightful Faroese national.

83. Candida Moss and Jeremy Schipper (eds), 'Introduction', in Candida Moss and Jeremy Schipper (eds), *Disability Studies and Biblical Literature* (New York: Palgrave Macmillan, 2011), 6.

84. Iris Young 'Foreword', in Marian Corker and Tom Shakespeare (eds), *Disability/Postmodernity: Embodying Disability Theory* (London: Continuum, 2002), p. xii.

85. My emphasis. Olyan, *Disability*, 7–8.

86. Amos Yong, 'Review of Jeremy Schipper and Candida R. Moss; eds., Disability Studies and Biblical Literature', *H-Net Reviews* (2012). Available online at <https://www.hnet.org/reviews/showrev.php?id=35031>.
87. Yong, 'Review'.
88. Fiorenza and Richards, 'Introduction', 4.
89. David Howes and Constance Classen, 'Sounding Sensory Profiles', in David Howes (ed.), *The Varieties of Sensory Experience* (Toronto: University of Toronto Press, 1991), 257–88.
90. Pheme Perkins, 'Commentaries: Windows to the Text', *Theology Today*, 46 (1990), 398.
91. Moore and Sherwood, *Invention*, 113.
92. Kevin J. Vanhoozer (ed.), *Dictionary for Theological Interpretation of the Bible* (Grand Rapids, Mich.: Baker Books, 2005), 124.
93. Gordon Fee, 'Reflections on Commentary Writing', *Theology Today*, 46 (1990), 389.
94. Birch, 'Impairment', 185.
95. Sathianathan Clarke, 'Viewing the Bible through the Ears and Eyes of Subalterns in India', *BibInt* 10 (2002), 262.
96. Clarke, 'Viewing the Bible', 263.
97. Clarke, 'Viewing the Bible', 264.
98. Martin, *Pedagogy*, 5.
99. Martin, *Pedagogy*, 7.
100. Martin, *Pedagogy*, 7.
101. Christopher Tilley, *Body and Image: Explorations in Landscape Phenomenology* (Walnut Creek, Calif.: Left Coast Press, 2008), 28–9.
102. Musa Dube, *Postcolonial Feminist Interpretation of the Bible* (St Louis, Mo.: Chalice Press, 2000), 195.
103. Stephen Tyler, 'On Being Out of Words', *CultAnth* 2 (1986), 135.
104. Tyler, 'Being Out of Words', 135.
105. Tyler, 'Being Out of Words', 137.
106. Hannah Lewis, *Deaf Liberation Theology* (Aldershot: Ashgate, 2007), 120.
107. Peter McDonough discussed in Lewis, *Deaf*, 118.
108. Janet Lees, 'Enabling the Body', in Avalos *et al.*, *This Abled Body*, 162.
109. Lees, 'Enabling', 169.
110. Holly Toensing, 'Living among the Tombs: Society, Mental Illness and Self-Destruction in Mark 5: 1–20', in Avalos *et al.*, *This Abled Body*, 131.
111. Toensing, 'Living', 131.
112. Toensing, 'Living', 133.
113. Toensing, 'Living', 143.

114. Constance Classen, 'Traveling without Sightseeing: Exploring Alternative Modes of Cross-Cultural Engagement', in Patrick Devlieger *et al.* (eds), *Blindness and the Multi-Sensorial City* (Antwerp: Garant, 2006), 261–72.
115. David Mitchell and Sharon Snyder, 'Jesus Thrown Everything Off Balance: Disability and Redemption in Biblical Literature', in Avalos *et al.*, *This Abled Body*, 173–83, 175.
116. Mitchell and Snyder, 'Jesus Thrown', 175.
117. See Zeba Crook, 'Structure versus Agency in Studies of the Biblical Social World: Engaging with Louise Lawrence', *JSNT* 29 (2007), 251–75, and Louise Lawrence, 'Structure, Agency and Ideology: A Response to Zeba Crook', *JSNT* 29 (2007), 277–86.
118. Seth Schwartz, *Were the Jews a Mediterranean Society? Reciprocity and Solidarity in Ancient Judaism* (Princeton and Oxford: Princeton University Press, 2010), 24.
119. Lees, 'Enabling', 164.

CHAPTER 2

1. 'Do you still not perceive or understand?...Do you have eyes and fail to see?' (Mark 8: 17–18, see also Matt. 13: 15); 'The eye is the lamp of the body. So if your eye is healthy, your whole body will be full of light; but if your eye is unhealthy, your whole body will be full of darkness' (Matt. 6: 22–3; Luke 6: 34–6, see also Matt. 5: 14; Luke 2: 32; John 3: 20, etc.).
2. Deshen, *Blind*, 2.
3. *Oxford English Dictionary*. See also Naomi Schor 'Blindness as Metaphor', *Differences: A Journal of Feminist Cultural Studies*, 11 (1999), 76–105, and J. Joseph Grigely, 'Blindness and Deafness as Metaphors: An Anthological Essay', *Journal of Visual Culture*, 5 (2006), 227–41.
4. Pierre Fontanier, cited in Schor, 'Blindness', 77.
5. Mitchell and Snyder, *Narrative*, 53.
6. Mitchell and Snyder, *Narrative*, 47–9.
7. Mitchell and Snyder, *Narrative*, 49.
8. CD 1: 8–11, see Saul Olyan's discussion of Qumran literature and the portrayal of physical defects therein. Olyan, *Disability*, 102–10.
9. Olyan, *Disability*, 51.
10. Lawrence, *Ethnography*, 113–41.
11. Robert H. Gundry, *Matthew, A Commentary on his Literary and Theological Art* (Grand Rapids, Mich.: William Eerdmans Publishing Co., 1982), 307.

12. Warren Carter, *Matthew and the Margins: A Sociopolitical and Religious Reading* (New York: Orbis Books, 2000), 319.

13. Carter, *Matthew*, 451.

14. The saying regarding the teacher and pupil and the log in one's own eye (Mark 6: 40–1), which immediately follows, cautions the addressee not to assume too high a status, or too readily deal out judgement on others.

15. Elizabeth Struthers Malbon, *In the Company of Jesus: Characters in Mark's Gospel* (Louisvill, Ky.e: Westminster John Knox Press, 2000), 211.

16. Willem S. Vorster, *Speaking of Jesus: Essays on Biblical Language, Gospel Narrative and the Historical Jesus* (Leiden: Brill, 1998), 430.

17. Marcus Borg, *Reading the Bible Again for the First Time* (New York: Harper Collins, 2001), 45–6.

18. Bruce Morrill, *Divine Worship and Human Healing: Liturgical Theology at the Margins of Life and Death* (New York: Liturgical Press, 2009), 92–3.

19. Herman Ridderbos, *The Gospel According to John: A Theological Commentary* (Grand Rapids, Mich.: William Eerdmans, 1997), 336.

20. John Painter, *Mark's Gospel: Worlds in Conflict* (Oxford: Routledge, 1997), 152.

21. Mosche Barasch, *Blindness: The History of a Mental Image in Western Thought* (New York: Routledge, 2001), 46.

22. George Lakoff and Mark Johnson, *Metaphors we Live by* (Chicago: University of Chicago Press, 1980), 3.

23. Julia Todolí, 'Disease Metaphors in Urban Planning', *CADAAD* 1 (2007), 51.

24. Paul Ricoeur, 'The Metaphorical Process as Cognition, Imagination, and Feeling', *Critical Inquiry*, 5 (1978), 143–59.

25. Mary Douglas, *Purity and Danger: An Analysis of Concepts of Pollution and Taboo* (New York: Praeger, 1966).

26. See Dale Martin, *The Corinthian Body* (New Haven: Yale University Press, 1995), 38–60.

27. Andreas Musolff, 'What Role do Metaphors Play in Racial Prejudice? The Function of Anti-Semitic Imagery in Hitler's "Mein Kampf"', *Patterns of Prejudice*, 41 (2007), 21. On a similar theme see Felicity Rash, *The Language of Violence: Adolf Hitler's Mein Kampf* (New York: Peter Lang, 2006).

28. Mitchell and Snyder, *Narrative*, 16.

29. Mikeal Parsons, *Body and Character in Luke and Acts: The Subversion of Physiognomy in Early Christianity* (Grand Rapids, Mich.: Baker Academic Press, 2006). See also Bruce Malina and Jerome Neyrey, *Portraits of Paul: An Archaeology of Ancient Personality* (Louisville, Ky.: Westminster John Knox Press, 1996).

30. Dale Allison, 'The Eye is the Lamp of the Body (Matthew 6: 22–3 = Luke 11: 34–6)', *NTS* 33 (1987), 61–83.

31. Joel Marcus, 'A Note on Markan Optics', *NTS* 45 (1999), 250–6.

32. Charles Hartsock, 'Sight and Blindness as an Index of Character in Luke-Acts and its Cultural Milieu', Ph.D. thesis (2007), 74, 180–2. Available online at <https://beardocs.baylor.edu/bitstream/2104/5058/3/Chad_Hartsock_phd.pdf>. See also Charles Hartsock, *Sight and Blindness in Luke-Acts: The Use of Physical Features in Characterization* (Leiden and Boston: Brill, 2008).

33. John H. Elliott, 'The Evil Eye in the First Testament: The Ecology and Culture of a Pervasive Belief', in David Jobling, Peggy Day, and Gerald Sheppard (eds), *The Bible and the Politics of Exegesis* (Cleveland: Pilgrim Press, 1991), 149. See also William D. Davies and Dale C. Allison, *A Critical and Exegetical Commentary on the Gospel According to Saint Matthew* (New York: T. & T. Clark International, 2004), 635.

34. Schor, 'Blindness', 77.

35. Schor, 'Blindness', 103.

36. Stanley Hauerwas, 'Community and Diversity: The Tyranny of Normality', in John Swinton (ed.), *Critical Reflections on Stanley Hauerwas' Theology of Disability* (Binghampton, NY: Haworth Pastoral Press, 2004), 37–43.

37. Barasch, *Blindness*, 8–9.

38. Simi Linton, *Claiming Disability: Knowledge and Identity* (Albany, NY: New York University Press, 1998), 25.

39. Barasch, *Blindness*, 9.

40. Liat Ben-Moshe, 'Infusing Disability in the Curriculum: The Case of Saramago's Blindness', *Disability Studies Quarterly*, 26 (2006). Available online at <http://dsq-sds.org/article/view/688/865>.

41. Birch, 'Impairment', 195.

42. See particularly, John Hull, *In the Beginning there was Darkness: A Blind Person's Conversations with the Bible* (London: SCM Press, 2001).

43. John Hull, 'Open Letter from a Blind Disciple to a Sighted Saviour: Text and Discussion', in Martin O'Kane (ed.), *Borders, Boundaries and the Bible* (Sheffield: Sheffield Academic Press 2001), 161.

44. Hull, *In the Beginning*, 50.

45. Hull, 'Open', 159.

46. Hull, 'Open', 159.

47. Hull, 'Open', 160.

48. He contends: 'It is when I am being led by a sighted person that I sometimes have bad experiences'. Hull, 'Open', 160.

49. Hull, 'Open', 162.

50. Hull, 'Open', 162.
51. Hull, 'Open', 168.
52. Hull, 'Open', 168.
53. Hull, *In the Beginning*, 170.
54. Hull, 'Open', 171.
55. Sandy Resendes, 'The World at your Fingertips: Understanding Blindness', MA thesis, Concordia University (2004), 175–6. Available online at <http://spectrum.library.concordia.ca/7908/1/MQ91106.pdf>.
56. See Deshen, *Blind*, also Elaine Bass Jenks's work on alternative ethnography. She is a parent of a visually impaired boy and tells of how frequently sighted people set the rules for interaction, making no accommodation at all for those who cannot make 'eye contact'. Elaine Bass Jenks, 'Sighted, Blind and In Between', in Robin Patric Clair (ed.), *Expressions of Ethnography: Novel Approaches to Qualitative Methods* (Albany, NY: State University of New York Press, 2003), 129.
57. Deshen, *Blind*, 16.
58. Deshen, *Blind*, 32.
59. Morna Hooker, *The Gospel According to Mark* (London: A. & C. Black, 1991), 253.
60. Deshen, *Blind*, 37.
61. Deshen, *Blind*, 38.
62. Davis, *Enforcing*, 12.
63. Mitchell and Snyder, *Narrative*, 35.
64. Mitchell and Snyder, *Narrative*, 35.
65. Georgina Kleege, *Sight Unseen* (New Haven: Yale University Press, 1999), 1.
66. Kleege, *Sight*, 5.
67. Kleege, *Sight*, 14. This is salutary reading in reference to the ancient world where a variety of sight impairments were widespread. Given this fact, is it really true that the label 'blind' would have universally encompassed everyone suffering from visual impairments within the gospels? Maybe it was just those subjugated peoples who were blinded after battle or those who were forced to beg, or those excluded from participation in cultic rituals that were in the minds of the evangelists when constructing ableist discourses and negative metaphors. On this theme see also Edward Wheatley, *Stumbling Blocks Before the Blind: Medieval Constructions of Disability* (Ann Arbor, Mich.: University of Michigan Press, 2010), 15.
68. Kleege, *Sight*, 96.
69. Susannah Mintz, 'Invisible Disability: Georgina Kleege's Sight Unseen', *NWSAJ* 14 (2002), 161.

70. Mintz, 'Invisible', 160.

71. Jennifer Koosed and Darla Schumm's study of blindness in the Gospel of John significantly notes in this regard how, later in the Thomas episode, a positive retrieval of a blindness metaphor is at play in Jesus' statement: 'Have you believed because you have seen me? Blessed are those who have not seen, yet have come to believe' (John 20: 29). Here, in their opinion, 'the connection in John between literally and symbolically seeing is broken. The tensions in the narrative between these two poles— whole bodies represent whole spirits and broken bodies can contain whole spirits—are never resolved. Rather, they serve to destabilize each other and also redeem each other.' See Jennifer Koosed and Darla Schumm, 'Out of the Darkness: Examining the Rhetoric of Blindness in the Gospel of John', *DSQ* 25 (2005). Available online at <http://www.dsq-sds.org>.

72. James Resseguie, 'John 9: A Literary Critical Analysis', in Mark Stibbe (ed.), *The Gospel of John as Literature* (Leiden: Brill, 1993), 115–16.

73. Cornelius Bennema, *Encountering Jesus: Character Studies in the Gospel of John* (Milton Keynes: Paternoster, 2009), 143.

74. Patricia Vieira, *Seeing Politics Otherwise: Vision in Latin American and Iberian Fiction* (Toronto: University of Toronto Press, 2011), 4.

75. Barasch, *Blindness*, 10.

76. Mary, Beavis, 'From the Margin to the Way: A Feminist Reading of the Story of Bartimaeus', *JFSR* 14 (1998), 27.

77. Barasch, *Blindness*, 10.

78. As outlined in Chapter 1, I have explored a similar ambivalence, even challenge, to the sight-centricity of the gospels. See Lawrence, 'Exploring the Sense-Scape', 387–97.

79. Mark Paterson, 'Seeing with the Hands, Touching with the Eyes: Vision, Touch and the Enlightenment Spatial Imaginary', *SenSoc* 1 (2006), 225–42.

80. Mintz, 'Invisible', 155–77.

81. Oliver Sacks, *An Anthropologist on Mars* (New York: Alfred Knopf, 1996), 109.

82. Kleege, *Sight*, 86–7.

83. My emphasis. John Duncan Derrett, 'Trees Walking: Prophecy and Christology', in John Duncan Derrett, *Studies in the New Testament*, iii (Leiden: Brill, 1982), 111.

84. My emphasis. Derrett, 'Trees', 111.

85. My emphasis. Derrett, 'Trees', 122–3.

86. Mintz, 'Invisible', 155–77.

87. Hannah Macpherson, 'Articulating Blind Touch: Thinking through the Feet', *SenSoc* 4 (2009), 188.

88. Lakshmi Fjord, 'Disasters, Race, and Disability: [Un]Seen through the Political Lens on Katrina', *Journal of Race and Policy*, 3 (2007). Available online at <http://cardcanhelp.org/wp-content/uploads/resources/Disasters%20Race%20Disability%20%7BLakshmi%20Fjord%7D.pdf>.

89. My emphasis. Parsons, *Body*, 145.

90. Sidonie Smith and Julia Watson, *Reading Autobiography: A Guide for Interpreting Life Narratives* (Minneapolis, Minn.: University of Minnesota Press, 2010), 59.

91. Lorraine Code, cited in Vivian May and Beth Ferri, 'Fixated on Ability', *Prose Studies*, 27 (2005), 133.

92. Geraldine Pratt, cited in May and Ferri, 'Fixated', 134.

93. Elizabeth Edwards and Kaushik Bhaumik, 'Introduction', in Elizabeth Edwards and Kaushik Bhaumik (eds), *Visual Sense: A Cultural Reader* (Oxford: Berg 2008), 11.

94. 'for the blind, as for many oral peoples, the world exists in large part through its movements and sounds; these are what give the world presence and life'. Classen, 'Travelling', 267.

95. Georgina Kleege, 'Helen Keller and the Empire of the Normal', *AmQ* 52 (2000), 323.

96. Homi Bhabha, cited in David Bolt, 'From Blindness to Visual Impairment: Terminological Typology and the Social Model of Disability', *Disability and Society*, 20 (2005), 540.

CHAPTER 3

1. <http://www.script-o-rama.com/movie_scripts/c/children-of-a-lesser-god-script.html>.This example is used in Michael Davidson's essay, 'Hearing Things: The Scandal of Speech in Deaf Performance', in H-Dirksen L. Bauman, Heidi M. Rose, and Jennifer L. Nelson (eds), *Signing the Body Poetic: Essays on American Sign Language Literature* (Los Angeles: University of California Press, 2006), 216–33. I have been inspired by this essay in a number of ways when writing this chapter.

2. Davidson, 'Hearing', 216.

3. Leland Ryken *et al.* (eds) *Dictionary of Biblical Imagery* (Downers Grove, Ill.: Intervarsity Press, 1998), 223. In Mark's Gospel, the ear is oft-times the primary sensory medium. Forms of hear, heed, and understand occur 40 times in Mark's Gospel. Reports about Jesus' deeds are frequently 'heard' by others (2: 1; 3: 8; 3: 21; 5: 27; 6: 14, 55; 7: 25; 10: 47), Jesus summons people to 'listen' to his teachings (4: 3; 6: 2; 7: 14) and, in the parable of the sower, hearing is characterized as the primary faculty by which people encounter the seed of the word (4: 15). Discipleship is

characterized as delivering a message (6: 11) and Mark's God petitions people to 'Listen' to his beloved son (9: 7). Jesus points to the primacy of all the commandments as the *shema*, prefaced by the imperative to 'Hear' (12: 29). Accordingly the organ of the ear features three times in Mark as a metaphor for spiritual [in]cognition ('ears to hear': 4: 9, 23; 8: 18).

4. The NIV titles the section 'Jesus Heals a Deaf and Mute Man', The NKJV has 'Jesus Heals a Deaf-Mute', The NLT and English Bible for the Deaf do not mention muteness (presumably resisting the negative connotations of the word) and rather opt to entitle the story simply as 'Jesus Heals a Deaf Man'.

5. The World Federation of the Deaf offer the following definitions on their website: 'Deaf-Mute: "Mute" means silent and without voice. This label is technically inaccurate, since deaf and hard of hearing people generally have functioning vocal chords. Because deaf and hard of hearing people use various methods of communication other than or in addition to using their voices, they are not truly mute. True communication occurs when one's message is understood by others, and they can respond in kind.' 'Deaf and Dumb: A relic from the medieval English era, this is the granddaddy of all negative labels pinned on deaf and hard of hearing people....The term is offensive to deaf and hard of hearing people for a number of reasons. One, deaf and hard of hearing people are by no means "silent" at all. They use sign language, lip-reading, vocalizations, and so on to communicate. Communication is not reserved for hearing people alone, and using one's voice is not the only way to communicate. Two, "dumb" also has a second meaning: stupid. Deaf and hard of hearing people have encountered plenty of people who subscribe to the philosophy that if you cannot use your voice well you don't have much else "upstairs," and have nothing going for you. Obviously, this is incorrect, ill-informed, and false. Deaf and hard of hearing people have repeatedly proved that they have much to contribute to the society at large.' See <http://www.wfdeaf.org/faq>.

6. Shifra Kisch, '"Deaf Discourse": The Social Construction of Deafness in a Bedouin Community', *MedAnth* 27 (2008), 285.

7. James Kyle and Bernice Woll, *Sign Language: The Study of Deaf People and their Language* (Cambridge: Cambridge University Press, 1988), 5.

8. Cheris Kramarae, *Women and Men Speaking: Frameworks for Analysis* (Rowley, Mass.: Newbury House, 1981), 1.

9. Beavis, *Mark*, 124.

10. Lewis, *Deaf*, 109.

11. Hooker, *Mark*, 184–6; Robert A. Guelich, *Mark 1–8* (Dallas, Tex.: Word Books, 1989), 391.

12. Hare, *Mark*, 87.
13. Guelich, *Mark*, 397.
14. Bas van Iersel, *Mark: A Reader-Response Commentary* (Sheffield: Sheffield Academic Press, 1998), 252.
15. A similar conclusion is reached by William Lane when he states the man had 'learned to be passive in life'. William Lane, *The Gospel According to Mark* (Grand Rapids, Mich.: Eerdmans Publishing Co., 1974), 266.
16. Daniel Harrington e.g. submits that '*kwfos* can have several meanings: unable to speak, unable to hear or both'. Harrington, *Matthew*, 132.
17. Using the now outlawed term 'dumb' with some hint of associations with 'intellectual inability' see Hooker, *Mark*, 186; Hugh Anderson, *The Gospel of Mark* (London: Oliphants, 1976), 193; John Painter, *Mark's Gospel: Worlds in Conflict* (London: Routledge, 1997), 116.
18. My emphasis. Robert H. Gundry, *Commentary on the New Testament* (Grand Rapids, Mich.: Baker Academic, 2010).
19. Martha Edwards, 'Deaf and Dumb in Ancient Greece', in Lennard Davis (ed.), *The Disability Studies Reader* (London: Routledge, 1997), 29.
20. Edwards, 'Deaf', 31.
21. Edwards, 'Deaf', 32.
22. Edwards, 'Deaf', 36.
23. Aristotle, *Historia Animalium*, cited in Christian Laes 'Silent Witnesses: Deaf-Mutes in Graeco-Roman Antiquity', *CW* 104 (2011), 460.
24. Pseudo-Aristotelian *Problemata*, cited in Laes, 'Silent', 460.
25. Laes, 'Silent', 452.
26. Laes, 'Silent', 455.
27. Laes, 'Silent', 455.
28. Laes, 'Silent', 472. Hector Avalos comes to a similar conclusion in his sensory-critical survey of the Deuteronomic history which in his opinion promotes a sustained 'sonic theology', perhaps because covenants in the Ancient Near East were usually 'heard'. Yahweh is accordingly 'heard' by the people, but not seen. See Avalos, 'Introducing Sensory Criticism', 59.
29. Amos Yong, *Theology and Down Syndrome: Reimagining Disability in Late Modernity* (Waco, Tex.: Baylor University Press, 2007), 28.
30. Robert Guelich identifies it as a *hapax legomenon*. Guelich, *Mark*, 394.
31. See Hooker, *Mark*, 186, also Adela Yarbro Collins, *Mark: A Commentary*, *Hermeneia* (Minneapolis, Minn.: Fortress Press, 2007), 376.
32. Robert Bratcher and Eugene Nida, *A Translator's Handbook on the Gospel of Mark* (Leiden: Brill, 1961), 241.
33. Hooker, *Mark*, 186.

34. Marie Noonan Sabin, *The Gospel According to Mark* (Collegeville, Minn.: Order of St Benedict, 2006), 68.

35. Stein, *Mark*, 360.

36. Lane, *Mark*, 267.

37. Lane, *Mark*, 267.

38. Ben Witherington, *The Gospel of Mark: A Socio-Historical Commentary* (Grand Rapids, Mich.: William Eerdmans Publishing Co., 2001), 234. William Lane notes a similar point but goes on to anachronistically diagnose the condition as 'a spasmodic condition of the tongue'. This seems to be reading far too much into an ancient and distant term though. Lane, *Mark*, 266.

39. D. Edmond Hiebert even suggests that we may be witnessing Jesus' use of signed language in this passage. See D. Edmond Hiebert, *The Gospel of Mark: An Expositional Commentary* (Greenville, SC: Bob Jones University Press, 1994), 213.

40. Clayton David Robinson, 'The Laying on of Hands, with Special Reference to the Reception of the Holy Spirit in the New Testament', Fuller Theological Seminary PhD dissertation (2008), 102. Available online at <http://books.google.co.uk/books/about/The_Laying_on_of_Hands_with_Special_Refe.html?id=h8rf5MOuPUAC&redir_esc=y>.

41. Susan Gregory, 'Deafness in Fiction', in Susan Gregory and Gillian Hartley (eds), *Constructing Deafness* (London: Pinter Publishers, 1991), 294–300.

42. Reynolds, *Vulnerable*, 15.

43. I use the term 'conversation' quite specifically to demonstrate the process of sounding out the formerly muted and silenced.

44. My emphasis. Tony Booth, 'Challenging Conceptions of Integration', in Gregory and Hartley, *Constructing*, 157.

45. Harlan Lane, 'Ethnicity, Ethics, and the Deaf-World', *Journal of Deaf Studies and Deaf*, 10 (2005). Available online at <http://jdsde.oxfordjournals.org/cgi/content/abstract/10/3/29>.

46. Paddy Ladd, *Understanding Deaf Culture: In Search of Deafhood* (Clevedon: Multilingual Matters, 2003), 8.

47. Lewis, *Deaf*, 32.

48. Davis, *Enforcing*, 77.

49. Susan Burch, 'Deaf Poet's Society: Subverting the Hearing Paradigm', *Literature and Medicine*, 16 (1997), 121.

50. Burch, 'Deaf', 121–2.

51. Kanta Kochhar-Lindgren, 'Hearing Difference across Theatres: Experimental, Disability and Deaf Performance', *Theatre Journal*, 58 (2006), 417.

52. Kochhar-Lindgren, 'Hearing', 423–4.

53. Burch, 'Deaf', 125.

54. Wayne Morris, *Theology without Words: Theology in the Deaf Community* (Aldershot: Ashgate, 2008), p. xiii.

55. Morris, *Theology*, p. xiii.

56. Christian Laes, 'Silent Witnesses: Deaf-Mutes in Graeco-Roman Antiquity', *CW* 104 (2011), 468.

57. Edwards, 'Deaf', 34.

58. Brenda Joe Brueggemann, 'Delivering Disability, Willing Speech', in Carrie Sandahl and Philip Auslander (eds), *Bodies in Commotion: Disability and Performance* (Ann Arbor, Mich.: University of Michigan Press, 2005), 17.

59. Kochhar-Lindgren, 'Hearing', 429.

60. Gundry, *Mark*, 384.

61. Edwards, 'Deaf', 32.

62. Alva Steffler, *Symbols of the Christian Faith* (Grand Rapids, Mich.: Eerdmans Publishing Co., 2002), 111.

63. George Veditz cited in Carol Padden and Tom Humphries, *Deaf in America: Voices from a Culture* (Cambridge, Mass.: Harvard University Press, 1988), 2. Peter C. Hauser *et al.* similarly comment on the visuality of Deaf sensory experience. See Peter C. Hauser, Amanda O'Hearn, Michael McKee, Anne Steider, and Denise Thew, 'Deaf Epistemology: Deafhood and Deafness', *American Annals of the Deaf* 154 (2010), 486–7.

64. Davidson, 'Hearing', 222.

65. Kochhar-Lindgren, 'Hearing', 430.

66. Davidson, 'Hearing', 222.

67. Kochhar-Lindgren, 'Hearing', 430.

68. A number of different reasons why this 'foreign' term (there is debate over its origin in Aramaic or Hebrew) features within the narrative are given by commentators. These range from Jesus exhibiting a deep emotional attachment to the man, to him offering a robust and powerful prayer to God for assistance in the healing. Others see the term as a typical evocation in Hellenistic magical techniques, and thus see the redaction and deletion of this very 'earthy' healing by later evangelists due to the embarrassing parallels it holds with such therapies. For a listing of these diverse theories see Stein, *Mark*, 330.

69. George Aichele, *Jesus Framed* (London: Routledge, 1996), 61

70. Nina Sun Eidsheim's discussion of Juliana Snapper's Five Fathoms Opera Project in which the artist sings underwater in order to show sound's movement through a variety of material media vividly shows the corporeal

nature of sound. Nina Sun Eidsheim, 'Sensing Voice: Materiality and the Lived Body in Singing and Listening', *SenSoc* 6 (2011), 133–55.

71. Padden and Humphries, *Deaf*, 93.
72. Michele Friedner and Stefan Helmreich, 'Sound Studies Meets Deaf Studies', *SenSoc* 7 (2012), 72–86.
73. Stanley Hauerwas, 'Community and Diversity: The Tyranny of Normality', in John Swinton (ed.), *Critical Reflections on Stanley Hauerwas' Theology of Disability* (Binghampton, NY: Haworth Pastoral Press, 2004), 37.
74. Davis, *Enforcing*, 115.
75. Kochhar-Lindgren, 'Hearing', 436.
76. Davidson, 'Hearing', 219.
77. Richard Senghas and Leila Monaghan, 'Signs of their Times: Deaf Communities and the Culture of Language', *Annual Review of Anthropology*, 31 (2002), 83.
78. Harlan Lane, 'Ethnicity, Ethics, and the Deaf-World', *Journal of Deaf Studies*, 10 (2005). Available online at <http://jdsde.oxfordjournals.org/cgi/content/abstract/10/3/29>.
79. Ladd, *Understanding*, 16.
80. Carol Padden, 'The Deaf Community and the Culture of Deaf People', in Susan Gregory and Gillian Hartley (eds), *Constructing Deafness* (London: Pinter Publishers, 1991), 42–3.
81. Howard Clark Kee, 'Magic and Messiah', in Jacob Neusner, Ernest S. Frerichs, and Paul Virgil McCracken Flesher (eds), *Religion, Science, and Magic: In Concert and in Conflict* (New York: Oxford University Press, 1989), 138.
82. Like Sarah in our opening vignette he may see the performance of speech as an oppressive subversion of his d/Deaf world.
83. Davidson, 'Hearing', 219.
84. Burch, 'Deaf', 132.
85. Susannah B. Mintz, 'The Art of Joseph Grigely: Deafness, Conversation, Noise', *JLCDS* 6 (2012), 5.
86. Petra Kuppers, cited in Kochhar-Lindgren, 'Hearing', 420–1.
87. H. Dirksen and L. Bauman, 'Toward a Poetics of Vision, Space and the Body: Sign Language and Literary Theory', in Davis, *Disability*, 315.
88. Lewis, *Deaf*, 146–8.

CHAPTER 4

1. Greek literature sustains the perception of women as permeable and 'leaky'. It is said that, unlike the mouth, the vagina cannot voluntarily be closed, it rather leaks, unprovoked, a variety of fluids. This 'leakiness' also

became symbolic on a moral level. In the words of Holt Parker, 'the weak ignorant or feminine soul is like the weak, leaky feminine body'. See Holt Parker, 'Women in Medicine', in Sharon James and Sheila Dillon (eds), *A Companion to Woman in the Ancient World* (Oxford: Wiley-Blackwell, 2012), 111. The image of the bleeding woman as 'leaky' is also taken up by Candida Moss in her article on this passage. See Candida Moss, 'The Man with the Flow of Power: Porous Bodies in Mark 5: 25–34', *JBL* 129/3 (2010), 507–19.

2. Sundar Sarukkai, 'Phenomenology of Untouchability', *Economic and Political Weekly*, 37 (2009), 43.

3. Sarukkai, 'Phenomenology', 43. A similar point is made by Rosa Maria Perez when she states 'the word does not define those who cannot be touched, but those who cannot touch'. Rosa Maria Perez, *Kings and Untouchables: A Study of the Caste System in Western India* (New Delhi: Chronicle Books, 2004), 9.

4. 'Untouchability' has of course been officially abolished in Indian society, but the customs and prejudice experienced by out-castes, scheduled castes, or Dalits (a transgressive and politically activist label, literally meaning 'broken'), as ethnographies attest, still continues.

5. See James Scott, *Weapons of the Weak: Everyday Forms of Peasant Resistance* (New Haven: Yale University Press, 1987).

6. Craig Evans e.g. states that 'in Jesus' day, touching a leper was unthinkable, for the leper was viewed as unclean. To touch the leper was to be defiled. But purity flows from Jesus to the leper, healing the disease and restoring the man to a state of purity.' Craig A. Evans, *Matthew: New Cambridge Bible Commentary* (Cambridge: Cambridge University Press, 2012), 184–5.

7. Cecelia Wassen, 'Jesus and the Hemorrhaging Woman in Mark 5: 24–34: Insights from Purity Laws from the Dead Sea Scrolls', in Raija Sollamo, Anssi Voitila, and Jutta Jokiranta (eds), *Scripture in Transition: Essays on Septuagint, Hebrew Bible, and Dead Sea Scrolls in Honour of Raija Sollamo* (Leiden: Brill, 2008), 641–60.

8. Wassen, 'Jesus', 644.

9. James Crossley, *The Date of Mark's Gospel* (London: T. & T. Clark, 2004), 90.

10. Twelftree, *Jesus*, 63.

11. 'To be a Brahmin is to be an untouchable, a permanent untouchable. For most Brahmins there are only moments of untouchability and they do not have the discipline or practice to reach this state of permanent untouchability. But for the most exalted spiritual leaders the moments of untouchability are permanent. In fact, being a permanent untouchable,

one that is passed on hereditarily, is what distinguishes these Brahmin spiritual leaders.' See Sarukkai, 'Phenomenology', 43.

12. Louis Dumont, *Homo Hierarchicus: The Caste System and its Implications* (Chicago: University of Chicago Press, 1970).

13. Dumont, *Homo*, 56.

14. Jerome Neyrey, 'Readers Guide to Clean/Unclean, Pure/Polluted, and Holy/Profane: The Idea and System of Purity'. Available online at <http://nd.edu/~jneyrey1/purity.html>.

15. Mary Douglas, *Purity and Danger* (London: Routledge & Kegan Paul, 1966).

16. Douglas, *Purity*, 5.

17. Stein, *Mark*, 105.

18. Stein, *Mark*, 105.

19. David deSilva, *Honor, Patronage, Kinship and Purity: Unlocking New Testament Culture* (Downers Grove, Ill.: Intervarsity Press, 2000), 284.

20. Mary Healy, *Gospel of Mark* (Grand Rapids, Mich.: Baker Academic, 2008), 100.

21. Thus, as Gabriele Alex maintains, 'pollution structures the encounters between persons and acts as a matrix of movement within a geographical and social space, thereby regulating the encounters between persons'. Gabriele Alex, 'A Sense of Belonging and Exclusion: Touchability and Untouchability in Tamil Nadu', *Ethnos*, 73 (2008), 529.

22. Peniel Rajkumar, *Dalit Theology and Dalit Liberation: Problems, Paradigms and Possibilities* (Aldershot: Ashgate, 2010), 15–16.

23. Pilch, *Healing*, 52.

24. Clifton Black, *Mark: Abingdon New Testament Commentary* (Nashville, Tenn.: Union Methodist Publishing House, 2011).

25. 'Waxler (1981) discusses how people "learn to become lepers [*sic*]" by being socialized into the discriminatory models around them...They were inscribed onto flesh per the original definition of stigma, a permanent mark, cut or burned on the skin of people so as to publicly brand them as members of a socially discredited group.' See Ronald Barrett, 'Self-Mortification and the Stigma of Leprosy in Northern India', *MedAnth* 19 (2005), 225.

26. deSilva, *Honor*, 284.

27. Susan Haber, *'They Shall Purify Themselves': Essays on Purity in Early Judaism* (Atlanta, Ga.: Society of Biblical Literature, 2008), 136.

28. Margaret Trawick, 'Wandering Lost: A Landless Laborer's Sense of Place and Self', in Arjun Appadurai, Frank J. Korom, and Margaret Ann Mills (eds), *Gender, Genre and Power in South Asian Expressive Traditions* (Philadelphia: University of Pennsylvania Press, 1991), 228.

29. Anupama Rao, *The Caste Question: Dalits and the Politics of Modern India* (Berkeley-Los Angeles: University of California Press, 2009), 8. Gerald Berreman, in his book, *Caste and Other Inequalities* (Meerut: Folklore Institute, 1979), likewise criticized Dumont for putting all emphasis on purity, when actually the real differential was political and economic power. The upper castes had abundant goods and security, by contrast the untouchables were weak and wanting.

30. Gerald Berreman, 'The Brahmanical View of Caste', *Contributions to Indian Sociology*, 5 (1971), 23.

31. Berreman, *Caste*, 162.

32. Isabelle Clark-Decès also chastises Dumont for ignoring colonial history in his analysis of Indian structure. She writes, 'How could he fail to see that the modern state was anything but weak or subordinate to the ritual purity of Brahmin priests? How could he persist talking about the superiority of pure castes when…governmental institutions…actively stripped Brahmins of their dominance?' Isabelle Clark-Decès, *The Encounter Never Ends: A Return to the Field of Tamil Rituals* (Albany, NY: State University of New York Press, 2007), 8.

33. Jonathan Klawans, 'Moral and Ritual Purity', in Amy-Jill Levine, Dale C. Allison, and John Dominic Crossan (eds), *The Historical Jesus in Context* (Princeton: Princeton University Press, 2006), 267.

34. Also 'real' religion in Jewish traditions was likely quite different from 'official' religion of the elites, as this relies on scholarly dichotomies of official/popular religions that Francesca Stavrakopoulou has recently critiqued. See Francesca Stavrakopoulou, '"Popular" Religion and "Official" Religion: Practice, Perception, Portrayal', in Francesca Stavrakopoulou and John Barton (eds), *Religious Diversity in Ancient Israel and Judah* (London and New York: T. & T. Clark International, 2010), 37–58.

35. Alex, 'Sense of Belonging', 528.

36. Richard H. Davis, 'Ethnosociology', in Sushil Mittal and Gene Thursby (eds), *Studying Hinduism: Key Concepts and Methods* (New York: Routledge, 2008), 131.

37. Elizabeth Harvey (ed.), *Sensible Flesh: On Touch in Early Modern Culture* (Philadelphia: University of Pennsylvania Press, 2003), 2.

38. Yasumasa Sekine, *Pollution, Untouchability and Harijans* (Jaipur: Rawat Publications, 2011), p. xv.

39. Sekine, *Pollution*, p. xv.

40. Sekine, *Pollution*, p. xv.

41. Sekine, *Pollution*, p. xvii.

42. Sekine, *Pollution*, 25.

43. Lynn Vincentnathan's work on untouchability as subculture looks at social tactics, including manipulating higher caste relationships through passive avoidance and withdrawal, defiance and protest. She also explores spheres of manipulation in intracaste relationships. Lynn Vincentnathan, *Harijan Subculture and Self-Esteem Management in a South Indian Community* (Madison, Wis.: University of Wisconsin Press, 1987).

44. Jim Drobnick, *The Smell Culture Reader* (Oxford: Berg, 2006), 14.

45. Smith, *Sensing*, 59.

46. Gale Largey and Rod Watson, 'The Sociology of Odors', *American Journal of Sociology*, 77 (1972), 1024.

47. Winnifred Menninghaus, *Disgust: The Theory and History of a Strong Sensation* (Albany, NY: State University of New York Press, 2003), 1.

48. Nicole Shikin, *Animal Capital: Rendering Life in Biopolitical Times* (Minneapolis, Minn.: University of Minnesota Press, 2009), 56.

49. Shikin, *Animal*, 56.

50. Julia Kristeva, *Powers of Horror: An Essay on Abjection* (New York: Columbia University Press, 1982), 65.

51. Rachel Newall, 'The Thanksgiving of Women After Childbirth: A Blessing in Disguise', in Mavis Kirkham (ed.), *Exploring the Dirty Side of Women's Health* (Oxford: Routledge, 2007), 40.

52. Susan B. Miller, *Disgust: The Gatekeeper Emotion* (Hillsdale, NJ: The Analytic Press), 181.

53. Jerry Toner, *Popular Culture in Ancient Rome* (Cambridge: Polity Press, 2009), 124. See also David S. Potter, 'Odor and Power in the Roman Empire', in James Porter (ed.), *Constructions of the Classical Body* (Ann Arbor, Mich.: University of Michigan Press, 1999), 183.

54. Susan Ashbrook, 'On Holy Stench: When the Odor of Sanctity Sickens', *Studia Patristica*, 35 (2001), 99.

55. Constance Classen, David Howes, and Anthony Synnott, *Aroma: The Cultural History of Smell* (London: Routledge, 1994), 38.

56. Toner, *Popular*, 129.

57. William Ian Miller, *The Anatomy of Disgust* (Cambridge, Mass.: Harvard University Press, 1997), 67.

58. Smith, *Sensing*, 60.

59. Theophrastus, *The Characters* (Boston: Federic Hill, 1831), 47.

60. Toner reveals that in the Roman world a common means of distancing the mentally ill was to throw stones at them. Toner, *Popular*, 75. Legion's self-mutilation is perhaps an even more arresting image of his isolation and social marginality.

61. Rikki Watts, *Isaiah's New Exodus and Mark* (Tübingen: Mohr Siebeck, 1997), 158.

62. See also the comment on Lazarus' smelly corpse in John 11: 39; however perfuming the cadaver was also important as were incense offerings at tombs. Indeed there is archaeological evidence to support this with fragrance bottles being located in Jewish tombs. See Laurie Brink and Deborah Green (eds), *Commemorating the Dead: Texts and Artifacts in Context* (Berlin: Walter de Gruyter, 2008).

63. Despite the near-complete ignoring of olfactory dimensions of mainstream biblical scholarship on this character, one particular sermon on Legion creates his sensuous identity: 'Legion before Christ was a walking pollutant. He was nude and unkempt. That's visual pollution. He cried out night and day. That's noise pollution. And he must have smelled horribly. That's odour pollution. But after Christ saved him, Legion obviously began to practice better hygiene [!]. He had no doubt bathed, for we see him in the end clothed and in his right mind sitting at the feet of Jesus.' David Kalas, Frank Honeycutt, Stephen Crotts, and Robert Cueni, *Sermons on the Gospel Readings* (Lima, O.: CSS Publishing Co., 2003), i. 240.

64. Plutarch, 'Questiones Convivales IV', tr. H. B. Hoffleit, *Plutarch's Moralia VIII*, Loeb Classical Library (Cambridge, Mass.: Harvard University Press, 1969), 351–9.

65. Some question whether the bleeding is uterine and offer some alternatives including nosebleeds. See Mary Rose D'Angelo, 'Gender and Power in the Gospel of Mark: The Daughter of Jairus and the Woman with the Flow of Blood', in John Cavadini (ed.), *Miracles in Jewish and Christian Antiquity: Imagining Truth* (Notre Dame, Ind.: University of Notre Dame Press, 1999), 101–2 also Amy-Jill Levine, 'Discharging Responsibility: Matthean Jesus, Biblical Law and Hemorrhaging Women', in Mark Allan Powell and David Bauer (eds), *Treasures New and Old: New Essays in Matthean Studies* (Atlanta, Ga.: Scholars Press, 1996), 384. The majority of commentators however do see it as a uterine flow though. The fact that the healing is narrated in terms of the drying up of a flow of blood seems to bring to mind Leviticus 12 where similar terminology is used about the cessation of vaginal bleeding.

66. Marilyn Skinner, 'Sex', in Daniel Garrison (ed.), *A Cultural History of the Human Body in Antiquity* (Oxford: Berg, 2010), 69.

67. See Isa. 30: 22; Ezek. 7: 19–20, 22: 10, 36: 17; Lam. 1: 8, 17; Ezra 9: 11. For associated discussion on these negative symbolics see Sharon Faye Koren, 'The Menstruant as "Other" in Medieval Judaism and Christianity', *Nashim: A Journal of Jewish Women's Studies and Gender Issues*, 17 (2009), 33–59.

68. Classen *et al.*, *Aroma*, 38.

69. Classen *et al.*, *Aroma*, 38.
70. Shane Butler, 'The Scent of a Woman', *Arethusa*, 43 (2010), 87–112.
71. Mark Moore and John Weece, *The Power of Jesus* (Joplin, Mo.: College Press Publishing, 2002), 37. In a similar vein Prathia Hall notes, 'no wonder Jesus related to women so differently. He was neither queasy nor offended by the fountain of blood....Her fountain of seemingly endless, painful, foul-smelling flow dried up, because she touched his clothes.' See Prathia L. Hall, 'Sermon: Encounters with Jesus from Dying to Life Mark 5: 21–43', in Cleophus Larue (ed.), *Power in the Pulpit* (Louisville, Ky.: Westminster John Knox Press, 2002), 70.
72. Rao, *Caste*, 9.
73. Ashis Nandy, 'Humiliation: The Politics and Cultural Psychology of the Limits of Human Degradation' in Elleke Boehmer and Rosinka Chaudhuri (eds), *The Indian Postcolonial: A Critical Reader* (Oxford: Routledge, 2010), 263.
74. REB (in text) and NRSV (in footnote) both represent the 'anger' rendering.
75. Twelftree, *Jesus*, 62.
76. An oft–cited Human Rights Watch report on the Dalit plight states: 'More than one-sixth of India's population, some 160 million people, live a precarious existence, shunned by much of society because of their rank as untouchables or Dalits—literally meaning "broken" people—at the bottom of India's caste system. Dalits are discriminated against, denied access to land, forced to work in degrading conditions, and routinely abused at the hands of the police and of higher-caste groups that enjoy the state's protection. In what has been called "hidden apartheid" entire villages in many Indian states remain completely segregated by caste. National legislations and constitutional protections serve only to mask the social realities of discrimination and violence faced by those living below the "pollution line".' *Broken People: Caste Violence Against India's 'Untouchables'* (New York: Human Rights Watch, 1999), 1–2.
77. Rao, *Caste*, p. xiii.
78. Constance Classen, *Worlds of Sense: Exploring the Senses in History and Across Cultures* (London: Routledge, 1993), 103.
79. Silvia Schroer and Thomas Staubli, *Body Symbolism in the Bible* (Collegeville, Minn.: Liturgical Press, 2001), 94–6.
80. Susan Bayly, *Caste, Society and Politics in India from the Eighteenth Century to the Modern Age* (Cambridge: Cambridge University Press, 1999), 339.
81. Most commentators opt for Jesus actually healing the man of his skin condition and see the latter command to go and show himself to a priest

as a fulfilment of religious conferral of the man as 'cleansed'. See Stein, *Mark*, 105.

82. Sarukkai, 'Phenomenology', 44.

83. Sarukkai, 'Phenomenology', 44.

84. Halvor Moxnes, *Putting Jesus in his Place: A Radical Vision of Household and Kingdom* (Louisville, Ky.: Westminster John Knox Press, 2003), 140.

85. Christian Strecker avers that possession as performance often enacts behaviour which culture views as 'demonic'. See Christian Strecker, 'Jesus and the Demoniacs', in Wolfgang Stegemann, Bruce Malina, and Gerd Theissen (eds), *The Social Setting of Jesus and the Gospels* (Minneapolis, Minn.: Fortress Press, 2002), 122.

86. See Paul Stoller, *Embodying Colonial Memories: Spirit Possession, Power and the Hauka in West Africa* (New York: Routledge, 1995) for more on this theme.

87. Richard Horsley, *Jesus and the Powers: Conflict, Covenant and the Hope of the Poor* (Minneapolis, Minn.: Augsburg Fortress, 2011), 128.

88. Barbara Sutton, 'Naked Protest: Memories of Bodies and Resistance at the World Social Forum', *JIWS* 8 (2007), 143.

89. Brett Lunceford, *Naked Politics: Nudity, Political Action and the Rhetoric of the Body* (Plymouth: Lexington Books, 2012), 7.

90. Sandra L. Gravett, Karla G. Bohmbach, F. V. Greifenhagen, and Donald Polaski, *An Introduction to the Hebrew Bible: A Thematic Approach* (Louisville, Ky.: Westminster John Knox Press, 2008), 189.

91. Gravett *et al.*, *Introduction*, 189.

92. Adeline Marie Masquelier, *Dirt, Undress, and Difference: Critical Perspectives on the Body's Surface* (Bloomington, Ind.: Indiana University Press, 2005), 7.

93. <http://www.deccanherald.com/content/82745/protesting–dalits–smear–themselves–human.html>.

94. Adeline Marie Masquelier also cites the dirty protests of the IRA female prisoners, who protested against the British who wanted to criminalize them, with urine, faeces, and menstrual blood. They accordingly disrupted neat boundaries between savagery and civilization and used their bodily fluids as powerful tools of non-violent resistance. See Masquelier, *Dirt*, 7.

95. Laura Donaldson, 'Gospel Hauntings: The Postcolonial Demons of New Testament Criticism', in Stephen D. Moore and Fernando Segovia (eds), *Postcolonial Biblical Criticism: Interdisciplinary Intersections* (London: T. & T. Clark, 2005), 104.

96. Sharyn Echols Dowd, *Reading Mark: A Literary and Theological Commentary on the Second Gospel* (Macon, Ga.: Smyth & Helwys Publishing, 2001), 57.

97. Muriel Orevillo-Montenegro, *The Jesus of Asian Women* (Darya Ganj, New Delhi: Logos Press, 2009), 64.
98. Alex, 'Sense of Belonging', 530.
99. F. Scott Spencer, *Dancing Girls, Loose Ladies, and Women of the Cloth: The Women in Jesus' Life* (New York: Continuum, 2004), 59.
100. Rao, *Caste*, 70.
101. Rao, *Caste*, 70.
102. Spencer, *Dancing*, 60.
103. Spencer, *Dancing*, 60.
104. Moss, 'The Man', 507–19.
105. Gopal Guru, 'Rejection of Rejection: Foregrounding Self-Respect', in Gopal Guru (ed.), *Humiliation: Claims and Context* (Oxford: Oxford University Press, 2009), 222.
106. Susan Wendell, *The Rejected Body: Feminist Philosophical Reflections on Disability* (New York and London: Routledge, 1996), 61.
107. Ravindra S. Khare, 'The Body, Sensoria, and Self of the Powerless: Remembering/Re-Membering Indian Untouchable Women', *NLH* 26/1 (1995), 162.
108. Gopal Guru, 'Introduction', in Guru, *Humiliation*, 14.
109. Guru, 'Introduction', 9.

CHAPTER 5

1. Anne Fadiman, *The Spirit Catches you and you Fall Down: A Hmong Child, Her American Doctors, and the Collision of Two Cultures* (New York: Farrar, Straus, & Giroux, 1997).
2. Fadiman, *Spirit*, 262.
3. My emphasis. Janelle Taylor, 'The Story Catches you and you Fall Down: Tragedy, Ethnography and Cultural Competence', *MedAnth* 17 (2003), 159–81.
4. Taylor, 'The Story', 179.
5. Taylor, 'The Story', 166.
6. Taylor, 'The Story', 179.
7. Taylor, 'The Story', 173–4.
8. My emphasis. Taylor, 'The Story', 174.
9. Taylor, 'The Story', 173–4.
10. Ronald Comer and Elizabeth Gould, *Psychology around us* (Hoboken, NJ: John Wiley & Son, 2011), 161.
11. Mark Osteen, 'Autism and Representation: A Comprehensive Introduction', in Mark Osteen (ed.), *Autism and Representation* (London: Taylor & Francis, 2008), 3.

12. Stuart Murray, *Representing Autism: Culture, Narrative, Fascination* (Liverpool: Liverpool University Press, 2008), 8.

13. Anne Louise Chappell, 'Still Out in the Cold: People with Learning Difficulties and the Social Model of Disability', in Tom Shakespeare (ed.), *The Disability Reader: Social Science Perspectives* (London: Cassell, 1998), 213.

14. Bryan Good, *Medicine, Rationality and Experience: An Anthropological Perspective* (Cambridge: Cambridge University Press, 1994), 157.

15. Chris A. Faircloth, 'Revisiting Thematisation in the Narrative Study of Epilepsy', Sociology of Health and Illness, 21 (1999), 222.

16. Good, *Medicine*, 136.

17. Good, *Medicine*, 158.

18. John R. Donahue and Daniel J. Harrington, *The Gospel of Mark* (Minneapolis, Minn.: Liturgical Press, 2002), 281.

19. Davies and Allison, *Matthew*, 721.

20. M. Eugene Boring and Fred B. Craddock, *The People's New Testament Commentary* (Louisville, Ky.: Westminster John Knox Press, 2009), 216.

21. <http://oxforddictionaries.com/definition/english/diagnosis>.

22. Frederick J. Gaiser, *Healing in the Bible: Theological Insight for Christian Ministry* (Grand Rapids, Mich.: Baker Academic, 2010), 138.

23. Steven Schachter and Lisa Andermann, *Epilepsy in our World: Stories of Living with Seizures from around the World* (Oxford: Oxford University Press, 2008), 3.

24. Schachter and Andermann, *Epilepsy*, 4.

25. 'Epileptic' appears in NRSV and NIV; 'Lunatic' appears in the JB and KJV.

26. John Wilkinson, 'The Case of an Epileptic Boy', *ET* 79 (1967), 40–1. Similarly, whilst Nicole Kelley in her review of epilepsy in ancient Christianity is careful to contextualize the phenomenon in ancient views of seizures, she still cannot completely resist the medicalizing shift and states that 'the boy's condition [is described] in terms that are consistent with the epileptic syndrome now known as toni-clonic seizures: he loses the ability to speak, falls down, foams at the mouth, grinds his teeth and becomes rigid during each episode'. See Nicole Kelley, '"The Punishment of the Devil was Apparent in the Torment of Human Body": Epilepsy in Ancient Christianity', in Candida Moss and Jeremy Schipper (eds), *Disability Studies and Biblical Literature* (New York: Palgrave Macmillan, 2011), 209.

27. My emphasis. John Meier, *A Marginal Jew: Rethinking the Historical Jesus* ii (New York: Doubleday, 1994), 655.

28. Veena Das and Ranendra K. Das, 'How the Body Speaks: Illness and the Lifeworld among the Urban Poor', in João Biehl, Byron Good,

and Arthur Kleinmann (eds), *Subjectivity: Ethnographic Investigations* (Berkeley, Calif.: University of California Press, 2007), 70.

29. John Pilch, *Healing in the New Testament: Insights from Medical Anthropology* (Minneapolis, Minn.: Augsburg Fortress, 2000), 19.

30. C. P. Panayiotopoulos, *A Clinical Guide to Epileptic Syndromes and their Treatment* (London: Springer Healthcare Ltd, 2010), 1.

31. Lars-Chri Hydén and Jens Brockmeier, 'Introduction: From the Retold to the Performed Story', in Lars-Chri Hydén and Jens Brockmeier (eds), *Health, Illness and Culture: Broken Narratives* (New York: Taylor & Francis, 2008), 7.

32. Oliver Sacks, *The Man Who Mistook his Wife for a Hat* (New York: Harper & Row, 1987), pp. vii–viii.

33. My emphasis, Rory C. Foster, *Studies in the Life of Christ: Introduction, the Early Period, the Middle Period, the Final Week* (Joplin, Mo.: Baker Book House, 1971), 745.

34. James Keir Howard, *Disease and Healing in the New Testament* (Lanham, Md.: University Press of America, 2001), 113–14.

35. Donald Capp, *Jesus the Village Psychiatrist* (Louisville, Ky.: Westminster John Knox Press, 2008), 97.

36. Capp, *Jesus*, 97.

37. Capp, *Jesus*, 99.

38. Capp, *Jesus*, 102.

39. Capp, *Jesus*, 103.

40. Capp, *Jesus*, 104.

41. Owsei Temkin, *The Falling Sickness: A History of Epilepsy from the Greeks to the Beginnings of Modern Neurology* (Baltimore, Md.: Johns Hopkins University Press, 1994), 115.

42. Temkin, *Falling*, 115.

43. Donahue and Harrington, *Mark*, 281.

44. Graham H. Twelftree, *Jesus the Miracle Worker: A Historical and Theological Study* (Downers Grove, Ill.: Intervarsity Press, 1999), 89.

45. Foster, *Studies*, 745.

46. Joel Marcus, *Mark 8–16*, Anchor Yale Bible Commentaries, 27 (New Haven: Yale University Press, 2009), 652.

47. Marcus, *Mark 8–16*, 653.

48. Harrington, *Matthew*, 259.

49. J. M. Ross, 'Epileptic or Moonstruck', *BT* 29 (1978), 126–8.

50. Ann Jacoby, Dee Snape, and Gus Baker, 'Social Aspects: Epilepsy, Stigma and Quality of Life', in Jerome Engel and Timothy A. Pedley (eds), *Epilepsy: A Comprehensive Textbook* (Philadelphia: Lippincott, Williams & Wilkins, 2008), 2229.

51. Plutarch, *Quaestiones Convivales* 658e–f.
52. Carter, *Matthew*, 353.
53. Carter, *Matthew*, 353.
54. Carter, *Matthew*, 353.
55. Kelley, 'Punishment', 219.
56. Kelley, 'Punishment', 215.
57. Capp, *Jesus*, 93.
58. Lars-Chri Hydén and Jens Brockmeier, 'Introduction: From the Retold to the Performed Story', in Hydén and Brockmeier, *Health*, 7.
59. Hydén and Brockmeier, 'Introduction', 7.
60. Gay Becker, *Disrupted Lives: How People Create Meaning in a Chaotic World* (Berkeley, Calif.: University of California Press, 1997), 17.
61. James M. Wilce 'Medical Discourse', *ARA* 38 (2009), 200.
62. Joseph Schneider and Peter Conrad, *Having Epilepsy: The Experience and Control of Illness* (Philadelphia: Temple University Press, 1985).
63. Chris A. Faircloth, 'Revisiting Thematisation in the Narrative Study of Epilepsy', *Sociology of Health and Illness,* 21 (1999), 210.
64. Faircloth, 'Revisiting', 210.
65. Faircloth, 'Revisiting', 210.
66. Good, *Medicine*, 138.
67. Good, *Medicine*, 153.
68. Good, Medicine, 162.
69. Arthur Kleinmann, *Suffering, Healing and the Human Condition* (New York: Basic Books, 1988), 49.
70. Das and Das, 'How the Body', 67.
71. Hydén and Brockmeier, 'Introduction', 7.
72. John Coulehan, 'The Word is an Instrument of Healing', *Literature and Medicine,* 10 (1991), 112.
73. Mircea Eliade, *Shamanism: Archaic Techniques of Ecstasy* (Princeton: Princeton University Press, 1970), 511.
74. Arthur Frank, *The Wounded Story Teller: Body, Illness and Ethics* (Chicago: University of Chicago Press, 1997), 2. On this theme see also Madonne Miner, 'Making up the Stories as we Go along: Men, Women and Narratives of Disability', in David Mitchell and Sharon L. Snyder (eds), *The Body and Physical Difference: Discourses of Disability* (Ann Arbor, Mich.: University of Michigan Press, 1997), 293.
75. Linda C. Garro and Cheryl Mattingly, 'Narrative as Construct and Construction', in Linda C. Garro and Cheryl Mattingly (eds), *Narrative and the Cultural Construction of Illness and Healing* (Berkeley-Los Angeles: University of California Press, 2000), 5.

76. John Pilch, 'The Transfiguration of Jesus: An Experience of Alternate Reality', in Philip Esler (ed.), *Modelling Early Christianity* (London: Routledge, 1995), 47–64. See also Louise Lawrence, *Reading with Anthropology: Exhibiting Aspects of New Testament Religion* (Milton Keynes: Paternoster Press, 2005), 35–54.

77. William C. Placher, *Mark* (Louisville, Ky.: Westminster John Knox Press, 2010), 131.

78. A. E. Harvey, *A Companion to the New Testament* (Cambridge: Cambridge University Press, 2004), 151.

79. Gundry, *Mark*, 487.

80. Schachter and Andermann, *Epilepsy*, 2.

81. Hippocrates, cited in Emmanouil Magiorkinis, Kalliopi Sidiropoulou, and Aristidis Diamantis, 'Hallmarks in the History of Epilepsy: From Antiquity till the Twentieth Century', *EpilepsyBehav.* 17 (2010), 103.

82. Galen cited in Temkin, *Falling*, 36.

83. Aretaeus of Cappadocia discussed in Magiorkinis *et al.*, 'Hallmarks', 104.

84. Eric Sorensen, *Possession and Exorcism in the New Testament and Early Christianity* (Tübingen: Mohr Siebeck, 2002), 107.

85. Sorensen, *Possession*, 107.

86. Hippocrates, discussed in Magiorkinis *et al.*, 'Hallmarks', 103.

87. Annette Weissenrieder, *Images of Illness in the Gospel of Luke: Insights of Ancient Medical Texts* (Tübingen: Mohr Siebeck, 2003), 269.

88. Weissenrieder, *Images*, 279.

89. Weissenrieder, *Images*, 281.

90. Antigone Samellas, *Alienation: The Experience of the Eastern Mediterranean (50–600 A.D.)* (Bern: Peter Lang, 2010), 172.

91. John Christopher Thomas, *The Devil, Disease and Deliverance: Origins of Illness in New Testament Thought* (Sheffield: Sheffield Academic Press, 1998), 153.

92. Hippocrates discussed in Magiorkinis *et al.*, 'Hallmarks', 103.

93. Deborah Kirklin, 'The Search for Meaning in Modern Medicine', in Knut Stene-Johansen and Frederick Tygstrup (eds), *Illness in Context* (Amsterdam: Rodopi, 2010), 28.

94. Jeannette Stirling, *Representing Epilepsy: Myth and Matter* (Liverpool: Liverpool University Press, 2010), 25.

95. Samellas, *Alienation*, 201.

96. Sanjeev V. Thomas and Aparna Nair, 'Confronting the Stigma of Epilepsy', *AIAN* 14 (2011), 158–63.

97. Graham Scambler and Anthony Hopkins, 'Being Epileptic: Coming to Terms with Stigma', *Sociology of Health and Illness*, 8 (2008), 26–43.

98. Louise Jilek-Aall, 'Forty Years of Experience with Epilepsy', in Schachter and Andermann, *Epilepsy*, 33.

99. Louise Jilek-Aall, 'Forty', 35.

100. Peter Bolt, *Jesus' Defeat of Death: Persuading Mark's Early Readers* (Cambridge: Cambridge University Press, 2003), 232.

101. Bolt, *Jesus*, 232.

102. Jeannine Brown, *The Disciples in Narrative Perspective* (Atlanta, Ga.: Society of Biblical Literature, 2002), 65.

103. Robert C. Tannehill, *Abingdon New Testament Commentary—Luke* (Nashville, Tenn.: Abingdon Press, 1996), 163.

104. David L. Turner, *Matthew* (Grand Rapids, Mich.: Baker Academic, 2008), 424.

105. Frank, *Wounded*, 131.

106. Frank, *Wounded*, 131.

107. Jonathan Imber, *Trusting Doctors: The Decline of Moral Authority in American Medicine* (Princeton: Princeton University Press, 2008), 124.

108. Frank, *Wounded*, 131.

109. Brian Brown, Paul Crawford, and Ronald Carter, *Evidence-Based Health Communication* (Maidenhead: Open University Press, 2006), 70.

110. Toby Ballou Hamilton, 'Narrative Reasoning', in Barbara A. Boyt Schell and John W. Schell (eds), *Clinical and Professional Reasoning in Occupational Therapy* (Baltimore, Md.: Lippincott, Williams & Wilkins, 2008), 149.

111. Samellas, *Alienation*, 154.

112. Christopher D. Marshall, *Faith as a Theme in Mark's Narrative* (Cambridge: Cambridge University Press, 1989), 116.

113. Stirling, *Representing*, 97.

114. Susan Reynolds Whyte, 'Constructing Epilepsy: Images and Contexts in East Africa', in Benedicte Ingstad and Susan Whyte (eds), *Disability and Culture* (Berkeley-Los Angeles: University of California Press, 1995), 228.

115. Wilkinson, 'Case', 42.

116. John Dominic Crossan, *The Historical Jesus: The Life of a Mediterranean Jewish Peasant* (London: Harper Collins, 1992), 336–7; Pilch, *Healing*, 19–38.

117. Bert Jan Lietaert Peerbolte and Michael Labahn, *Wonders Never Cease: The Purpose of Narrating Miracle Stories in the New Testament and its Religious Environment* (London: T. & T. Clark, 2006), 124.

118. Lane, *Mark*, 334–5.

119. Meier, *Marginal Jew*, 671.

120. Joseph Schneider and Peter Conrad, *Having Epilepsy: The Experience and Control of Illness* (Philadelphia: Temple University Press, 1983), 24.

121. Sabine Lucas, *Bloodlines of the Soul* (Lincoln: iUniverse Books, 2005), 185.

122. 'morbus comitialis', in Guenter Kraemer, *Epilepsy from A—Z: Dictionary of Medical Terms* (Stuttgart: Georg Thieme Verlag, 1996).

123. Samellas, *Alienation*, 153.

124. Stirling, *Representing*, 25.

125. Stirling, *Representing*, 97.

126. Stirling, *Representing*, 97.

127. Schachter and Andermann, *Epilepsy*, 9.

128. Nora L. Jones, 'Embodied Ethics: From the Body as Specimen and Spectacle to the Body as Patient', in Frances Mascia-Less (ed.), *A Companion to the Anthology of Bodies/Embodiment* (Chichester: Willey-Blackwell Publishing, 2011), 82.

129. Laura Ackerman Sherwood, 'A Counterstory to Master Narratives for Persons with Disability', Ph.D. thesis (Regents University, 2009), 66. Available online at <http://books.google.co.uk/books?id=hI5nJW5WC7IC&printsec=frontcover&source=gbs_ge_summary_r&cad=0#v=onepage&q&f=false>.

130. Frank, *Wounded*, 131–2.

CONCLUSION

1. Theo Peters, 'Foreword', in Olga Bogdashina, *Autism and the Edges of the Known World: Sensitivities Language and Constructed Reality* (London: Jessica Kingsley Publishers, 2010), 10.

2. Avrahami, *Senses*, 221.

3. Fiona Campbell, *Contours of Ableism: The Production of Disability and Abledness* (New York: Palgrave Macmillan, 2009), 198.

4. Campbell, *Contours*, 4.

5. Davis, *Enforcing*, 2.

6. Paul Harpur, 'From Disability to Ability: Changing the Phrasing of the Debate' *Disabilty and Society*, 27 (2012), 329.

7. Robert McRuer, *Crip Theory: Cultural Signs of Queerness and Disability* (Albany, NY: New York University Press, 2006), 9.

8. Campbell, *Contours*, 6.

9. Fiona Campbell, 'Stalking Ableism: Using Disability to Expose "Abled" Narcissism', in Dan Goodley, Bill Hughes, and Lennard Davis

(eds), *Disability and Social Theory: New Developments and Directions* (New York: Palgrave Macmillan, 2012), 227.

10. Adrian Thatcher, *God, Sex and Gender: An Introduction* (Chichester: John Wiley & Son, 2011), 255.

11. Thatcher, *God*, 255.

12. Eiesland, *Disabled*, 101

13 Deborah Creamer, *Disability and Christian Theology: Embodied Limits and Constructive Possibilities* (Oxford: Oxford University Press, 2009), 112–13.

14. Creamer, *Disability*, 113.

15. Creamer, *Disability*, 113

16 Susan Peters, 'Is there a Disability Culture? A Syncretisation of Three Possible World Views', *Disability and Society*, 15 (2000), 585.

17. Winnie Dunn, *Living Sensationally: Understanding your Senses* (London: Jessica Kingsley Publishers 2008), 16.

| *Works Cited*

Abu Lughod, Lila, *Veiled Sentiments*. Berkeley-Los Angeles: University of California Press, 2000.

Aichele, George, *Jesus Framed*. London: Routledge, 1996.

Alex, Gabriele, 'A Sense of Belonging and Exclusion: "Touchability" and "Untouchability" in Tamil Nadu', *Ethnos*, 73 (2008): 523–43.

Allison, Dale, 'The Eye is the Lamp of the Body (Matthew 6: 22–3 = Luke 11: 34–6)', *NTS* 33 (1987): 61–83.

Anderson, Hugh, *The Gospel of Mark*. London: Oliphants, 1976.

Anupama, Rao, *The Caste Question: Dalits and the Politics of Modern India*. Berkeley-Los Angeles: University of California Press, 2009.

Appadurai, Arjun, 'Introduction: Commodities and the Politics of Value', in Arjun Appadurai (ed.), *The Social Life of Things: Commodities in Cultural Perspective*. Cambridge: Cambridge University Press, 1986.

Ashbrook, Susan, 'On Holy Stench: When the Odor of Sanctity Sickens', *Studia Patristica*, 35 (2001): 90–101.

Avalos, Hector, 'Introducing Sensory Criticism in Biblical Studies: Audiocentricity and Visiocentricity', in Hector Avalos, Sarah Melcher, and Jeremy Schipper (eds), *This Abled Body: Rethinking Disabilities in Biblical Studies*. Atlanta, Ga.: Society of Biblical Literature, 2007, 31–46.

Avalos, Hector, Sarah Melcher, and Jeremy Schipper, 'Introduction', in Hector Avalos, Sarah Melcher, and Jeremy Schipper (eds), *This Abled Body: Rethinking Disabilities in Biblical Studies*. Atlanta, Ga.: Society of Biblical Literature, 2007, 1–9.

Avrahami, Yael, *The Senses of Scripture: Sensory Perception in the Hebrew Bible*. London: T. & T. Clark, 2012.

Barasch, Mosche, *Blindness: The History of a Mental Image in Western Thought*. New York: Routledge, 2001.

Bar-Ilan, Meir, 'Illiteracy in the Land of Israel in the First Centuries C.E.'. Available online at <http://faculty.biu.ac.il/~barilm/illitera.html>.

Barrett, Ronald, 'Self-Mortification and the Stigma of Leprosy in Northern India', *MedAnth* 19 (2005): 216–30.

Bayly, Susan, *Caste, Society and Politics in India from the Eighteenth Century to the Modern Age*. Cambridge: Cambridge University Press, 1999.

Beavis, Mary, 'From the Margin to the Way: A Feminist Reading of the Story of Bartimaeus', *JFSR* 14 (1998): 19–39.

Becker, Gay, *Disrupted Lives: How People Create Meaning in a Chaotic World*. Berkeley-Los Angeles: University of California Press, 1997.

Ben-Moshe, Liat, 'Infusing Disability in the Curriculum: The Case of Saramago's Blindness', *DSQ* 26 (2006). Available online at <http://dsq-sds.org/article/view/688/865>.

Bennema, Cornelius, *Encountering Jesus: Character Studies in the Gospel of John*. Milton Keynes: Paternoster, 2009.

Berreman, Gerald, 'The Brahmanical View of Caste', *Contributions to Indian Sociology*, 5 (1971): 16–23.

——— *Caste and Other Inequalities*. Meerut: Folklore Institute, 1979.

Birch, Bruce, 'Impairment as a Condition in Biblical Scholarship', in Hector Avalos, Sarah Melcher, and Jeremy Schipper (eds), *This Abled Body: Rethinking Disabilities in Biblical Studies*. Atlanta, Ga.: Society of Biblical Literature, 2007, 185–95.

Black, Clifton, *Mark: Abingdon New Testament Commentary*. Nashville, Tenn.: Union Methodist Publishing House, 2011.

Bolt, David, 'From Blindness to Visual Impairment: Terminological Typology and the Social Model of Disability', *DisabSoc* 20 (2005): 539–52.

Bolt, Peter, *Jesus' Defeat of Death: Persuading Mark's Early Readers*. Cambridge: Cambridge University Press, 2003.

Borg, Marcus, *Reading the Bible Again for the First Time*. New York: Harper Collins, 2001.

Boring, M. Eugene, and Fred B. Craddock, *The People's New Testament Commentary*. Louisville, Ky.: Westminster John Knox Press, 2009.

Bratcher, Robert, and Eugene Nida. *A Translator's Handbook on the Gospel of Mark*. Leiden: Brill, 1961.

Brink, Laurie, and Deborah Green (eds), *Commemorating the Dead: Texts and Artifacts in Context*. Berlin: Walter de Gruyter, 2008.

Brown, Brian, Paul Crawford, and Ronald Carter, *Evidence-Based Health Communication* Maidenhead: Open University Press, 2006.

Brown, Jeannine, *The Disciples in Narrative Perspective*. Atlanta, Ga.: Society of Biblical Literature, 2002.

Brueggemann, Brenda Joe, 'Delivering Disability, Willing Speech', in Carrie Sandahl and Philip Auslander (eds), *Bodies in Commotion: Disability and Performance*. Ann Arbor, Mich.: University of Michigan Press, 2005.

Burch, Susan, 'Deaf Poet's Society: Subverting the Hearing Paradigm', *Literature and Medicine*, 16 (1997): 121–34.

Butler, Shane, 'The Scent of a Woman', *Arethusa*, 43 (2010): 87–112.

Campbell, Fiona, *Contours of Ableism: The Production of Disability and Abledness*. New York: Palgrave Macmillan, 2009.

—— 'Stalking Ableism: Using Disability to Expose "Abled" Narcissism', in Dan Goodley, Bill Hughes, and Lennard Davis (eds), *Disability and Social Theory: New Developments and Directions*. New York: Palgrave Macmillan, 2012, 212–30.

Capp, Donald, *Jesus the Village Psychiatrist*. Louisville, Ky.: Westminster John Knox Press, 2008.

Carp, Richard, 'Hearing, Smelling, Tasting, Feeling, Seeing: The Role of the Arts in Making Sense Out of the Academy', *Issues in Integrative Studies*, 13 (1995): 25–36. Available online at <http://libres.uncg.edu/ir/asu/f/Carp_Richard_1995_Hearing.pdf>.

Carter, Warren, *Matthew and the Margins: A Sociopolitical and Religious Reading*. New York: Orbis Books, 2000.

Chappell, Anne Louise, 'Still Out in the Cold: People with Learning Difficulties and the Social Model of Disability', in Tom Shakespeare (ed.), *The Disability Reader: Social Science Perspectives*. London: Cassell, 1998, 211–20.

Clark Kee, Howard. 'Magic and Messiah', in Jacob Neusner, Ernest S. Frerichs, and Paul Virgil McCracken Flesher (eds), *Religion, Science, and Magic: In Concert and in Conflict*. New York: Oxford University Press, 1989, 121–41.

Clark-Decès, Isabelle, *The Encounter Never Ends: A Return to the Field of Tamil Rituals*. New York: State University of New York Press, 2007.

Clarke, Sathianathan, 'Viewing the Bible through the Ears and Eyes of Subalterns in India'. *BibInt* 10 (2002): 245–66.

Classen, Constance, *Worlds of Sense: Exploring the Senses in History and across Cultures*. London: Routledge, 1993.

——. 'Foundations for an Anthropology of the Senses', *ISSJ* 49 (1997): 401–12.

——. 'Traveling without Sightseeing: Exploring Alternative Modes of Cross-Cultural Engagement', in Patrick Devlieger, Frank Renders, Huberet Froyen, and Kristel Wildiers (eds), *Blindness and the Multi-Sensorial City*. Antwerp: Garant, 2006, 261–72.

Classen, Constance, David Howes, and Anthony Synnott, *Aroma: The Cultural History of Smell*. London: Routledge, 1994.

Collins, Adela Yarbro, *Mark: A Commentary. Hermeneia*. Minneapolis: Fortress Press, 2007.

Comer, Ronald, and Elizabeth Gould. *Psychology around us*. Hoboken, NJ: John Wiley & Son, 2011.

Conquergood, Dwight, 'Performance Studies, Interventions and Radical Research', *Drama Review*, 46 (2002): 145–56.

Corker, Marian, and Tom Shakespeare (eds), *Disability/ Postmodernity: Embodying Disability Theory*. London: Continuum, 2002.

Coulehan, John, 'The Word is an Instrument of Healing', *Literature and Medicine*, 10 (1991): 111–29.

Couser, G. Thomas, *Signifying Bodies: Disability in Contemporary Life Writing*. Ann Arbor, Mich.: University of Michigan Press, 2009.

Creamer, Deborah, *Disability and Christian Theology: Embodied Limits and Constructive Possibilities*. Oxford: Oxford University Press, 2009.

Crook, Zeba, 'Structure versus Agency in Studies of the Biblical Social World: Engaging with Louise Lawrence', *JSNT* 29 (2007): 251–75.

Crossan, John Dominic, *The Historical Jesus: The Life of a Mediterranean Jewish Peasant*. London: Harper Collins, 1992, 336–7.

Crossley, James, *The Date of Mark's Gospel*. London: T. & T. Clark, 2004.

—— *Jesus in an Age of Terror: Scholarly Projects for a New American Century*. London: Equinox, 2008.

D'Angelo, Mary Rose, 'Gender and Power in the Gospel of Mark: The Daughter of Jairus and the Woman with the Flow of Blood', in John Cavadini (ed.), *Miracles in Jewish and Christian Antiquity: Imagining Truth*. Notre Dame, Ind.: University of Notre Dame Press, 1999, 83–109.

Das, Veena, and Ranendra K. Das, 'How the Body Speaks: Illness and the Lifeworld among the Urban Poor', in João Biehl, Byron Good, and Arthur Kleinmann (eds), *Subjectivity: Ethnographic Investigations*. Berkeley and Los Angeles: University of California Press, 2007, 66–97.

Davidson, Michael, 'Hearing Things: The Scandal of Speech in Deaf Performance', in H.-Dirksen L. Bauman, Heidi M. Rose, and Jennifer L. Nelson (eds), *Signing the Body Poetic: Essays on American Sign Language Literature*. Berkeley-Los Angeles: University of California Press, 2006, 216–33.

Davies, William D., and Dale C. Allison, *A Critical and Exegetical Commentary on the Gospel According to Saint Matthew*. New York: T. & T. Clark International, 2004.

Davis, Lennard, 'Introduction', in Lennard Davis (ed.), *The Disability Studies Reader*. New York: Routledge, 1997, 1–8.

Davis, Richard H., 'Ethnosociology', in Sushil Mittal and Gene Thursby (eds), *Studying Hinduism: Key Concepts and Methods*. New York: Routledge, 2008, 125–38.

de Pina-Cabral, João, 'The Mediterranean as a Category of Regional Comparison: A Critical View', *CA* 30 (1989): 399–406.

Derrett, John Duncan, 'Trees Walking: Prophecy and Christology', in John Duncan Derrett, *Studies in the New Testament*, iii. Leiden: Brill, 1982, 107–29.

Deshen, Shlomo, *Blind People: The Private and Public Life of Sightless Israelis.* Albany, NY: State University of New York Press, 1992.

deSilva, David, *Honor, Patronage, Kinship and Purity: Unlocking New Testament Culture.* Downers Grove, Ill.: Intervarsity Press, 2000.

Donahue, John R., and Daniel J. Harrington. *The Gospel of Mark.* Minneapolis, Minn.: Liturgical Press, 2002.

Donaldson, Laura, 'Gospel Hauntings: The Postcolonial Demons of New Testament Criticism', in Stephen D. Moore and Fernando Segovia (eds), *Postcolonial Biblical Criticism: Interdisciplinary Intersections.* London: T. & T. Clark, 2005, 97–113.

Douglas, Mary, *Purity and Danger: An Analysis of Concepts of Pollution and Taboo.* New York: Praeger, 1966.

Dowd, Sharyn Echols, *Reading Mark: A Literary and Theological Commentary on the Second Gospel.* Macon, Ga.: Smyth & Helwys Publishing, 2001.

Drobnick, Jim, *The Smell Culture Reader.* Oxford: Berg, 2006.

Dube, Musa, *Postcolonial Feminist Interpretation of the Bible.* St Louis, Mo.: Chalice Press, 2000.

Dumont, Louis, *Homo Hierarchicus: The Caste System and its Implications.* Chicago: University of Chicago Press, 1970.

Dunn, Winnie, *Living Sensationally: Understanding Your Senses.* London: Jessica Kingsley Publishers, 2008.

Edwards, Elizabeth, and Kaushik Bhaumik, 'Introduction', in Elizabeth Edwards and Kaushik Bhaumik (eds), *Visual Sense: A Cultural Reader.* Oxford: Berg, 2008, 3–15.

Edwards, Martha, 'Deaf and Dumb in Ancient Greece', in Lennard Davis (ed.), *The Disability Studies Reader.* London: Routledge, 1997, 29–51.

Eidsheim, Nina Sun, 'Sensing Voice: Materiality and the Lived Body in Singing and Listening', *Senses and Society,* 6 (2011): 133–55.

Eiesland, Nancy, *The Disabled God: Toward a Liberatory Theology of Disability.* Nashville, Tenn.: Abingdon Press, 1994.

Eliade, Mircea, *Shamanism: Archaic Techniques of Ecstasy.* Princeton: Princeton University Press, 1970.

Elliott, John H., 'The Evil Eye in the First Testament: The Ecology and Culture of a Pervasive Belief', in David Jobling, Peggy Day, and Gerald Sheppard (eds), *The Bible and the Politics of Exegesis.* Cleveland: Pilgrim Press, 1991, 147–59.

Engel, Jerome, and Timothy A. Pedley (eds), *Epilepsy: A Comprehensive Textbook.* Philadelphia: Lippincott, Williams & Wilkins, 2008, 2229–36.

Evans, Craig A., *Matthew: New Cambridge Bible Commentary.* Cambridge: Cambridge University Press, 2012, 184–5.

Fadiman, Anne, *The Spirit Catches you and you Fall Down: A Hmong Child, her American Doctors, and the Collision of Two Cultures.* New York: Farrar, Straus & Giroux, 1997.

Faircloth, Chris, 'Revisiting Thematisation in the Narrative Study of Epilepsy', *Sociology of Health and Illness,* 21 (1999): 209–27.

Fee, Gordon, 'Reflections on Commentary Writing', *Theology Today,* 46 (1990): 387–92.

Fjord, Lakshmi, 'Disasters, Race, and Disability: [Un]Seen through the Political Lens on Katrina', *Journal of Race and Policy,* 3 (2007). Available online at <http://cardcanhelp.org/wp-content/uploads/resources/Disasters%20Race%20Disability%20%7BLakshmi%20Fjord%7D.pdf>.

Fontaine, Carol, 'Roundtable Discussion', in Alice Bach (ed.), *Women in the Hebrew Bible: A Reader.* New York: Routledge, 1999, 438–9.

Foster, Rory C., *Studies in the Life of Christ: Introduction, the Early Period, the Middle Period, the Final Week.* Joplin, Mo.: Baker Book House, 1971.

Frank, Arthur, *The Wounded Story Teller: Body, Illness and Ethics.* Chicago: University of Chicago Press, 1997.

Friedner, Michele, and Stefan Helmreich. 'Sound Studies Meets Deaf Studies', *Senses and Society,* 7 (2012): 72–86.

Gaiser, Frederick J., *Healing in the Bible: Theological Insight for Christian Ministry.* Grand Rapids, Mich.: Baker Academic, 2010.

Garro, Linda C., and Cheryl Mattingly, 'Narrative as Construct and Construction', in Linda C. Garro and Cheryl Mattingly (eds), *Narrative and the Cultural Construction of Illness and Healing.* Berkeley-Los Angeles: University of California Press, 2000, 1–49.

Geertz, Clifford, *The Interpretation of Cultures.* New York: Basic Books, 1973.

Goffman, Erving, *Stigma: Notes on the Management of a Spoiled Identity.* Englewood Cliffs, NJ: Prentice-Hall, 1963.

Good, Bryan, *Medicine, Rationality and Experience: An Anthropological Perspective.* Cambridge: Cambridge University Press, 1994.

Grace, Nora Ellen, *Everyone Here Spoke Sign-Language: Hereditary Deafness on Martha's Vineyard.* Cambridge, Mass.: Harvard University Press, 1985.

Gravett, Sandra L., Karla G. Bohmbach, F. V. Griefenhagen, and Donald Polaski, *An Introduction to the Hebrew Bible: A Thematic Approach.* Louisville, Ky.: Westminster John Knox Press, 2008.

Green, Gill, *The End of Stigma? Changes in Social Experience of Long-Term Illness.* Oxford: Routledge, 2009.

Gregory, Susan, 'Deafness in Fiction', in Susan Gregory and Gillian Hartley (eds), *Constructing Deafness.* London: Pinter Publishers, 1991, 294–300.

Grigely, Joseph, 'Blindness and Deafness as Metaphors: An Anthological Essay', *Journal of Visual Culture,* 5 (2006): 227–41.

Gundry, Robert, *Matthew, A Commentary on his Literary and Theological Art*. Grand Rapids, Mich.: William Eerdmans Publishing Company, 1982.

—— *Commentary on the New Testament* (Grand Rapids, Mich.: Baker Academic, 2010).

Guru, Gopal, 'Introduction', in Gopal Guru (ed.), *Humiliation: Claims and Context*. Oxford: Oxford University Press, 2009, 1–19.

—— 'Rejection of Rejection: Foregrounding Self-Respect', in Gopal Guru (ed.), *Humiliation: Claims and Context*. Oxford: Oxford University Press, 2009, 209–25.

Haber, Susan, *'They Shall Purify Themselves': Essays on Purity in Early Judaism*. Atlanta, Ga.: Society of Biblical Literature, 2008.

Hall, Prathia L., 'Sermon: Encounters with Jesus from Dying to Life Mark 5: 21–43', in Cleophus Larue (ed.), *Power in the Pulpit*. Louisville, Ky.: Westminster John Knox Press, 2002, 67–73.

Hamilton, Toby Ballou, 'Narrative Reasoning', in Barbara A. Boyt Schell and John W. Schell (eds), *Clinical and Professional Reasoning in Occupational Therapy*. Baltimore, Md.: Lippincott, Williams and Wilkins, 2008, 125–68.

Harpur, Paul, 'From Disability to Ability: Changing the Phrasing of the Debate', *Disability and Society*, 27 (2012): 325–37.

Hartsock, Charles, 'Sight and Blindness as an Index of Character in Luke-Acts and its Cultural Milieu', Ph.D. Thesis (2007). Available online at <https://beardocs.baylor.edu/bitstream/2104/5058/3/Chad_Hartsock_phd.pdf>.

—— *Sight and Blindness in Luke-Acts: The Use of Physical Features in Characterization*. Leiden and Boston: Brill, 2008.

Harvey, A. E., *A Companion to the New Testament*. Cambridge: Cambridge University Press, 2004.

Harvey, Elizabeth (ed.), *Sensible Flesh: On Touch in Early Modern Culture*. Philadelphia: University of Pennsylvania Press, 2003.

Hauerwas, Stanley, 'Community and Diversity: The Tyranny of Normality', in John Swinton (ed.), *Critical Reflections on Stanley Hauerwas' Theology of Disability*. Binghampton, NY: Haworth Pastoral Press, 2004, 37–43.

Hauser, Peter C., Amanda O'Hearn, Michael McKee, Anne Steider, and Denise Thew, 'Deaf Epistemology: Deafhood and Deafness', American Annals of the Deaf, 154 (2010): 486–92.

Healy, Mary, *Gospel of Mark*. Grand Rapids, Mich.: Baker Academic, 2008.

Herzfeld, Michael, 'The Horns of the Mediterraneanist Dilemma', *AmEthn* 11 (1984): 439–54.

—— *Anthropology: Theoretical Practice in Culture and Society*. Oxford: Blackwell Publishers, 2001.

Hiebert, D. Edmond, *The Gospel of Mark: An Expositional Commentary*. Greenville, SC: Bob Jones University Press, 1994.

Hooker, Morna, *The Gospel According to Mark*. London: A. & C. Black, 1991.

Horsley, Richard, *Jesus and the Powers: Conflict, Covenant and the Hope of the Poor*. Minneapolis, Minn.: Augsburg Fortress, 2011.

Howard, James Keir, *Disease and Healing in the New Testament*. Lanham, Md.: University Press of America, 2001.

Howes, David, 'Controlling Textuality: A Call for a Return to the Senses', *Anthropologica*, 32 (1990): 55–73.

———— *Sensual Relations: Engaging the Senses in Culture and Social Theory*. Ann Arbor, Mich.: University of Michigan Press, 2003.

Howes, David, and Constance Classen, 'Sounding Sensory Profiles', in David Howes (ed.). *The Varieties of Sensory Experience*. Toronto: University of Toronto Press, 1991, 257–88.

———— 'Doing Sensory Anthropology'. Available online at <http://www.sensorystudies.org/sensorial-investigations-2/doing-sensory-anthropology>.

Hull, John, 'Open Letter from a Blind Disciple to a Sighted Saviour: Text and Discussion', in Martin O'Kane (ed.), *Borders, Boundaries and the Bible*. Sheffield: Sheffield Academic Press, 2001, 154–77.

———— *In the Beginning there was Darkness: A Blind Person's Conversations with the Bible*. London: SCM Press, 2001.

Human Rights Watch Report, *'Broken People: Caste Violence Against India's 'Untouchables'*. New York: Human Rights Watch, 1999.

Hydén, Lars-Chri, and Jens Brockmeier, 'Introduction: From the Retold to the Performed Story', in Lars-Chri Hydén and Jens Brockmeier (eds), *Health, Illness and Culture: Broken Narratives*. New York: Taylor & Francis, 2008, 1–17.

Imber, Jonathan. *Trusting Doctors: The Decline of Moral Authority in American Medicine*. Princeton: Princeton University Press, 2008.

Jacoby, Ann, Dee Snape, and Gus Baker, 'Social Aspects: Epilepsy, Stigma and Quality of Life', in Jerome Engel, Timothy A. Pedley, Jean Alcardi, Solomon Moshé, and Marc A. Dichter (eds.), *Epilepsy: A Comprehensive Textbook*. Philadelphia: Lippincott, Williams & Wilkins, 2008, 2229–36.

Jenks, Elaine Bass, 'Sighted, Blind and In Between' in Robin Patric Clair (ed.), *Expressions of Ethnography: Novel Approaches to Qualitative Methods*. Albany, NY: State University of New York Press, 2003, 126–37.

Jilek-Aall, Louise, 'Forty Years of Experience with Epilepsy', in Steven Schachter and Lisa Andermann (eds), *Epilepsy: Stories of Living with Seizures from Around the World*. Oxford: Oxford University Press, 2008, 33–47.

Jones, Nora L., 'Embodied Ethics: From the Body as Specimen and Spectacle to the Body as Patient', in Frances Mascia-Lees (ed.), *A Companion to the*

Anthology of Bodies/Embodiment. Chichester: Willey-Blackwell Publishing, 2011, 72–85.

Jütte, Robert, *A History of the Senses: From Antiquity to Cyberspace.* Cambridge: Polity Press, 2005.

Just, Roger, 'On the Ontological Status of Honour', in Joy Hendry and C. W. Watson (eds), *An Anthropology of Indirect Communication.* London and New York: Routledge, 2001, 34–49.

Kalas, David, Frank Honeycutt, Stephen Crotts, and Robert Cueni. *Sermons on the Gospel Readings,* i. Lima, O.: CSS Publishing Co., 2003.

Kalimi, Isaac, 'Human and Musical Sounds and their Hearing Elsewhere as a Literary Device in the Biblical Narratives', *VT* 60 (2010): 565–70.

Kasnitz, Devva, and Shuttleworth, Russell, 'Semiotics and Dis/Ability: Interrogating Categories of Difference', in Linda J. Rogers and Beth Swadener (eds), *Anthropology and Disability.* Albany, NY: State University of New York Press, 2001, 19–41.

Keating, Elizabeth, and R. Neill Hadder, 'Sensory Impairment', *ARA* 39 (2010): 115–29.

Kelley, Nicole, '"The Punishment of the Devil was Apparent in the Torment of Human Body": Epilepsy in Ancient Christianity', in Candida Moss and Jeremy Schipper (eds), *Disability Studies and Biblical Literature.* New York: Palgrave Macmillan, 2011, 205–21.

Khare, Ravindra S., 'The Body, Sensoria, and Self of the Powerless: Remembering/Re-Membering Indian Untouchable Women', *NLH* 26/1 (1995): 147–68.

Kirklin, Deborah, 'The Search for Meaning in Modern Medicine', in Knut Stene-Johansen and Frederick Tygstrup (eds), *Illness in Context* Amsterdam: Rodopi, 2010, 15–36.

Kisch, Shifra, '"Deaf Discourse": The Social Construction of Deafness in a Bedouin Community', *MedAnth* 27 (2008): 283–313.

Klawans, Jonathan, 'Moral and Ritual Purity', in Amy-Jill Levine, Dale C. Allison, and John Dominic Crossan (eds), *The Historical Jesus in Context.* Princeton: Princeton University Press, 2006, 266–84.

Kleege, Georgina, *Sight Unseen.* New Haven: Yale University Press, 1999.

——— 'Helen Keller and the Empire of the Normal', *AmQ* 52 (2000): 322–5.

Kleinmann, Arthur, *Suffering, Healing and the Human Condition.* New York: Basic Books, 1988.

Kochhar-Lindgren, Kanta, 'Hearing Difference across Theatres: Experimental, Disability and Deaf Performance', *Theatre Journal,* 58 (2006): 417–36.

Koosed, Jennifer, and Schumm, Darla, 'Out of the Darkness: Examining the Rhetoric of Blindness in the Gospel of John', *DSQ* 25 (2005). Available online at <http://www.dsq-sds.org>.

Koren, Sharon Faye, 'The Menstruant as "Other" in Medieval Judaism and Christianity', *Nashim: A Journal of Jewish Women's Studies and Gender Issues,* 17 (2009): 33–59.

Kraemer, Guenter, *Epilepsy from A–Z: Dictionary of Medical Terms.* Stuttgart: Georg Thieme Verlag, 1996.

Kramarae, Cheris, *Women and Men Speaking: Frameworks for Analysis.* Rowley, Mass.: Newbury House, 1981.

Kristeva, Julia, *Powers of Horror: An Essay on Abjection.* New York: Columbia University Press, 1982.

Kuppers, Petra, *Disability and Contemporary Performance: Bodies on the Edge.* London: Routledge, 2004.

Kurek-Chomycz, Dominika, 'The Fragrance of her Perfume: The Significance of Sense Imagery in John's Account of the Anointing in Bethany', *NovT* 52 (2010): 334–54.

—— 'Spreading the Sweet Scent of the Gospel as the Cult of the Wise: Sapiential Background of Paul's Olfactory Metaphor in 2 Cor 2: 14–16', in Christian Eberhart (ed.), *Ritual and Metaphor: Sacrifice in the Bible.* Atlanta, Ga.: Society of Biblical Literature, 2011, 115–34.

Kyle, James, and Bernice Woll, *Sign Language: The Study of Deaf People and their Language.* Cambridge: Cambridge University Press, 1988.

Ladd, Paddy, *Understanding Deaf Culture: In Search of Deafhood.* Clevedon: Multilingual Matters, 2003.

Laes, Christian, 'Silent Witnesses: Deaf-Mutes in Graeco-Roman Antiquity', *CW* 104 (2011): 451–73.

Lakoff, George, and Mark Johnson, *Metaphors we Live by.* Chicago: University of Chicago Press, 1980.

Lane, Harlan, 'Ethnicity, Ethics, and the Deaf-World', *Journal of Deaf Studies,* 10 (2005). Available online at <http://jdsde.oxfordjournals.org/cgi/content/abstract/10/3/29>.

Lane, William, *The Gospel According to Mark* (Grand Rapids, Mich.: Eerdmans Publishing Co., 1974).

Largey, Gale, and Rod Watson, 'The Sociology of Odors', *American Journal of Sociology,* 77 (1972): 1021–34.

Lawrence, Louise, *An Ethnography of the Gospel of Matthew.* Tübingen: Mohr Siebeck, 2003.

—— *Reading with Anthropology: Exhibiting Aspects of New Testament Religion.* Milton Keynes: Paternoster Press, 2005.

—— 'Structure, Agency and Ideology: A Response to Zeba Crook', *JSNT* 29 (2007): 277–86.

—— 'Exploring the Sense-Scape of the Gospel of Mark', *JSNT* 33 (2011): 387–97.

Lee, Dorothy, 'The Gospel of John and the Five Senses', *JBL* 129 (2010): 115–27.

Lees, Janet, 'Enabling the Body', in Hector Avalos, Sarah Melcher, and Jeremy Schipper (eds), *This Abled Body: Rethinking Disabilities in Biblical Studies*. Atlanta, Ga.: Society of Biblical Literature, 2007, 161–71.

Levine, Amy-Jill, 'Discharging Responsibility: Matthean Jesus, Biblical Law and Hemorrhaging Women', in Mark Allan Powell and David Bauer (eds), *Treasures New and Old: New Essays in Matthean Studies*. Atlanta, Ga.: Scholars Press, 1996, 379–97.

Lewis, Hannah, *Deaf Liberation Theology*. Aldershot: Ashgate, 2007.

Linton, Simi, *Claiming Disability: Knowledge and Identity*. Albany, NY: New York University Press, 1998.

Lucas, Sabine, *Bloodlines of the Soul*. Lincoln: iUniverse Books, 2005.

Lunceford, Brett, *Naked Politics: Nudity, Political Action and the Rhetoric of the Body*. Plymouth: Lexington Books, 2012.

Macpherson, Hannah, 'Articulating Blind Touch: Thinking through the Feet'. *Senses and Society*, 4 (2009): 179–93.

Magiorkinis, Emmanouil, Kalliopi Sidiropoulou, and Aristidis Diamantis, 'Hallmarks in the History of Epilepsy: From Antiquity till the Twentieth Century', *EpilepsyBehav*, 17 (2010): 103–8.

Malbon, Elizabeth Struthers, *In the Company of Jesus: Characters in Mark's Gospel*. Louisville, Ky.: Westminster John Knox Press, 2000.

Malina, Bruce, *The New Testament World: Insights from Cultural Anthropology*, 3rd edn. Louisville, Ky.: Westminster John Knox [1981] 2001.

—— *Windows on the World of Jesus: Time Travel to Ancient Judea*. Louisville, Ky.: Westminster John Knox Press, 1993.

—— and Jerome Neyrey, *Portraits of Paul: An Archaeology of Ancient Personality*. Louisville, Ky.: Westminster John Knox Press, 1996.

—— and Richard Rohrbaugh, *Social-Science Commentary on the Synoptic Gospels*, 2nd edn. Minneapolis, Minn.: Fortress Press, 2003.

—— *Social-Science Commentary on the Gospel of John*. Minneapolis, Minn.: Fortress Press, 1998.

Malul, Meier, *Knowledge, Control and Sex: Studies in Biblical Thought, Culture, and Worldview*. Tel Aviv-Jaffa: Archaeological Center Publication, 2002.

Marcus, Joel, 'A Note on Markan Optics', *NTS* 45 (1999): 250–6.

—— *Mark 8–16*, Anchor Yale Bible Commentaries, 27. New Haven: Yale University Press, 2009.

Marshall, Christopher D., *Faith as a Theme in Mark's Narrative*. Cambridge: Cambridge University Press, 1989.

Martin, Dale, *The Corinthian Body*. New Haven: Yale University Press, 1995.

Martin, Dale, *Pedagogy of the Bible: An Analysis and Proposal.* Louisville, Ky.: Westminster/John Knox, 2008.

Masquelier, Adeline Marie, *Dirt, Undress, and Difference: Critical Perspectives on the Body's Surface.* Bloomington, Ind.: Indiana University Press, 2005.

May, Vivian, and Beth Ferri, 'Fixated on Ability', *Prose Studies,* 27 (2005): 120–40.

McRuer, Robert, and Michael Berube, *Crip Theory: Cultural Signs of Queerness and Disability.* New York: New York University Press, 2006.

Meier, John, *A Marginal Jew: Rethinking the Historical Jesus,* ii. New York: Doubleday, 1994.

Menninghaus, Winnifred, *Disgust: The Theory and History of a Strong Sensation.* Albany, NY: State University of New York Press, 2003.

Miller, Susan B., *Disgust: The Gatekeeper Emotion.* Hillsdale, NJ: The Analytic Press, 2004.

Miller, William Ian, *The Anatomy of Disgust.* Cambridge, Mass.: Harvard University Press, 1997.

Miner, Madonne, 'Making up the Stories as we Go Along: Men, Women and Narratives of Disability', in David Mitchell and Sharon L. Snyder (eds), *The Body and Physical Difference: Discourses of Disability.* Ann Arbor, Mich.: University of Michigan Press, 1997, 283–95.

Mintz, Susannah, 'Invisible Disability: Georgina Kleege's Sight Unseen', *NWSAJ* 14 (2002): 155–77.

—— 'The Art of Joseph Grigely: Deafness, Conversation, Noise', *JLCDS* 6 (2012): 1–16.

Mitchell, David, and Sharon Snyder, *Narrative Prosthesis: Disability and the Dependencies of Discourse.* Ann Arbor, Mich.: University of Michigan Press, 2000.

—— 'Jesus Thrown Everything Off Balance: Disability and Redemption in Biblical Literature', in Hector Avalos, Sarah Melcher, and Jeremy Schipper (eds), *This Abled Body: Rethinking Disabilities in Biblical Studies.* Atlanta, Ga.: Society of Biblical Literature, 2007, 173–83.

Moore, Mark, and John Weece, *The Power of Jesus.* Joplin, Mo.: College Press Publishing, 2002.

Moore, Stephen, and Yvonne Sherwood. *The Invention of the Biblical Scholar: A Critical Manifesto.* Minneapolis, Minn.: Augsburg Fortress, 2011.

Morrill, Bruce, *Divine Worship and Human Healing: Liturgical Theology at the Margins of Life and Death.* New York: Liturgical Press, 2009.

Morris, Wayne, *Theology without Words: Theology in the Deaf Community.* Aldershot: Ashgate, 2008.

Moss, Candida, 'The Man with the Flow of Power: Porous Bodies in Mark 5: 25–34', *JBL* 129/3 (2010): 507–19.

—— and Jeremy Schipper (eds), *Disability Studies and Biblical Literature*. New York: Palgrave Macmillan, 2011, 1–11.

Moxnes, Halvor, *Putting Jesus in his Place: A Radical Vision of Household and Kingdom*. Louisville, Ky.: Westminster John Knox Press, 2003.

Murray, Stuart, *Representing Autism: Culture, Narrative, Fascination*. Liverpool: Liverpool University Press, 2008.

Musolff, Andreas, 'What Role do Metaphors Play in Racial Prejudice? The Function of Anti-Semitic Imagery in Hitler's "Mein Kampf"', *Patterns of Prejudice*, 41 (2007): 21–43.

Nandy, Ashis, 'Humiliation: The Politics and Cultural Psychology of the Limits of Human Degradation', in Elleke Boehmer and Rosinka Chaudhuri (eds), *The Indian Postcolonial: A Critical Reader*. Oxford: Routledge, 2010, 261–75.

Newall, Rachel, 'The Thanksgiving of Women After Childbirth: A Blessing in Disguise', in Mavis Kirkham (ed.), *Exploring the Dirty Side of Women's Health*. Oxford: Routledge, 2007, 38–52.

Newell, Christopher, 'Disabled Theologies and the Journeys of Liberation to Where our Names Appear', *FemTh* 15 (2007): 322–45.

Neyrey, Jerome, 'Readers Guide to Clean/Unclean, Pure/Polluted, and Holy/Profane: The Idea and System of Purity'. Available online at <http://nd.edu/~jneyrey1/purity.html>.

Olyan, Saul, 'The Ascription of Physical Disability as a Stigmatizing Strategy in Biblical Iconic Polemics', *JHS* 9 (2003): 1–15. Available online at <http://www.jhsonline.org/Articles/article_116.pdf>.

—— *Biblical Mourning: Ritual and Social Dimensions*. Oxford: Oxford University Press, 2004.

—— *Disability in the Hebrew Bible: Interpreting Mental and Physical Differences*. Cambridge: Cambridge University Press, 2008.

Orevillo-Montenegro, Muriel, *The Jesus of Asian Women*. Darya Ganj, New Delhi: Logos Press, 2009.

Osteen, Mark (ed.), *Autism and Representation*. London: Taylor & Francis, 2008.

—— 'Autism and Representation: A Comprehensive Introduction', in Mark Osteen (ed.), *Autism and Representation*. London: Taylor and Francis, 2008, 1–47.

Padden, Carol, 'The Deaf Community and the Culture of Deaf People', in Susan Gregory and Gillian Hartley (eds), *Constructing Deafness*. London: Pinter Publishers, 1991, 40–5.

—— and Tom Humphries, *Deaf in America: Voices from a Culture*. Cambridge, Mass.: Harvard University Press, 1988.

Painter, John, *Mark's Gospel: Worlds in Conflict*. Oxford: Routledge, 1997.

Palmer, Gary, and William Jankowiak, 'Performance and Imagination: Toward an Anthropology of the Spectacular and the Mundane', *CultAnth* 11 (1996): 225–58.

Panayiotopoulos, C. P., *A Clinical Guide to Epileptic Syndromes and their Treatment*. London: Springer Healthcare Ltd, 2010.

Papataxiarchis, Evthymios, 'Dealing with Disadvantage: Culture and the Gendered Self in the Politics of Locality', in Christian Bromberger and Dionigi Albera (eds), *L'Anthropologie et la Méditerranné: Unité, diversité et perspectives*. Paris: Éditions de la Maison des Sciences de l'Homme, 2001, 179–211.

Parker, Holt, 'Women in Medicine', in Sharon James and Sheila Dillon (eds), *A Companion to Woman in the Ancient World*. Oxford: Wiley-Blackwell, 2012, 107–24.

Parsons, Mikael, *Body and Character in Luke and Acts: The Subversion of Physiognomy in Early Christianity*. Grand Rapids, Mich.: Baker Academic Press, 2006.

Paterson, Mark, 'Seeing with the Hands, Touching with the Eyes: Vision, Touch and the Enlightenment Spatial Imaginary', *Senses and Society*, 1 (2006): 225–42.

Peerbolte, Bert Jan Lietaert, and Michael Labahn, *Wonders Never Cease: The Purpose of Narrating Miracle Stories in the New Testament and its Religious Environment*. London: T. & T. Clark, 2006.

Perez, Rosa Maria, *Kings and Untouchables: A Study of the Caste System in Western India.* New Delhi: Chronicle Books, 2004.

Perkins, Pheme, 'Commentaries: Windows to the Text', *Theology Today*, 46 (1990): 393–8.

Peters, Susan, 'Is there a Disability Culture? A Syncretisation of Three Possible World Views', *DisabSoc* 15 (2000): 583–601.

Peters, Theo, 'Foreword', in Olga Bogdashina. *Autism and the Edges of the Known World: Sensitivities Language and Constructed Reality.* London: Jessica Kingsley Publishers, 2010, 9–12.

Pilch, John, 'The Transfiguration of Jesus: An Experience of Alternate Reality', in Philip Esler (ed.), *Modelling Early Christianity*. London: Routledge, 1995, 47–64.

——— *Healing in the New Testament: Insights from Medical Anthropology*. Minneapolis, Minn.: Augsburg Fortress, 2000.

Pink, Sarah, *Doing Sensory Ethnography*. London: Sage 2009.

Pitt Rivers, Julian, 'Honour and Social Status', in John G. Peristiany (ed.). *Honour and Shame: The Values of Mediterranean Society.* Chicago: University of Chicago Press, 1965, 19–77.

Placher, William C., *Mark*. Louisville, Ky.: Westminster John Knox Press, 2010.

Plutarch, 'Questiones Convivales IV', tr. H. B. Hoffleit, *Plutarch's Moralia VIII*, Loeb Classical Library. Cambridge, Mass.: Harvard University Press, 1969.

Potter, David S., 'Odor and Power in the Roman Empire', in James Porter (ed.), *Constructions of the Classical Body*. Ann Arbor, Mich.: University of Michigan Press, 1999, 169–89.

Rajkumar, Peniel, *Dalit Theology and Dalit Liberation: Problems, Paradigms and Possibilities*. Aldershot: Ashgate, 2010.

Rash, Felicity, *The Language of Violence: Adolf Hitler's Mein Kampf* New York: Peter Lang, 2006.

Resendes, Sandy, 'The World at your Fingertips: Understanding Blindness', MA thesis, Concordia University (2004). Available online at <http://spectrum.library.concordia.ca/7908/1/MQ91106.pdf>.

Resseguie, James, 'John 9: A Literary Critical Analysis', in Mark Stibbe (ed.), *The Gospel of John as Literature*. Leiden: Brill, 1993, 115–22.

Reynolds, Thomas, *Vulnerable Communion: A Theology of Disability and Hospitality*. Grand Rapids, Mich.: Brazos Press, 2008.

Rhoads, David, 'Performance Criticism: An Emerging Methodology in Biblical Studies'. Available online at <http://www.sbl-site.org/assets/pdfs/Rhoads_Performance.pdf>.

Ricoeur, Paul, 'The Metaphorical Process as Cognition, Imagination, and Feeling', *Critical Inquiry*, 5 (1978): 143–59.

Ridderbos, Herman, *The Gospel According to John: A Theological Commentary*. Grand Rapids, Mich.: William Eerdmans, 1997.

Ritchie, Ian, 'The Nose Knows: Bodily Knowing in Isaiah 11: 3', *JSOT* 87 (2000): 59–73.

Robinson, Clayton David, 'The Laying on of Hands, with Special Reference to the Reception of the Holy Spirit in the New Testament', Fuller Theological Seminary Ph.D. dissertation (2008), 102. Available online at <http://books.google.co.uk/books/about/The_Laying_on_of_Hands_with_Special_Refe.html?id=h81f5MOuPUAC&redir_esc=y>.

Rodaway, Paul, *Sensuous Geographies: Body, Sense and Place*. London: Routledge, 1994.

Roeder, George, 'Coming to our Senses', *JAmHist* 81 (1994): 1112–22.

Ross, J. M., 'Epileptic or Moonstruck', *BT* 29 (1978): 126–8.

Ryken, Leland, James C. Wilhoit, and Tremper Longman III (eds), *Dictionary of Biblical Imagery*. Downers Grove, Ill.: Intervarsity Press, 1998.

Sabin, Marie Noonan, *The Gospel According to Mark*. Collegeville, Minn.: Order of St Benedict, 2006.

Sacks, Oliver, *The Man Who Mistook His Wife for a Hat.* New York: Harper & Row, 1987.

—— *An Anthropologist on Mars.* New York: Alfred Knopf, 1996.

Samellas, Antigone, *Alienation: The Experience of the Eastern Mediterranean (50–600 A.D.).* Bern: Peter Lang, 2010.

Sandahl, Carrie, and Philip Auslander, 'Introduction', in Carrie Sandahl and Philip Auslander (eds), *Bodies in Commotion: Disability and Performance.* Ann Arbor, Mich.: University of Michigan Press, 2005, pp. 1–11.

Sanjeev V., and Aparna Nair, 'Confronting the Stigma of Epilepsy', *AIAN* 14 (2011): 158–63.

Sarukkai, Sundar, 'Phenomenology of Untouchability', *Economic and Political Weekly,* 37 (2009): 39–48.

Scambler, Graham, and Anthony Hopkins, 'Being Epileptic: Coming to Terms with Stigma', *Sociology of Health and Illness,* 8 (2008): 26–43.

Schachter, Steven, and Lisa Andermann, *Epilepsy in our World: Stories of Living with Seizures from around the World.* Oxford: Oxford University Press, 2008.

Schipper, Jeremy, *Disability and Isaiah's Suffering Servant.* Oxford: Oxford University Press, 2011.

Schmidt, Leigh Eric, 'Hearing Loss', in Michael Bull and Les Back (eds), *The Auditory Culture Reader.* Oxford: Berg, 2003, 41–59.

Schneider, Joseph, and Peter Conrad, *Having Epilepsy: The Experience and Control of Illness.* Philadelphia: Temple University Press, 1985.

Schor, Naomi, 'Blindness as Metaphor', *Differences: A Journal of Feminist Cultural Studies,* 11 (1999): 76–105.

Schroer, Silvia, and Thomas Staubli, *Body Symbolism in the Bible.* Collegeville, Minn.: Liturgical Press, 2001.

Schüssler Fiorenza, Elisabeth, *Democratizing Biblical Studies: Toward an Emancipatory Educational Space* Louisville, Ky.: Westminster John Knox Press, 2009.

—— and Kent Harold Richards (eds), *Transforming Graduate Biblical Education: Ethos and Discipline.* Atlanta, Ga.: Society of Biblical Literature, 2010.

Schwartz, Seth, *Were the Jews a Mediterranean Society? Reciprocity and Solidarity in Ancient Judaism.* Princeton and Oxford: Princeton University Press, 2010.

Scott, James, *Weapons of the Weak: Everyday Forms of Peasant Resistance.* New Haven: Yale University Press, 1987.

Sekine, Yasumasa, *Pollution, Untouchability and Harijans.* Jaipur: Rawat Publications, 2011.

Senghas, Richard, and Leila Monaghan, 'Signs of their Times: Deaf Communities and the Culture of Language', ARA 31 (2002): 69–97.

Seremetakis, Nadia, *The Last Word Women, Death and Divination in Inner Mani.* Chicago: University of Chicago Press, 1991.

—— *The Senses Still: Memory and Perception as Material Culture in Modernity.* Boulder, Colo.: Westview, 1994.

Sherwood, Laura Ackerman, 'A Counterstory to Master Narratives for Persons with Disability', Ph.D. thesis, Regents University, 2009. Available online at <http://books.google.co.uk/books?id=hI5nJW5WC7IC&printsec=frontco ver&source=gbs_ge_summary_r&cad=0#v=onepage&q&f=false>.

Shikin, Nicole, *Animal Capital: Rendering Life in Biopolitical Times.* Minneapolis, Minn.: University of Minnesota Press, 2009.

Shiner, Whitney, *Proclaiming the Gospel: First-Century Performance of Mark.* Harrisburg, Pa.: Trinity Press International, 2003.

Shuttleworth, Russell, and Devva Kasnitz, 'The Cultural Context of Disability', in Gary Albrecht (ed.), *Encyclopedia of Disability.* Thousand Oaks, Calif.: Sage, 2005.

Skinner, Marilyn, 'Sex', in Daniel Garrison (ed.), *A Cultural History of the Human Body in Antiquity.* Oxford: Berg 2010, 67–82.

Smith, Mark, *Sensing the Past: Seeing, Hearing, Smelling, Tasting and Touching in History.* Berkeley-Los Angeles: University of California Press, 2007.

Smith, Sidonie, and Julia Watson. *Reading Autobiography: A Guide for Interpreting Life Narratives.* Minneapolis, Minn.: University of Minnesota Press, 2010.

Sorensen, Eric, *Possession and Exorcism in the New Testament and Early Christianity.* Tübingen: Mohr Siebeck, 2002.

Spencer, F. Scott, *Dancing Girls, Loose Ladies, and Women of the Cloth: The Women in Jesus' Life.* New York: Continuum, 2004.

Stavrakopoulou, Francesca, '"Popular" Religion and "Official" Religion: Practice, Perception, Portrayal', in Francesca Stavrakopoulou and John Barton (eds), *Religious Diversity in Ancient Israel and Judah.* London and New York: T. & T. Clark International, 2010, 37–58.

Steffler, Alva, *Symbols of the Christian Faith.* Grand Rapids, Mich.: Eerdmans Publishing Co., 2002.

Stirling, Jeannette, *Representing Epilepsy: Myth and Matter.* Liverpool: Liverpool University Press, 2010.

Stoller, Paul, *Embodying Colonial Memories: Spirit Possession, Power and the Hauka in West Africa.* New York: Routledge, 1995.

—— *Sensuous Scholarship.* Philadelphia: University of Pennsylvania Press, 1997.

Strecker, Christian, 'Jesus and the Demoniacs', in Wolfgang Stegemann, Bruce Malina, and Gerd Theissen (eds), *The Social Setting of Jesus and the Gospels*. Minneapolis, Minn.: Fortress Press, 2002, 117–33.

Sutton, Barbara, 'Naked Protest: Memories of Bodies and Resistance at the World Social Forum', *JIWS* 8 (2007): 139–48.

Tannehill, Robert C., *Abingdon New Testament Commentary—Luke*. Nashville, Tenn.: Abingdon Press, 1996.

Taylor, Janelle, 'The Story Catches you and you Fall Down: Tragedy, Ethnography and Cultural Competence', *Med Anth* 17 (2003): 159–81.

Temkin, Owsei, *The Falling Sickness: A History of Epilepsy from the Greeks to the Beginnings of Modern Neurology*. Baltimore, Md.: Johns Hopkins University Press, 1994.

Thatcher, Adrian, *God, Sex and Gender: An Introduction*. Chichester: John Wiley & Son, 2011.

Theophrastus, *The Characters*. Boston: Frederic Hill, 1831.

Thomas, John Christopher, *The Devil, Disease and Deliverance: Origins of Illness in New Testament Thought*. Sheffield: Sheffield Academic Press, 1998.

Thompson, Katherine, 'Library Rules: No Loud Yells, No Bad Smells'. Available online at <http://www.newser.com/story/56021/library-rules-no-loud-yells-no-bad-smells.html>.

Tilley, Christopher, *Body and Image: Explorations in Landscape Phenomenology*. Walnut Creek, Calif.: Left Coast Press, 2008.

Todolí, Julia, 'Disease Metaphors in Urban Planning', *CADAAD* 1 (2007): 51–60.

Toensing, Holly, 'Living among the Tombs: Society, Mental Illness and Self-Destruction in Mark 5: 1–20', in Hector Avalos, Sarah Melcher, and Jeremy Schipper (eds), *This Abled Body: Rethinking Disabilities in Biblical Studies*. Atlanta, Ga.: Society of Biblical Literature, 2007, 131–43.

Toner, Jerry, *Popular Culture in Ancient Rome*. Cambridge: Polity Press, 2009.

Trawick, Margaret, 'Wandering Lost: A Landless Laborer's Sense of Place and Self', in Arjun Appadurai, Frank J. Korom, and Margaret Ann Mills (eds), *Gender, Genre and Power in South Asian Expressive Traditions*. Philadelphia: University of Pennsylvania Press, 1991, 224–66.

Turner, David L., *Matthew*. Grand Rapids, Mich.: Baker Academic, 2008.

Twelftree, Graham H., *Jesus the Miracle Worker: A Historical and Theological Study*. Downers Grove, Ill.: Intervarsity Press, 1999.

Tyler, Stephen, 'On Being Out of Words' *CultAnth* 2 (1986): 131–7.

Vanhoozer, Kevin J. (ed.), *Dictionary for Theological Interpretation of the Bible*. Grand Rapids, Mich.: Baker Books, 2005.

van Iersel, Bas, *Mark: A Reader-Response Commentary*. Sheffield: Sheffield Academic Press, 1998.

Vieira, Patricia, *Seeing Politics Otherwise: Vision in Latin American and Iberian Fiction*. Toronto: University of Toronto Press, 2011.

Vincentnathan, Lynn, *Harijan Subculture and Self-Esteem Management in a South Indian Community*. Madison, Wis.: University of Wisconsin Press, 1987.

Vorster, Willem S., *Speaking of Jesus: Essays on Biblical Language, Gospel Narrative and the Historical Jesus*. Leiden: Brill, 1998.

Waskul, Dennis D., Vannini Phillip, and Janelle Wilson, 'The Aroma of Recollection: Olfaction, Nostalgia, and the Shaping of the Sensuous Self', *Senses and Society*, 4 (2009): 5–22.

Wassen, Cecelia, 'Jesus and the Hemorrhaging Woman in Mark 5: 24–34: Insights from Purity Laws from the Dead Sea Scrolls', in Raija Sollamo, Anssi Voitila, and Jutta Jokiranta (eds), *Scripture in Transition: Essays on Septuagint, Hebrew Bible, and Dead Sea Scrolls in Honour of Raija Sollamo*. Leiden: Brill, 2008, 641–60.

Watts, Rikki, *Isaiah's New Exodus and Mark*. Tübingen: Mohr Siebeck, 1997.

Weissenrieder, Annette, *Images of Illness in the Gospel of Luke: Insights of Ancient Medical Texts*. Tübingen: Mohr Siebeck, 2003.

Weitzman, Steven, 'Sensory Reform in Deuteronomy' in David Brakke, Michael Satlow, and Steven Weitzman (eds), *Religion and the Self in Antiquity*. Bloomington, Ind.: Indiana University Press, 2005, pp. 123–39.

Wendell, Susan, *The Rejected Body: Feminist Philosophical Reflections on Disability*. New York and London: Routledge, 1996.

Wheatley, Edward, *Stumbling Blocks Before the Blind: Medieval Constructions of Disability*. Ann Arbor, Mich.: University of Michigan Press, 2010.

Whyte, Susan Reynolds, 'Constructing Epilepsy: Images and Contexts in East Africa', in Benedicte Ingstad and Susan Whyte (eds), *Disability and Culture*. Berkeley-Los Angeles: University of California Press, 1995, 226–45.

Wilce, James M., 'Medical Discourse', *ARA* 38 (2009): 199–215.

Wilkinson, John, 'The Case of an Epileptic Boy', *ET* 79 (1967): 39–42.

Witherington, Ben, *The Gospel of Mark: A Socio-Historical Commentary*. Grand Rapids, Mich.: William Eerdmans Publishing Co., 2001.

Yong, Amos. *Theology and Down Syndrome: Reimagining Disability in Late Modernity*. Waco, Tex.: Baylor University Press, 2007.

—— 'Review of Jeremy Schipper and Candida R. Moss eds., Disability Studies and Biblical Literature', *H-Net Reviews* (2012). Available online at <https://www.hnet.org/reviews/showrev.php?id=35031>.

Young, Iris, 'Foreword', in Marian Corker and Tom Shakespeare (eds), *Disability/Postmodernity: Embodying Disability Theory*. London: Continuum, 2002, pp. xii–xiv.

Index to Sense and Stigma in the Gospels

Index to Biblical and Other Ancient Texts

CPSIA information can be obtained
at www.ICGtesting.com
Printed in the USA
FFHW011519150919
54966675-60681FF